Additional Practice Workbook

GRADE 5 TOPICS 1–16

enVision® Mathematics

Savvas Learning Company LLC, 15 East Midland Avenue, Paramus, NJ 07652

ISBN-13: 978-0-13-495380-9
ISBN-10: 0-13-495380-0
6 21

Grade 5 Topics 1–16

Name ______________________________

 Video  Practice  Tools Games

Additional Practice 1-1

Patterns with Exponents and Powers of 10

Another Look!

Patterns can help you multiply by powers of 10.

Find the product of 8×10^4.

Write the product in standard form.

The number of zeros in the product is the same as the exponent.

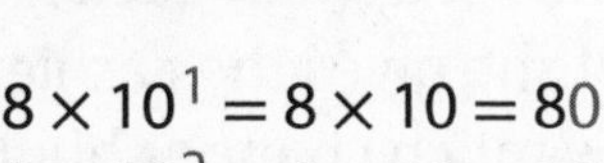

$8 \times 10^1 = 8 \times 10 = 80$
$8 \times 10^2 = 8 \times 10 \times 10 = 800$
$8 \times 10^3 = 8 \times 10 \times 10 \times 10 = 8{,}000$
$8 \times 10^4 = 8 \times 10 \times 10 \times 10 \times 10 = 80{,}000$

So, 8×10^4 written in standard form is 80,000.

1. Write $10 \times 10 \times 10 \times 10 \times 10 \times 10 \times 10$ with an exponent.

2. Write $6 \times 10 \times 10 \times 10 \times 10$ with an exponent.

3. How many zeros are in the standard form of 10^7? Write this number in standard form.

In **4–14**, find each product. Use patterns to help.

4. $4 \times 10^1 =$
$4 \times 10^2 =$
$4 \times 10^3 =$
$4 \times 10^4 =$

5. $7 \times 10 =$
$7 \times 100 =$
$7 \times 1{,}000 =$
$7 \times 10{,}000 =$

6. $5 \times 10^1 =$
$5 \times 10^2 =$
$5 \times 10^3 =$
$5 \times 10^4 =$

7. 3×10^1

8. 2×100

9. 3×10^4

10. $1{,}000 \times 9$

11. 6×10^2

12. 3×10^3

13. $10{,}000 \times 2$

14. 8×10^5

15. Explain how to find the number of zeros in the product for Exercise 14.

16. Maria saw 2×10^1 dogs in the park on Saturday. She saw twice as many dogs on Sunday as she saw on Saturday. How many dogs did she see over the two days?

17. **Number Sense** In which place is the digit in the number 5,341 that would be changed to form 5,841? How do the values of the two numbers compare?

18. **enVision® STEM** There are 2,000 pounds in a ton. How can you write 2,000 with an exponent?

Scientific notation is written as one digit times a power of ten.

19. Kay buys 12 pounds of apples. Each pound costs \$3. If she gives the cashier two \$20 bills, how much change should she receive?

20. **Model with Math** James practiced piano for 48 minutes. Alisa practiced for 5 times as long as James. How many minutes did Alisa practice? How many minutes in all did James and Alisa practice? Write an equation to model your work.

	?					
Alisa →	48	48	48	48	48	5 times as long
James →	48					

21. **Higher Order Thinking** George said that 6×10^3 is 180. Do you agree or disagree? If you disagree, explain the mistake that he made and find the correct answer.

Assessment Practice

22. Choose all the equations that are true.

- ☐ $10 \times 10 \times 10 \times 10 \times 10 = 100{,}000$
- ☐ $10 \times 10 \times 10 \times 10 \times 10 = 50$
- ☐ $10 \times 10 \times 10 \times 10 \times 10 = 50{,}000$
- ☐ $10 \times 10 \times 10 \times 10 \times 10 = 10^5$
- ☐ $10 \times 10 \times 10 \times 10 \times 10 = 50{,}000$

23. Choose all the equations that are true.

- ☐ $90{,}000 = 9 \times 1{,}000$
- ☐ $90{,}000 = 9 \times 10{,}000$
- ☐ $90{,}000 = 9 \times 10^4$
- ☐ $90{,}000 = 9 \times 10^5$
- ☐ $90{,}000 = 9 \times 10^6$

Name ______________________

Additional Practice 1-2

Understand Whole-Number Place Value

Another Look!

A place-value chart can help you write larger numbers. What are the various ways to write 92,888,100?

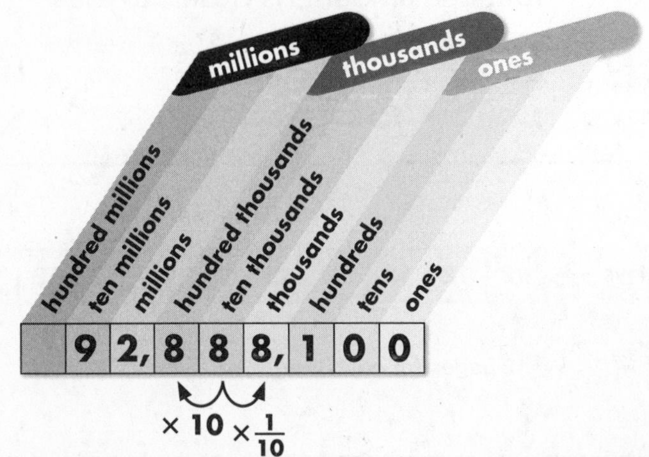

The value of the first 8 is $8 \times 100{,}000 = 800{,}000$, and the value of the second 8 is $8 \times 10{,}000 = 80{,}000$.

Expanded form: $(9 \times 10^7) + (2 \times 10^6) + (8 \times 10^5) + (8 \times 10^4) + (8 \times 10^3) + (1 \times 10^2)$

Standard form: 92,888,100

Number name: ninety-two million, eight hundred eighty-eight thousand, one hundred

1. Write 720,080 in expanded form with exponents.
   $(7 \times 10^5) +$

2. Write the number name for 43,080,700.

In **3–5**, write the values of the given digits.

3. the 2s in 42,256

4. the 9s in 9,905,482

5. the 4s in 305,444

6. Write 12,430,000 in expanded form.

7. Write 337,060 in expanded form using exponents.

8. Write the number name for 3,1<u>5</u>2,308.

   What is the value of the underlined digit?

9. Sue and Jonah chose numbers for a place-value game. Sue chose the number one hundred fifty-two thousand. Jonah chose five million for his number. Who chose the greater number? Explain.

10. **Higher Order Thinking** One day, total attendance at the state fair was 126,945. Round 126,945 to the nearest hundred thousand, nearest ten thousand, and nearest thousand. Which of these rounded amounts is closest to the actual attendance?

11. Maricko and her family went on a 10-day vacation. She read 12 pages in her book each day. How many total pages did she read while on vacation?

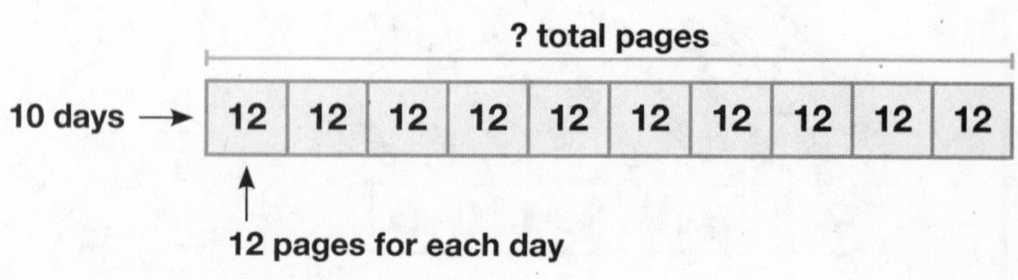

12. **Construct Arguments** Is the value of the first 5 in California's population 10 times as great as the value of the second 5? Explain.

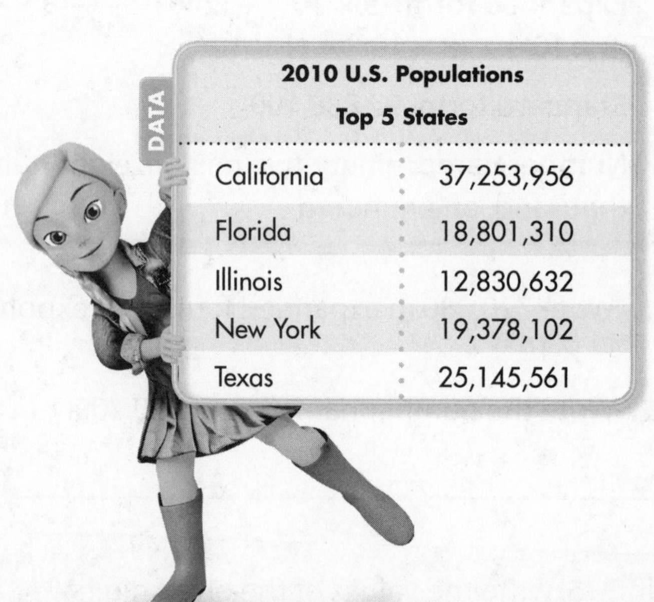

2010 U.S. Populations
Top 5 States

State	Population
California	37,253,956
Florida	18,801,310
Illinois	12,830,632
New York	19,378,102
Texas	25,145,561

13. **Number Sense** Write the population of Florida in expanded form using exponents.

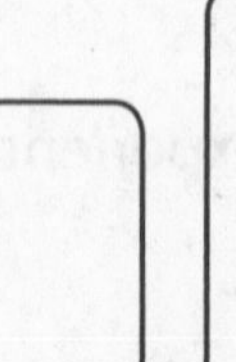

Assessment Practice

14. Joseph says that in the number 9,999,999, all the digits have the same value.

Part A

Is Joseph correct? Explain.

Part B

Describe the relationship between the values of the digits in the number.

Name ______________________

Video Practice Tools Games

Additional Practice 1-3
Decimals to Thousandths

Another Look!

Patterns can help you read and write decimals.

Decimal	Fraction	Number Name
0.1	$\frac{1}{10}$	One tenth
0.01	$\frac{1}{100}$	One hundredth
0.001	$\frac{1}{1,000}$	One thousandth

0.01 is 10 times as great as 0.001.

0.01 is $\frac{1}{10}$ as great as 0.1.

0.1 is 10 times as great as 0.01.

The value of each place-value position is 10 times the value of the place to its right and $\frac{1}{10}$ the value of the place to its left.

1. 0.08 is 10 times as great as __________.

2. 0.002 is $\frac{1}{10}$ of __________.

3. 0.5 is 10 times as great as __________.

4. 0.07 is $\frac{1}{10}$ of __________.

In **5–12**, write each decimal as a fraction.

5. 0.009 **6.** 0.105 **7.** 0.2 **8.** 0.025

9. 0.563 **10.** 0.31 **11.** 0.6 **12.** 0.004

In **13–20**, write each fraction as a decimal.

13. $\frac{8}{1,000}$ **14.** $\frac{63}{100}$ **15.** $\frac{984}{1,000}$ **16.** $\frac{29}{1,000}$

17. $\frac{111}{1,000}$ **18.** $\frac{3}{10}$ **19.** $\frac{6}{1,000}$ **20.** $\frac{5}{1,000}$

21. **Number Sense** Tommy is beginning a science experiment in the lab. The instructions call for 0.322 kilogram of potassium. Write 0.322 as a fraction.

22. Mt. McKinley is the highest mountain peak in North America with an elevation of 20,320 feet. What is the value of the digit 3 in 20,320?

23. **Construct Arguments** Jorge said that 0.029 can be written as $\frac{29}{100}$. Is he correct? Explain.

24. The area of the continent of North America is about 9,540,000 square miles. Write 9,540,000 in expanded form using exponents to show powers of 10.

25. What part of the entire square is shaded? Write your answer as a fraction and as a decimal.

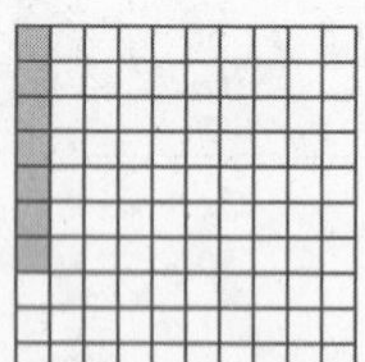

26. **Higher Order Thinking** Write the fractions $\frac{5}{10}$, $\frac{5}{100}$, and $\frac{5}{1,000}$ as decimals. How are the decimals related?

27. **Vocabulary** Complete the sentence using one of the words below.

power **base** **exponent**

The number 1,000,000 is a(n) ________ of 10.

28. **Algebra** In three months, Harold watched a total of 40 movies. If he watched 12 movies in June and 13 movies in July, how many movies did he watch in August? Write an equation using the variable *a* to model your work.

Assessment Practice

29. 0.003 is $\frac{1}{10}$ of which decimal?

Ⓐ 0.3

Ⓑ 0.03

Ⓒ 0.33

Ⓓ 0.333

30. 0.8 is 10 times as great as which decimal?

Ⓐ 0.08

Ⓑ 0.88

Ⓒ 0.008

Ⓓ 0.888

Name ____________________

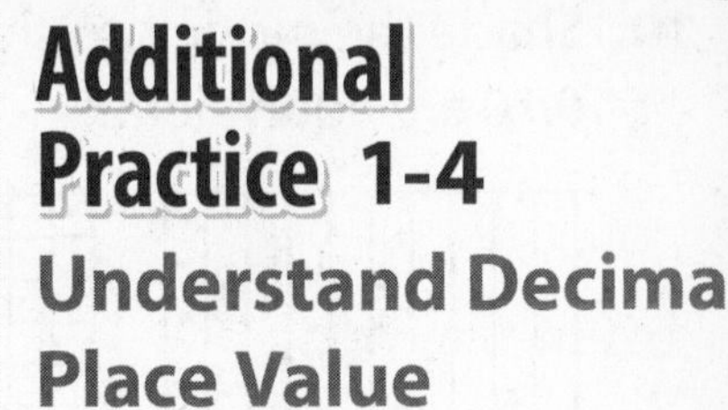

Another Look!

One of the largest ostrich eggs laid weighed 5.476 pounds. What is the value of the digit 6 in 5.476?

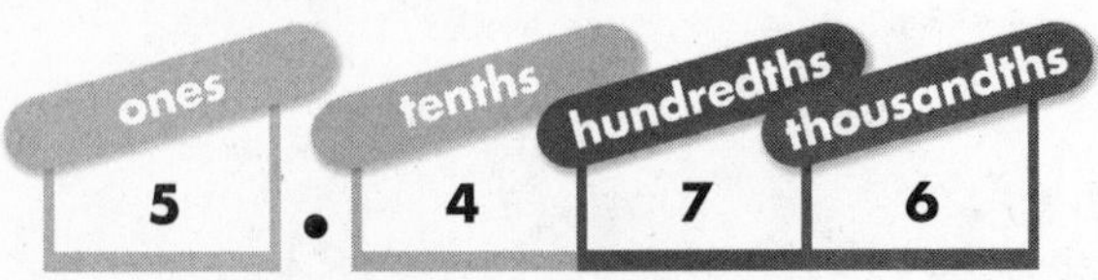

A place-value chart can show you the value of each digit in a decimal.

Standard Form: 5.476

Expanded Form: $(5 \times 1) + \left(4 \times \frac{1}{10}\right) + \left(7 \times \frac{1}{100}\right) + \left(6 \times \frac{1}{1{,}000}\right)$

Number Name: Five and four hundred seventy-six thousandths

The digit 6 is in the thousandths place, so the value is 0.006.

1. Complete the place-value chart for the following number. Write its number name and tell the value of the underlined digit.

6.3<u>2</u>4

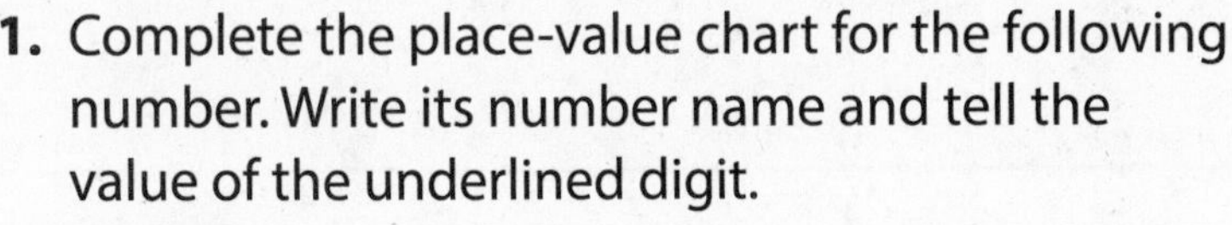

2. Write 863.141 in expanded form.

In **3–5**, write each number in standard form.

3. $(8 \times 1) + \left(5 \times \frac{1}{100}\right) + \left(9 \times \frac{1}{1{,}000}\right)$

4. $1 + 0.9 + 0.08 + 0.001$

5. Four hundred twenty-five and fifty-two hundredths

In **6–9**, write two decimals that are equivalent to the given decimal.

6. 5.300

7. 3.7

8. 0.9

9. 2.50

10. Shade the models to show that 0.7 and 0.70 are equivalent.

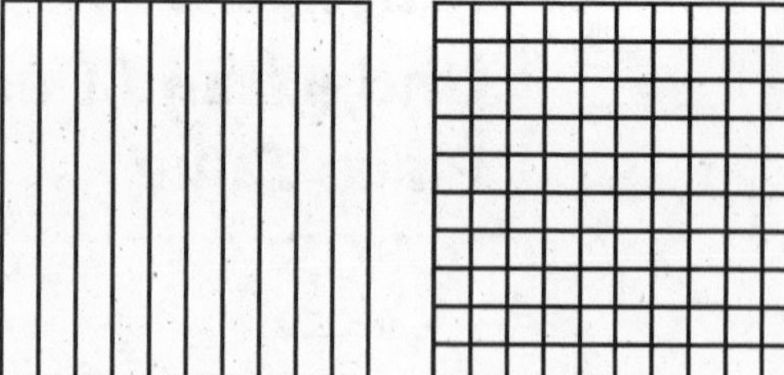

11. Marco has a piece of wood that measures $9 \times \frac{1}{10} + 6 \times \frac{1}{100} + 4 \times \frac{1}{1,000}$ meter. How can this measurement be written as a decimal?

12. There are 275 people in the movie theater. The same number of people are seated in each of the 5 different sections of the theater. How many people are seated in each section?

275 people

?	?	?	?	?

13. Construct Arguments Cheryl's softball batting average is 0.340, and Karin's is 0.304. Karin says they have the same average. What error did she make? Explain.

14. Number Sense Nico spent eight dollars and seventy-five cents on lunch. Which two items did Nico buy?

DATA

Lunch Menu

Item	Price
Hamburger	\$4.20
Chef Salad	\$4.50
Tuna Sandwich	\$4.05
Pizza	\$4.25

15. Higher Order Thinking Anthony drew a pentagon with each side measuring 6 inches. Carol drew a hexagon with each side measuring 5 inches. Which shape has a greater perimeter? Write an equation to help explain your answer.

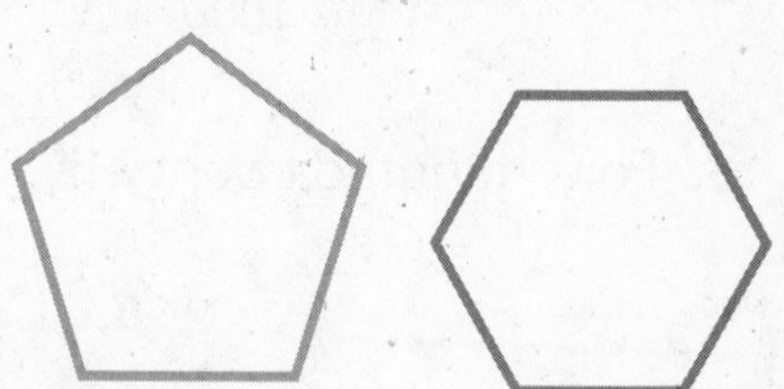

Assessment Practice

16. Find two decimals that are equivalent to $(8 \times 100) + \left(3 \times \frac{1}{10}\right) + \left(6 \times \frac{1}{100}\right)$. Write the decimals in the box.

8.36 800.36 800.036 800.306 8.360 800.360

Name ______________________

Additional Practice 1-5

Compare Decimals

Another Look!

Amanda completed a race in 8.016 minutes. Liz's time was 7.03 minutes, and Steve's time was 8.16 minutes. Order the times from least to greatest. Who won the race?

Remember, the winner of a race is the person who ran it in the least amount of time.

Write the numbers, lining up the decimal points. Start at the left. Compare digits of the same place value. 8.016 7.03 8.16 7.03 is the least.	Write the remaining numbers, lining up the decimal points. Start at the left. Compare. 8.016 8.16 8.16 is greater than 8.016.	Liz won the race! 7.03, 8.016, 8.16

1. Order the speeds from least to greatest.

2. Driver D had a speed between Driver A and Driver C. Write a possible speed for Driver D.

DATA

Driver	Average Speed (mph)
Driver A	145.155
Driver B	145.827
Driver C	144.809

In **3–8**, write >, <. or = for each ◯.

3. 7.539 ◯ 7.344

4. 9.202 ◯ 9.209

5. 0.75 ◯ 0.750

6. 4.953 ◯ 4.951

7. 1.403 ◯ 1.4

8. 3.074 ◯ 3.740

In **9–12**, order from greatest to least.

9. 9.129, 9.37, 9.3, 9.219

10. 0.012, 0.100, 0.001, 0.101

11. 5.132, 5.123, 5.312, 5.231

12. 62.905, 62.833, 62.950, 62.383

13. Write three different fractions that each match the shaded part of the drawing.

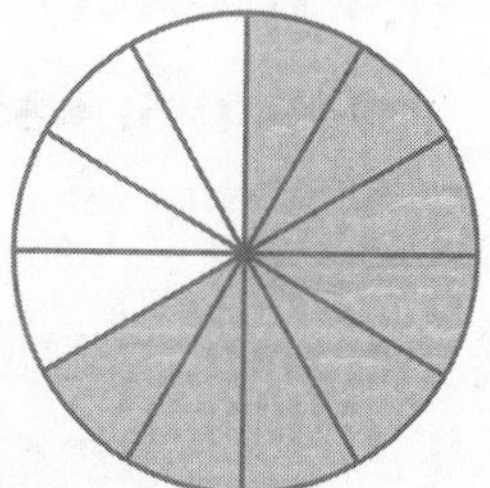

14. The total cost to stay one night at Sleepy Head Motel is $119 without breakfast and $142 with breakfast included. What is the difference in the cost for a one-night stay with and without breakfast?

$142	
$119	?

15. **Make Sense and Persevere** Tanya bought the least expensive brand of dog food. Eddie bought the most expensive brand of dog food. Which brand did each person buy?

DATA

Dog Food Sale

Brand	Price per bag
A	$12.49
B	$11.55
C	$12.09
D	$11.59

16. Why can it help to line up the decimal points before comparing and ordering numbers with decimals?

17. **Higher Order Thinking** The heights of four boys measured 152.0 cm, 150.75 cm, 149.5 cm, and 149.25 cm. Bradley is the tallest. Calvin is taller than Josh, but shorter than Mark. Josh is the shortest. What is Mark's height?

Assessment Practice

18. Which statements correctly compare two numbers?

- ☐ $28.435 < 28.431$
- ☐ $28.404 < 28.342$
- ☐ $28.430 < 28.431$
- ☐ $28.431 > 28.419$
- ☐ $28.42 > 28.404$

19. Michael averaged 22.075 points per game. Which numbers make the statement true?

$\square < 22.075$

- ☐ 21.9
- ☐ 22.08
- ☐ 23.06
- ☐ 22.07
- ☐ 22.079

Name ______________________

Video Practice Tools Games

Additional Practice 1-6

Round Decimals

Another Look!

An African Watusi steer's horn measures 95.25 centimeters around. What is 95.25 rounded to the nearest tenth?

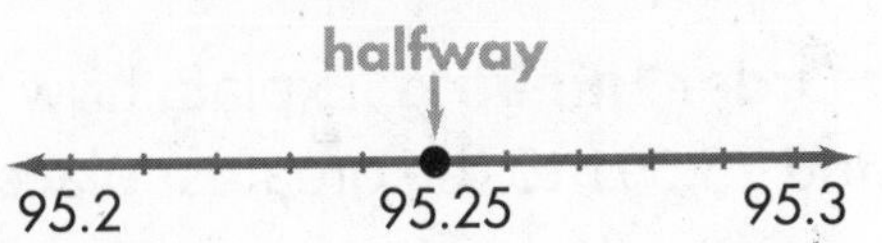

On a number line, 95.25 is halfway between 95.2 and 95.3.

Step 1	Step 2	Step 3
Find the rounding place. Look at the digit to the right of the rounding place. 95.$\underline{2}$5	If the digit is 5 or greater, increase the rounding digit by 1. If the digit is less than 5, the rounding digit stays the same. The digit to the right is 5, so increase the 2 in the tenths place to 3.	Drop the digits to the right of the rounding digit. 95.25 rounded to the nearest tenth is 95.3.

1. Ian mailed a package that weighed 5.63 pounds. What is the first step in rounding this number to the nearest tenth? What is the next step? What is 5.63 rounded to the nearest tenth?

In **2–5**, round each decimal to the nearest whole number.

2. 6.7 **3.** 12.1 **4.** 30.92 **5.** 1.086

In **6–13**, round each number to the place of the underlined digit.

6. 32.$\underline{6}$5 **7.** 3.2$\underline{4}$6 **8.** 41.$\underline{0}$73 **9.** 0.4$\underline{2}$4

10. 6.$\underline{0}$99 **11.** 6.$\underline{1}$3 **12.** 18$\underline{3}$.92 **13.** 905.2$\underline{5}$5

14. **Vocabulary** Complete the sentence using one of the words below.

power **base** **exponent**

In 10^6, the 10 is the ________.

15. **Be Precise** If the area of a park is exactly halfway between 2.4 and 2.5 acres, what is the area of the park?

16. Does the line appear to be a line of symmetry of the triangle? Explain.

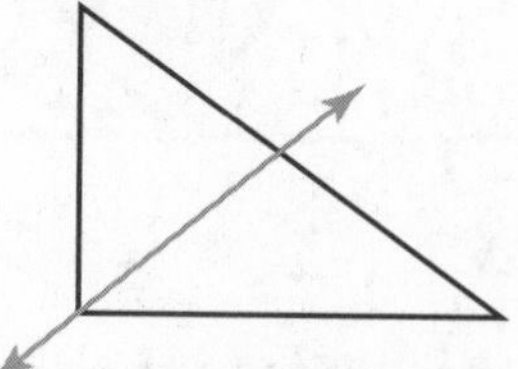

17. **Higher Order Thinking** Explain how you can round 25.691 to the greatest place.

18. A professional baseball team won 84 games this season. The team won 14 more games than it lost. There were no ties. How many games did the team lose? How many did it play?

?	
84	?

19. Rounded to the nearest dime, what is the greatest amount of money that rounds to \$105.40? What is the least amount of money that rounds to \$105.40? Explain your answers.

20. **enVision® STEM** The students in Mr. Bhatia's class measure the length of four bees. The students round the lengths to the nearest tenth. Whose bee has a length that rounds to 0.5 inch? 0.8 inch?

DATA

Student	Bee Lengths
Isabel	0.841 inch
Pablo	0.45 inch
Wendi	0.55 inch
Brett	0.738 inch

Assessment Practice

21. Find two numbers that round to 15.5 when rounded to the nearest tenth. Write the numbers in the box.

15.04 15.55 15.508 15.445 15.0 15.49

Name ______________________

Additional Practice 1-7
Look For and Use Structure

Another Look!

This grid is a part of a decimal number chart similar to the one on page 30 of the lesson. Write the missing number in each of the lettered squares.

Tell how you can use structure.

Analyze the number pattern to find the structure of the grid.
Use the pattern to write the missing numbers.

Moving down and left, the tenths increase by 1, and the hundredths decrease by 1.
The number in Box A is 0.34.
The number in Box B is 0.43.
The number in Box C is 0.61.

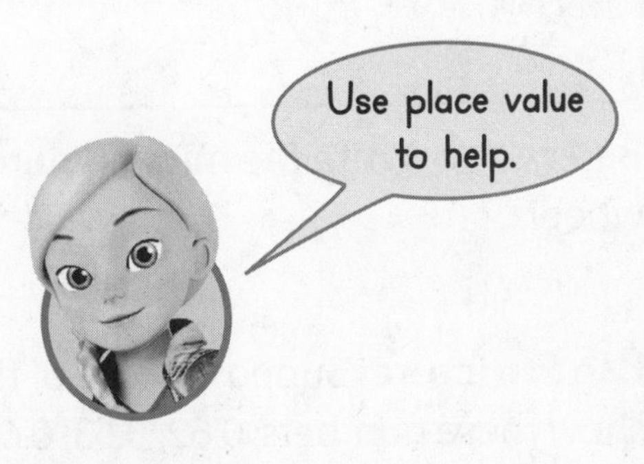

Use Structure

In **1–3**, each grid is a part of a decimal number chart similar to the one on page 30 of the lesson. Write the missing numbers.

1.

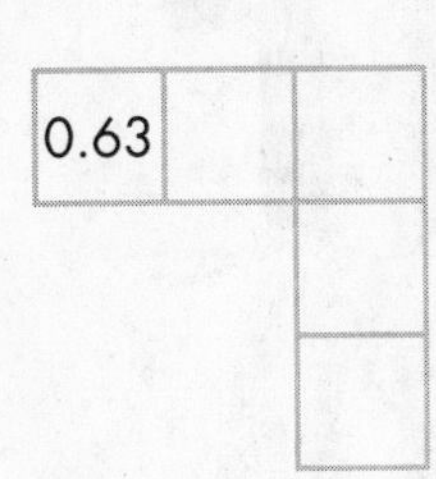

2.

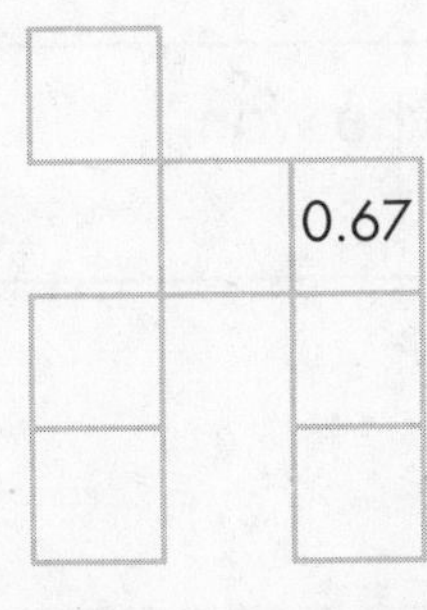

3.

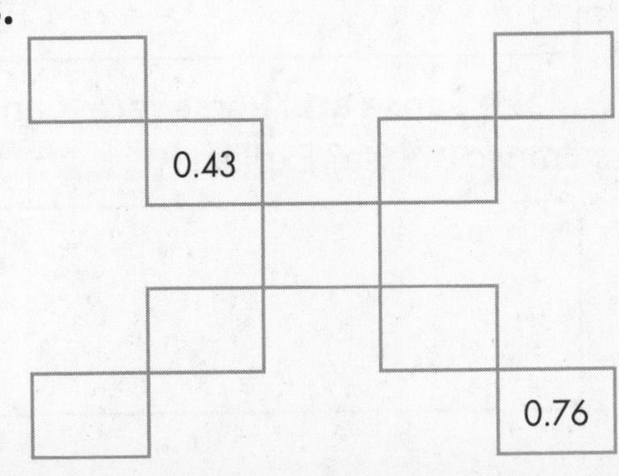

Performance Task

Decimal Wheels

Franco and Lisa are playing a game with decimal numbers. The first player to correctly write the missing numbers in each decimal wheel is the winner.

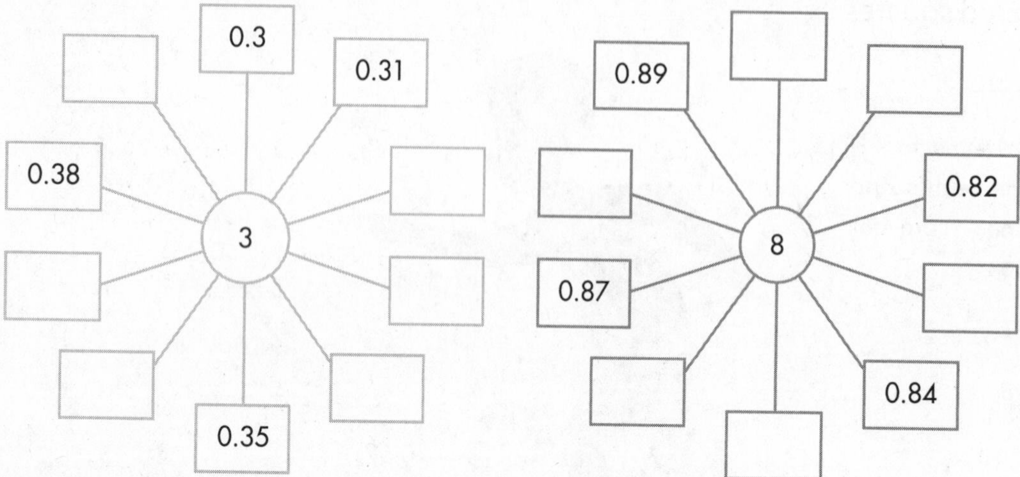

4. **Use Repeated Reasoning** Starting at the top, as you move clockwise around the wheel, how do the numbers change?

5. **Be Precise** Write the missing numbers in each decimal wheel.

6. **Use Structure** Suppose some of the boxes in a decimal wheel show these numbers: 0.62, 0.63, 0.67, and 0.69. Explain how to use structure to find the number that is written in the circle at the center of the decimal wheel.

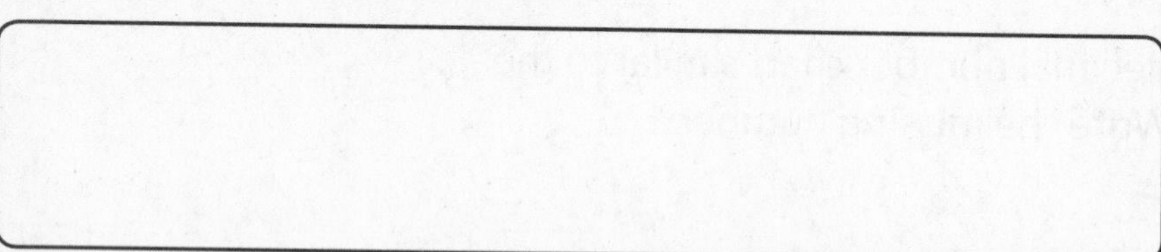

7. **Make Sense and Persevere** Can you tell who won, Franco or Lisa? Explain.

Thinking about decimal place value helps you understand the structure of decimal numbers.

Name ____________________

Additional Practice 2-1
Mental Math

Another Look!

You can use properties of addition, compatible numbers, or compensation to help you find the answers.

Use properties of addition to find 5.7 + 6 + 4.3.	Use compensation to find 12.7 + 0.9.	Use compensation to find 18.3 − 6.9.
5.7 + 6 + 4.3 Use the Commutative Property. 5.7 + 4.3 + 6 Add. 10 + 6 = 16	12.7 + 0.9. Add 0.1 to 0.9. 12.7 + 1 = 13.7 Subtract 0.1. 12.7 + 0.9 = 13.6	18.3 − 6.9. Add 0.1 to 6.9. 18.3 − 7 = 11.3 0.1 too much was subtracted. Add 0.1. 18.3 − 6.9 = 11.4

Leveled Practice In **1–15**, use properties and mental math to solve.

1. 275 + 180 + 120 =
275 + ______ =
______

2. 19.5 + 24 + 7.5 =
19.5 + ______ + 24 =
______ + 24 = ______

3. 87.2 − 25.9 =
87.2 − ______ = 61.2
______ + 0.1 = ______

4. 8.4 + 6.21 + 2.6

5. 7.35 + 1.47 + 9.65

6. 12.32 − 8

7. 75.25 − 11.92

8. 34.76 + 170 + 16.24

9. 54.3 − 19.74

10. 192.63 − 7.95

11. 201.96 + 38.7 + 0.84

12. 100.6 + 296.5

13. 421.2 − 305.8

14. 1,050 + 815 + 250

15. \$5.40 + \$8.70 + \$6.30

16. James is buying school supplies. He buys a notebook for $2.45, a package of mechanical pencils for $3.79, and an eraser for $1.55. Use mental math to find how much he spent in all.

17. Generalize How is using mental math to add with decimals like using mental math to add whole numbers? How is it different?

18. Isabel made the following graph to show the daily share price for Company XYZ. What was the change in the price from Monday to Friday?

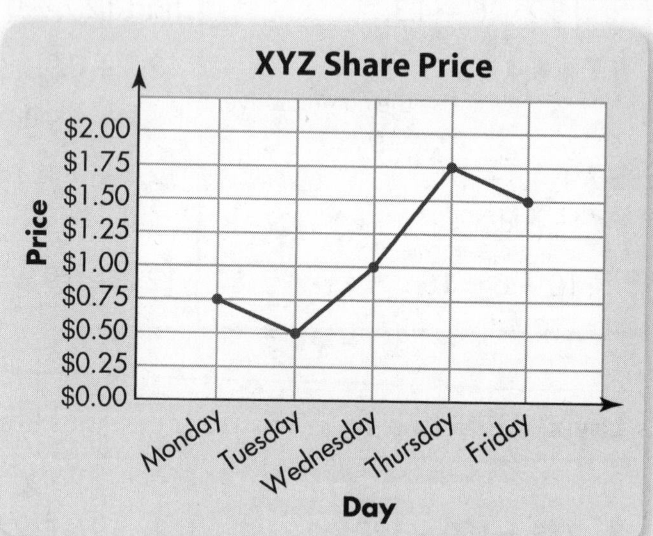

19. Higher Order Thinking Julia went to the supermarket and bought a dozen eggs, two pounds of bananas, and a jar of tomato sauce. A store coupon for $0.70 off any purchase does not appear on the receipt. If Julia used the coupon, how much did she spend in all?

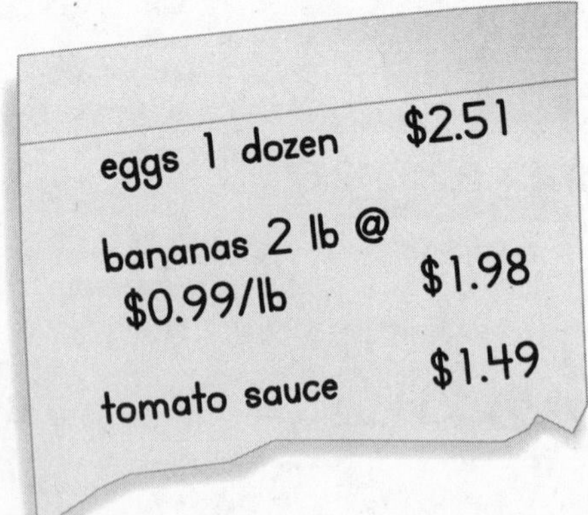

Assessment Practice

20. In a week Karry ran 9.3 miles and Tricia ran 4.4 miles. Use mental math to find how much farther Karry ran than Tricia. Explain how you determined the difference.

Name ____________________

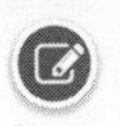

Games

Additional Practice 2-2

Estimate Sums and Differences

Another Look!

During one week, Mr. Graham drove a truck to four different towns to make deliveries. Estimate how far he drove in all. About how much farther did he drive on Wednesday than on Monday?

DATA

Mr. Graham's Mileage Log

Day	Cities	Mileage
Monday	Mansley to Mt. Hazel	243.5
Tuesday	Mt. Hazel to Perkins	303
Wednesday	Perkins to Alberton	279.1
Thursday	Alberton to Fort Maynard	277.4

Round each number to the nearest hundred.

243.5 → 200
303 → 300
279.1 → 300
+ 277.4 → + 300
1,100

Mr. Graham drove about 1,100 miles.

Estimate the difference to the nearest ten.

279.1 → 280
− 243.5 → − 240
40

Mr. Graham drove about 40 more miles on Wednesday than on Monday.

1. Marisol rode her bicycle each day for five days. Estimate how far she biked in all. Round each number to the nearest whole number.

12 + ____ + 18 + ____ + ____ = ____

She biked about ____ miles.

DATA

Marisol's Bike Rides

Day	Mileage
Monday	12.3
Tuesday	14.1
Wednesday	17.7
Thursday	11.8
Friday	15.2

2. About how much farther did she bike on Wednesday than on Thursday?

18 − ____ = ____

She biked about ____ more miles on Wednesday.

Estimate each sum or difference.

3. 19.7 − 6.9

4. 59 + 43.6

5. 5.82 + 1.69 + 2.3

6. 87.99 − 52.46

7. **enVision® STEM** About how many more inches of rain did Asheville get than Wichita? About how many more days did it rain in Asheville than Wichita?

DATA

Average Yearly Rainfall of U.S. Cities

City	Inches	Days
Asheville, North Carolina	47.71	124
Wichita, Kansas	28.61	85

8. Four friends made a bar graph to show how many baseball cards they collected over the summer.

About how many cards did they collect in all?

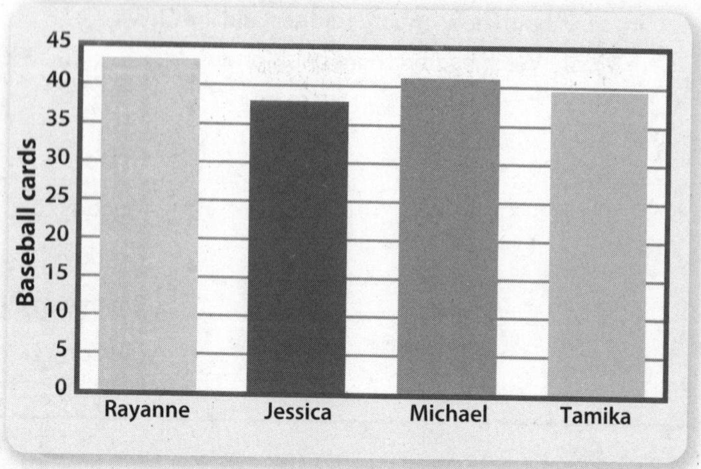

9. **Construct Arguments** Estimate the total weight of two boxes that weigh 9.4 pounds and 62.6 pounds using rounding and compatible numbers. Which estimate is closer to the actual total weight? Why?

10. **Higher Order Thinking** A gardener is estimating the amount of mulch needed for two garden beds. There is no room to store extra mulch. Is it better to estimate a greater or lesser amount than the mulch he needs? Why?

Assessment Practice

11. Martha bought an apple for $0.89 and a drink for $1.95. Which is the best estimate of how much money she spent?

Ⓐ $2.00

Ⓑ $3.00

Ⓒ $4.00

Ⓓ $5.00

12. Rachel bought a book for $5.49 and a game for $10.98. She paid with a $20 bill. Which is the best estimate of the amount of change she should receive?

Ⓐ $4

Ⓑ $6

Ⓒ $14

Ⓓ $16

Name ______________________

Additional Practice 2-3

Use Models to Add and Subtract Decimals

Another Look!

Find 0.22 + 0.17.

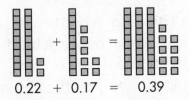

0.22 + 0.17 = 0.39

Step 1

Show 0.22 and 0.17 with place-value blocks.

Step 2

Combine the blocks.
Regroup if possible.

So, 0.22 + 0.17 = 0.39.

Find 0.61 − 0.42.

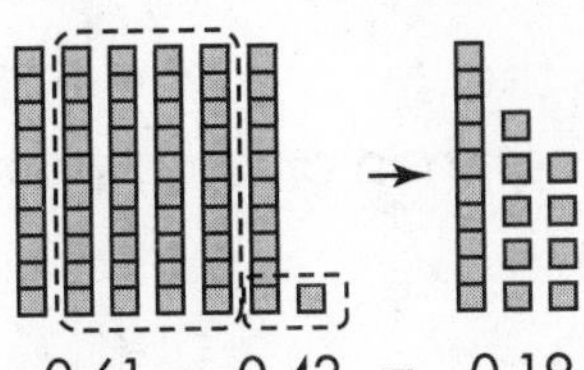

0.61 − 0.42 = 0.19

Step 1

Show 0.61 with place-value blocks.

Step 2

Regroup if necessary. Remove 0.42.

So, 0.61 − 0.42 = 0.19.

Count all the tenths and hundredths blocks to find the sum and circle and remove blocks to find the difference.

In **1–8**, use place-value blocks to add or subtract.

1. 0.27 + 0.19 = ____

2. 0.39 − 0.14 = ____

3. 0.68 − 0.24 = ____

4. 0.88 + 0.25 = ____

5. 2.88 − 0.59 = ____

6. 1.24 + 0.44 = ____

7. 0.96 + 1.05 = ____

8. 0.52 − 0.19 = ____

9. Write the number sentence that is shown by the place-value blocks to the right.

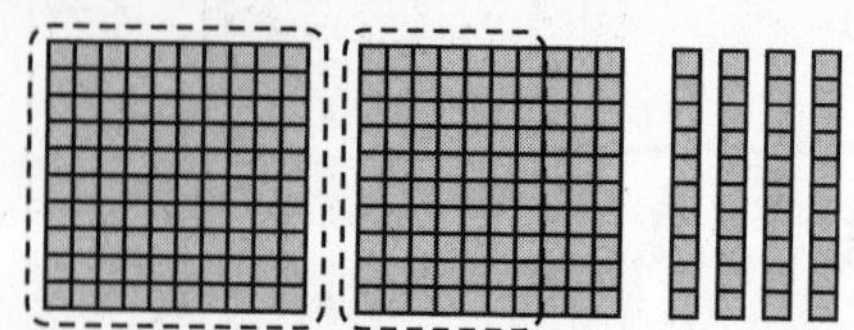

10. Construct Arguments Is the difference of 1.48 – 0.25 less than or greater than one? Explain.

11. Higher Order Thinking A bottle of perfume holds 0.55 fluid ounce. A bottle of cologne holds 0.2 fluid ounce. How many more fluid ounces does the bottle of perfume hold?

12. As part of his workout, Jamal does 2 sets of 25 push-ups. If he does this 10 times each month, how many push-ups does he do each month? Write an equation to show your work.

13. The smallest video camera in the world is 0.99 millimeter in diameter. Is the diameter of the video camera less than or great than 0.1 millimeter?

14. A restaurant bought 48.5 pounds of apples from a local orchard. The next month, the restaurant bought another 65.3 pounds of apples and 24.5 pounds of pears. How many pounds of fruit did the restaurant buy?

15. Write an expression that is represented by the model below.

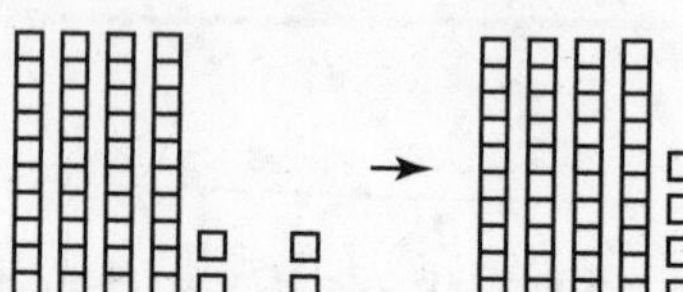

Assessment Practice

16. Each set of place-value blocks below represents a decimal.

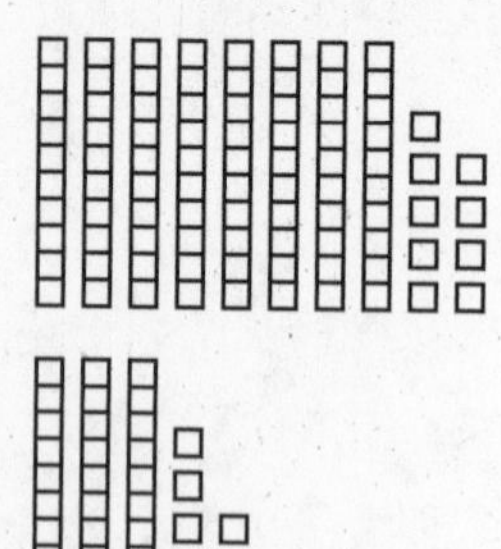

Part A

What is the sum of the decimals?

Part B

Explain how you found your answer.

Name ______________________________

Additional Practice 2-4
Add Decimals

Another Look!

A scientist used 0.62 milliliter of solution for an experiment and 0.56 milliliter of solution for a different experiment. How much solution did he use for the two experiments?

You can estimate first to be sure that your answer is reasonable. Both 0.62 and 0.56 are close to 0.5. So the answer will be close to 0.5 + 0.5 = 1.

Write the numbers, lining up the digits by place value. Include the zeros as place holders in the ones place.

ones .	tenths	hundredths
0 .	6	2
+ 0 .	5	6

Add by place value.

ones .	tenths	hundredths	
0 .	6	2	
+ 0 .	5	6	
.	0	8	(0.02 + 0.06)
1 .	1		(0.6 + 0.5)
1 .	1	8	

The scientist used 1.18 milliliters of solution.

Leveled Practice In **1–11**, use place value and properties of operations to find the sum.

1. 55.25 + 298 + 16.3

```
  55.25
   2.98
+ 16.30
```

2.

```
  37.2
 103.
+  8.52
```

3.

```
  2.97
+ 0.35
```

4.

```
  5.62
+ 7.99
```

5.

```
 23.59
+ 6.56
```

6. 13 + 7.69

7. 41.5 + 12.61

8. 39.48 + 26.7

9. 67.55 + 0.83

10. 88.8 + 4.27 + 78.95

11. 2.94 + 45 + 58.06

For **12** and **13**, use the table.

12. How much combined snowfall was there in Milwaukee and Oklahoma City?

13. What is the combined snowfall total for all three cities?

DATA

City	Snowfall (inches) in 2000
Milwaukee, WI	87.8
Baltimore, MD	27.2
Oklahoma City, OK	17.3

In science class, students weighed different amounts of clay. Carmen's weighed 4.361 ounces, Kim's weighed 2.704 ounces, Simon's weighed 5.295 ounces, and Angelica's weighed 8.537 ounces.

14. How many ounces of clay did Carmen and Angelica have in all?

15. How many ounces of clay did Kim and Simon have in all?

16. Three bags of beads have masses of 10.3 grams, 5.23 grams, and 3.74 grams. Complete the bar diagram to find the total mass of all the beads.

? grams of beads → ?

bag 1 ____ | bag 2 ____ | bag 3 ____

17. Reasoning Reilly adds 45.3 and 3.21. Should his sum be greater than or less than 48? Tell how you know.

18. Higher Order Thinking Patrick has a 600-meter skein of yarn. He used 248.9 meters of yarn to make a hat. Does he have enough yarn left to make a scarf that uses 354.03 meters of yarn? Explain.

Assessment Practice

19. Choose all expressions that are equal to 15.02.

- ☐ 12.96 + 2.06
- ☐ 0.56 + 14.64
- ☐ 2.62 + 12.4
- ☐ 1.22 + 1.8 + 12
- ☐ 1 + 0.5 + 13.8

20. Choose all expressions that are equal to 13.99.

- ☐ 13 + 0.9
- ☐ 6.25 + 3.9 + 3.84
- ☐ 4.635 + 9.355
- ☐ 8 + 5.99
- ☐ 10 + 3.09

Name ______________________

Practice

Video

Tools

Games

Additional Practice 2-5
Subtract Decimals

Another Look!

Mr. Montoya bought 3.5 pounds of ground beef. He used 2.38 pounds to make hamburgers. How much ground beef does he have left?

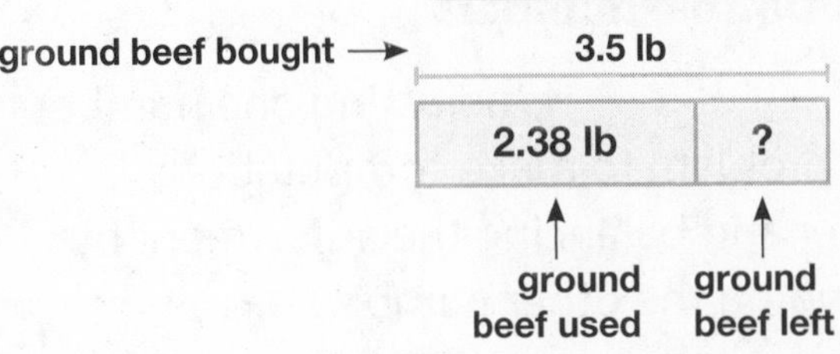

You can use a number line to subtract.

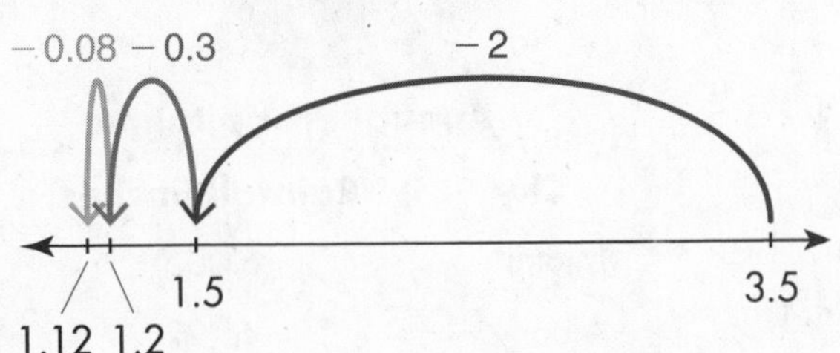

You can subtract using partial differences.

Find 3.5 − 2.38

$$
\begin{array}{rl}
3.50 & \\
-\ 2.00 & \text{subtract 2 ones} \\
\hline
1.50 & \\
-\ .30 & \text{subtract 3 tenths} \\
\hline
1.20 & \\
-\ .08 & \text{subtract 8 hundredths} \\
\hline
1.12 &
\end{array}
$$

3.5 − 2.38 = 1.12

1. Anya bought 1.4 pounds of peaches. She used 0.37 pound in a fruit salad. How much is left? Use the bar diagram to help you.

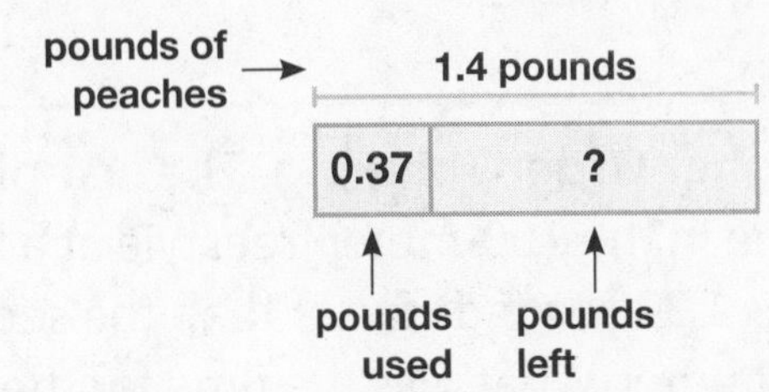

Leveled Practice In **2–7**, find the difference.

2. 82.7 − 5.59

3. 43.3 − 12.82

4. 7.28 − 4.9

5. $72.35 − $6.19

6. 1.24 − 0.92

7. 6.04 − 3.48

8. **Vocabulary** Complete the sentence using one of the terms below.

Commutative property
Compensation
Compatible numbers

__________ is adjusting one number in a problem to make computations easier and balancing the adjustment by changing the other number.

9. Describe the steps you would use to subtract 7.6 from 20.39.

In **10** and **11**, use the table.

10. **enVision® STEM** How much greater was Miami's annual rainfall than Albany's?

11. The annual rainfall in Albany is 0.33 inch less than the annual rainfall in Nashville. How much less rainfall did Nashville get than Miami? Show your work.

Annual Precipitation

City	Rainfall (inches)
Miami	61.05
Albany	46.92

12. **Model with Math** Lila would like to take a ceramics class. The class costs $120. She has saved $80 so far. Use the bar diagram to write and solve an equation to find the amount that Lila still needs.

$120	
$80	*d*

13. **Higher Order Thinking** The first-place swimmer's time in the 100-meter freestyle at a local swim meet was 1.32 seconds faster than the second-place swimmer. What was the time for the first-place swimmer? What was the difference in time between the second- and third-place swimmers?

100-m Freestyle

Finish	Time (seconds)
First	?
Second	49.33
Third	53.65

Assessment Practice

14. Circle the two subtraction problems that have a difference of 10.2.

12.05 – 2.03
16.29 – 6.09
36.1 – 25.9
22.09 – 21.07
10.82 – 9.8

Name ___________________

Practice Video Tools Games

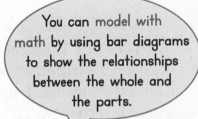

Additional Practice 2-6
Model with Math

Another Look!

For her birthday, Lucy received $20 from her aunt, $15 from her grandmother, and $32 from her cousins. She bought an e-book for $10.85. How much birthday money does Lucy have left?

Show how you can model this problem.

I can use bar diagrams and equations to represent and solve this problem.

How much money did Lucy receive?

? total money received

$20	$15	$32

$20 + $15 + $32 = $67 received

How much money does Lucy have left?

$67 total received

$10.85	? money left

$67.00 – $10.85 = $56.15 Lucy has $56.15 left.

You can model with math by using bar diagrams to show the relationships between the whole and the parts.

Model with Math

Jeffrey earned $65 doing yard work. He bought a pair of jeans for $31.25 and a sweatshirt for $16.50. He set aside the money left from his shopping trip to buy a gift for his cousin. How much money did he set aside for the gift?

1. What do you need to find before you can solve the problem?

2. Draw bar diagrams to represent the problem.

Remember, a bar diagram clearly shows how the quantities in the problem are related.

3. Write equations to represent the problem. Then solve the problem.

Performance Task

Snowfall

The total snowfall for last year was 36.4 inches. The graph shows snowfalls for 3 months last year and for the same 3 months this year. Find how much greater this year's 3-month snowfall was than last year's.

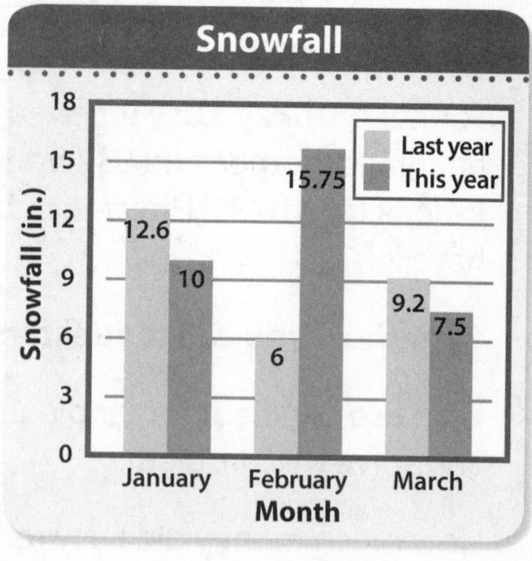

4. **Make Sense and Persevere** Do you need all of the information given to solve the problem? Explain.

5. **Model with Math** Draw bar diagrams to represent last year's total 3-month snowfall and this year's total 3-month snowfall. Then find the total 3-month snowfalls for each year.

6. **Model with Math** Write and solve an equation to find how much greater this year's 3-month snowfall was than last year's.

7. **Reasoning** Describe a way to determine how much more snow needs to fall so this year's total is 37.4 inches. Then find the answer.

When you model with math, you decide what steps need to be completed to find the final answer.

Name ______________________

Practice Video Tools Games

Additional Practice 3-1

Multiply Greater Numbers by Powers of 10

Another Look!

Patterns can help you multiply by powers of 10.

$53 \times 1 = 53$	$70 \times 1 = 70$
$53 \times 10 = 530$	$70 \times 10^1 = 700$
$53 \times 100 = 5{,}300$	$70 \times 10^2 = 7{,}000$
$53 \times 1{,}000 = 53{,}000$	$70 \times 10^3 = 70{,}000$
$53 \times 10{,}000 = 530{,}000$	$70 \times 10^4 = 700{,}000$

Look at the number of zeros or the exponent for the power of 10. Place that number of zeros on the end of the other factor.

1. To find $61 \times 1{,}000$, place _____ zeros on the end of _____ to form the product _______.

In **2–5**, use patterns to find each product.

2. 75×1
75×10
75×100
$75 \times 1{,}000$
$75 \times 10{,}000$

3. 50×1
50×10
50×100
$50 \times 1{,}000$
$50 \times 10{,}000$

4. 60×1
60×10^1
60×10^2
60×10^3
60×10^4

5. 18×1
18×10^1
18×10^2
18×10^3
18×10^4

In **6–9**, find each product.

6. 84×100

7. 90×10

8. 54×10^2

9. $10^3 \times 12$

In **10–15**, use reasoning to fill in the missing numbers.

10. $45 \times 10^3 =$ _______

11. $12{,}960 = 10^1 \times$ _______

12. $22 \times 10^{\_} = 220{,}000$

13. $10^4 \times 30 =$ _______

14. $10^{\_} \times 374 = 37{,}400$

15. $70{,}000 = 70 \times 10^{\_}$

16. **Construct Arguments** Ms. O'Malley's cousin lives 1,650 miles away. Ms. O'Malley won a gift card for 100 gallons of gas. If her car can travel 35 miles on each gallon, can she drive roundtrip to see her cousin on the free gas? Explain how you know.

17. Each beehive on Larson's Honey Farm usually produces 85 pounds of honey per year. About how many pounds of honey will 10^3 hives produce in a year?

18. A hotel chain is ordering new furnishings. What is the total cost of 1,000 sheet sets, 1,000 pillows, and 100 desk chairs?

DATA

Item	Price
Towel sets	$18
Sheet sets	$24
Pillows	$7
Desk chair	$114

19. Which number is greater: 87 or 13.688? How do you know?

20. **Higher Order Thinking** The weight of an elephant is 10^3 times the weight of a cat. If the elephant weighs 14,000 pounds, how many pounds does the cat weigh? How did you find the answer?

Assessment Practice

21. Which is equivalent to multiplying a number by 10^3?

Ⓐ multiplying by 30
Ⓑ multiplying by 1,000
Ⓒ multiplying by 10,000
Ⓓ multiplying by 10 twice

22. Which is equivalent to 5×10^4? Select all that apply.

☐ $5 \times 10{,}000$
☐ $5 \times 100{,}000$
☐ 5,000
☐ 50,000
☐ 50×10^3

Name ______________________

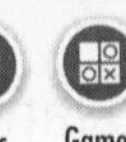
Practice Video Tools Games

Additional Practice 3-2
Estimate Products

Another Look!

Mrs. Carter orders new supplies for a hospital. About how much will it cost to purchase 14 pulse monitors?

DATA

Supplies	
Electronic thermometers	$19 each
Pulse monitors	$189 each
Pillows	$17 each
Telephones	$19 each

Use rounding to estimate.

Estimate 14 × 189.

You can round 14 to 10 and 189 to 200.

10 × 200 = 2,000

Use compatible numbers to estimate.

Estimate 14 × 189.

Replace 14 with 15 and 189 with 200.

15 × 200 = 3,000

The 14 pulse monitors will cost between $2,000 and $3,000.

1. About how much would it cost to buy 18 MP3 players? About how much would it cost to buy 18 CD/MP3 players?

DATA

Electronics Prices	
CD player	$74.00
MP3 player	$99.00
CD/MP3 player	$199.00
AM/FM radio	$29.00

In **2–15**, estimate each product.

2. 184 × 210
Round 184 to ______.
Round 210 to ______.
Multiply ______ × ______ = ______.

3. 77 × 412
Round 77 to ______.
Round 412 to ______.
Multiply ______ × ______ = ______.

4. 87 × 403

5. 19 × 718

6. 888 × 300

7. 352 × 20

8. 520 × 797

9. 189 × 46

10. 560 × 396

11. 498 × 47

12. 492 × 22

13. 928 × 89

14. 308 × 18

15. 936 × 410

16. Laura's family is going on a vacation. They will drive 4,180 miles over the next two weeks. About how many miles will they drive on average each week?

17. **Make Sense and Persevere** A bus service drives passengers between Milwaukee and Chicago every day. They travel from city to city 8 times each day. The distance between the two cities is 89 miles. In February, there are 28 days. The company's budget allows for 28,000 total miles for February. Do you think the budget is reasonable? Explain.

18. **Higher Order Thinking** Explain whether rounding or compatible numbers gives a closer estimate for the product below.

$48 \times 123 = 5{,}904$

19. A case of 24 pairs of the same kind of sports shoes costs a little more than $800. Explain whether $28 per pair with tax included is a good estimate of the price.

20. The number of Adult tickets is the same as the number of Child (age 5–12) tickets. A total of 38 tickets was purchased. What is the total cost of the tickets? Explain.

DATA

Ticket	Price (in $)
Adult	23
Child, age 5–12	17
Under 5	8

Assessment Practice

21. Which does **NOT** show a reasonable estimate of 360×439?

Ⓐ 100,000
Ⓑ 140,000
Ⓒ 160,000
Ⓓ 180,000

22. A club orders 124 T-shirts at a cost of $18 each. Which is the best estimate of the total cost of the order?

Ⓐ $1,000
Ⓑ $2,000
Ⓒ $3,000
Ⓓ $4,000

Name ______________________

Additional Practice 3-3
Multiply by 1-Digit Numbers

Another Look!

The steps below show one way to multiply 3-digit numbers by 1-digit numbers.

Step 1

Multiply the ones.
Regroup if necessary.

$$\begin{array}{r} {}^{1} \\ 154 \\ \times\ \ 4 \\ \hline 6 \end{array}$$

Step 2

Multiply the tens.
Add any extra tens.
Regroup if necessary.

$$\begin{array}{r} {}^{2\,1} \\ 154 \\ \times\ \ 4 \\ \hline 16 \end{array}$$

Step 3

Multiply the hundreds.
Add any extra hundreds.

$$\begin{array}{r} {}^{2\,1} \\ 154 \\ \times\ \ 4 \\ \hline 616 \end{array}$$

For **1–16**, find each product.

Remember to regroup if necessary.

1. $\begin{array}{r} 13 \\ \times\ 3 \\ \hline \end{array}$ 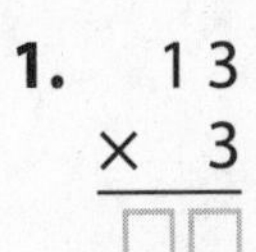

2. $\begin{array}{r} 17 \\ \times\ 7 \\ \hline \end{array}$ 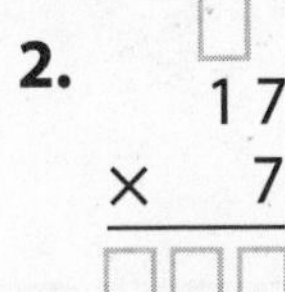

3. $\begin{array}{r} 741 \\ \times\ 3 \\ \hline \end{array}$ 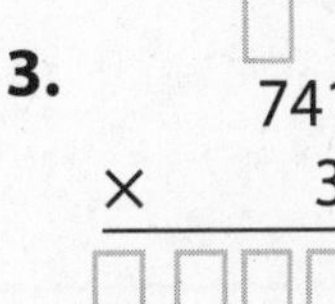

4. $\begin{array}{r} 587 \\ \times\ 3 \\ \hline \end{array}$ 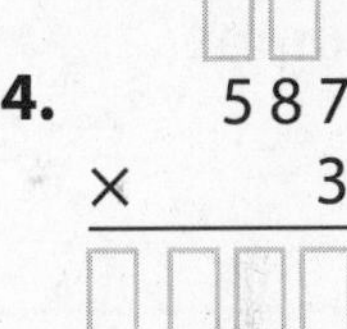

5. $\begin{array}{r} 413 \\ \times\ 6 \\ \hline \end{array}$

6. $\begin{array}{r} 625 \\ \times\ 6 \\ \hline \end{array}$

7. $\begin{array}{r} 36 \\ \times\ 5 \\ \hline \end{array}$

8. $\begin{array}{r} 731 \\ \times\ 9 \\ \hline \end{array}$

9. $\begin{array}{r} 88 \\ \times\ 5 \\ \hline \end{array}$

10. $\begin{array}{r} 52 \\ \times\ 8 \\ \hline \end{array}$

11. $\begin{array}{r} 352 \\ \times\ 3 \\ \hline \end{array}$

12. $\begin{array}{r} 159 \\ \times\ 5 \\ \hline \end{array}$

13. $\begin{array}{r} 164 \\ \times\ 5 \\ \hline \end{array}$

14. $\begin{array}{r} 19 \\ \times\ 8 \\ \hline \end{array}$

15. $\begin{array}{r} 478 \\ \times\ 2 \\ \hline \end{array}$

16. $\begin{array}{r} 862 \\ \times\ 7 \\ \hline \end{array}$

For **17–18**, use the table at the right.

17. What is the average length fingernails will grow in 12 months?

18. How much longer will hair grow than fingernails in 6 months?

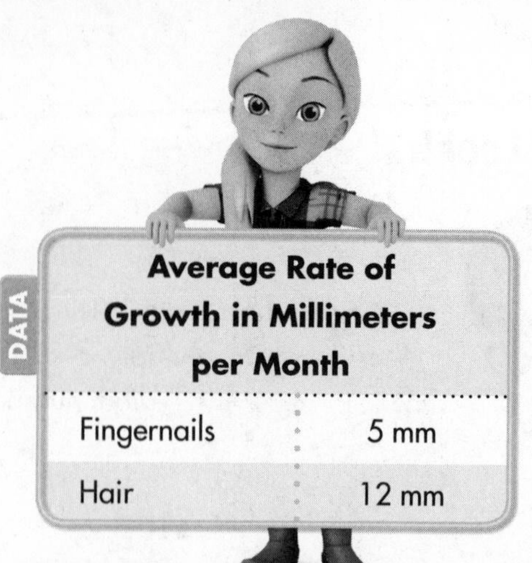

Average Rate of Growth in Millimeters per Month	
Fingernails	5 mm
Hair	12 mm

19. Derek rides in 3 motorcycle races. Each race is 150 miles. How many miles does Derek ride?

20. Walt averages 98 miles per hour in 4 races. If each race is 95 miles in length, how many miles did Walt drive in the races?

21. The Puerto Rico Trench has a depth of 30,246 feet. Write the numbers that are 10,000 less than and 10,000 greater than this number.

22. Which place value would you look at to compare 225,998 and 225,988?

23. **Critique Reasoning** Martin multiplied 423 by 7 and said the product is 2,841. Do Martin's calculations make sense? Explain.

24. **Higher Order Thinking** Tyrone has 6 times as many marbles as Pam. Pam has 34 marbles. Louis has 202 marbles. Who has more marbles, Tyrone or Louis? Explain.

25. Find the product.

$$\begin{array}{r} 651 \\ \times \quad 7 \\ \hline \end{array}$$

26. Find the product.

$$\begin{array}{r} 2{,}311 \\ \times \quad 6 \\ \hline \end{array}$$

Name ____________________

Practice Video Tools Games

Additional Practice 3-4
Multiply 2-Digit by 2-Digit Numbers

Another Look!

There are 24 cars in the Speedy Cup Series. Each car has 13 workers in the pit area. How many pit-area workers are at the race?

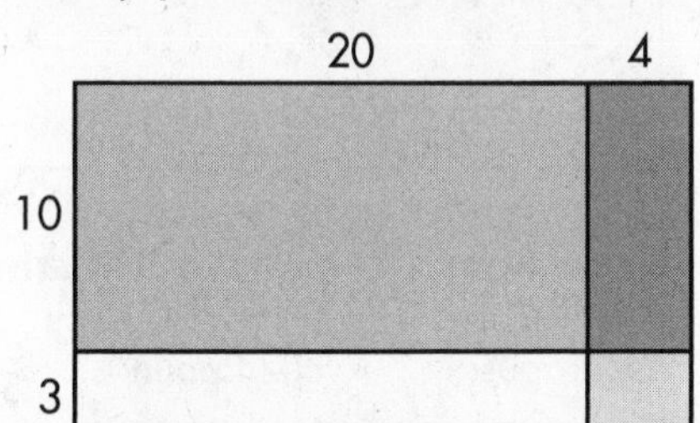

There is more than one way to multiply.

Use Partial Products

$$\begin{array}{r} 24 \\ \times\ 13 \\ \hline 12 \\ 60 \\ 40 \\ +\ 200 \\ \hline 312 \end{array}$$

Use the Standard Algorithm

Multiply by the ones. Regroup if necessary.

$$\begin{array}{r} \overset{1}{2}4 \\ \times\ 13 \\ \hline 72 \end{array}$$

Multiply by the tens. Regroup if necessary.

$$\begin{array}{r} \overset{1}{2}4 \\ \times\ 13 \\ \hline 72 \\ +\ 240 \\ \hline 312 \end{array}$$

Add the partial products.

There are 312 pit-area workers at the race.

For **1–10**, use the standard algorithm or partial products to find the product. Draw area models as needed.

You can use rounding or compatible numbers to estimate and check if your answer is reasonable.

1. $\begin{array}{r} 18 \\ \times\ 26 \\ \hline \square\square\square \\ +\ \square\square 0 \\ \hline \square\square\square \end{array}$

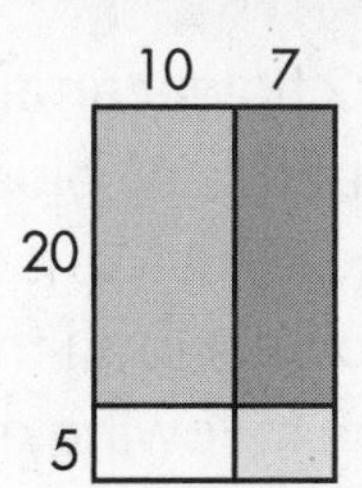

2. $\begin{array}{r} 17 \\ \times\ 25 \\ \hline \square\square \\ +\ \square\square 0 \\ \hline \square\square\square \end{array}$

3. $\begin{array}{r} 88 \\ \times\ 32 \\ \hline \end{array}$

4. $\begin{array}{r} 53 \\ \times\ 48 \\ \hline \end{array}$

5. $\begin{array}{r} 18 \\ \times\ 77 \\ \hline \end{array}$

6. $\begin{array}{r} 67 \\ \times\ 27 \\ \hline \end{array}$

7. $\begin{array}{r} 67 \\ \times\ 34 \\ \hline \end{array}$

8. $\begin{array}{r} 91 \\ \times\ 46 \\ \hline \end{array}$

9. $\begin{array}{r} 56 \\ \times\ 31 \\ \hline \end{array}$

10. $\begin{array}{r} 67 \\ \times\ 57 \\ \hline \end{array}$

11. An ultralight airplane tracked monarch butterflies migrating to Mexico during the month of September. There are 30 days in September. How many miles did the ultralight travel in September?

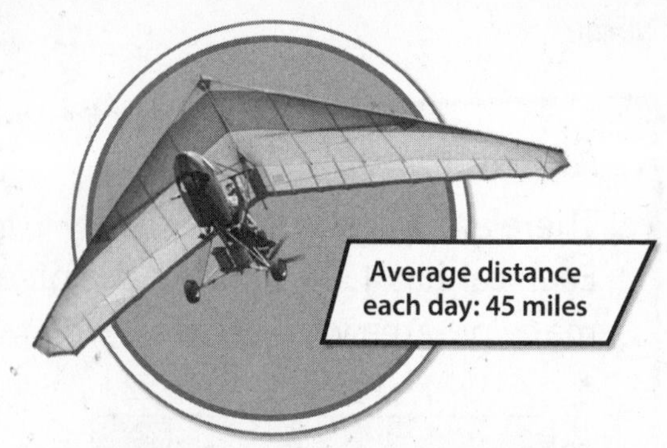

For **12–13**, use the table at the right.

12. How much do 21 bushels of sweet corn weigh?

13. How much do 18 bushels of asparagus and 7 bushels of carrots weigh?

DATA

Vegetable	Weight of 1 Bushel
Asparagus	24 pounds
Beets	52 pounds
Carrots	50 pounds
Sweet corn	35 pounds

14. Rob purchased a rug for his apartment. The rug is 72 inches by 96 inches. Calculate the area of the rug in square inches.

15. Higher Order Thinking Corina found $62 \times 22 = 1{,}042$. Is Corina's answer reasonable? Explain.

Assessment Practice

16. Maria has 92 flower arrangements. Each arrangement has 48 blue flowers and 50 yellow flowers. Maria calculates there are 9,016 flowers in all the arrangements. Which of the following expressions shows how to use an estimate to check Maria's calculation?

Ⓐ $90 + 50 + 50$

Ⓑ 90×10

Ⓒ $90 \times (50 + 50)$

Ⓓ $90 \times (50 \times 50)$

17. Without calculating, which of the following is a reasonable answer for 28×32?

Ⓐ 196

Ⓑ 496

Ⓒ 896

Ⓓ 12,096

Name ______________________

Additional Practice 3-5
Multiply 3-Digit by 2-Digit Numbers

Another Look!

Last year, 23 students in fifth grade were assigned a kindergarten student as a reading buddy. Each student read for 1 hour during each reading session and for a total of 128 sessions. How many hours in all did the fifth-grade students read?

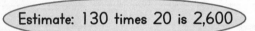

Step 1

Multiply by the ones. Regroup as needed.

$$\begin{array}{r} \overset{2}{1}28 \\ \times \quad 3 \\ \hline 384 \end{array}$$

Step 2

Multiply by the tens. Regroup as needed.

$$\begin{array}{r} \overset{1}{1}28 \\ \times \quad 20 \\ \hline 2{,}560 \end{array}$$

Step 3

Add to get the final product.

$$\begin{array}{r} 128 \\ \times \quad 23 \\ \hline \overset{1}{3}84 \\ +\,2{,}560 \\ \hline 2{,}944 \end{array}$$

The fifth-grade students read for 2,944 hours in all. The answer is reasonable because it is close to the estimate.

In **1–10**, find each product. Estimate to check that your answer is reasonable.

1. $\begin{array}{r} 282 \\ \times \quad 19 \\ \hline \end{array}$

← Multiply by the ones.

+ ← Multiply by the tens.

← Add the partial products.

2. $\begin{array}{r} 538 \\ \times \quad 46 \\ \hline \end{array}$

← Multiply by the ones.

+ ← Multiply by the tens.

← Add the partial products.

3. $\begin{array}{r} 395 \\ \times \quad 76 \\ \hline \end{array}$

4. $\begin{array}{r} 83 \\ \times \quad 57 \\ \hline \end{array}$

5. $\begin{array}{r} 628 \\ \times \quad 33 \\ \hline \end{array}$

6. $\begin{array}{r} 154 \\ \times \quad 35 \\ \hline \end{array}$

7. 682×25

8. 324×71

9. 158×6

10. 16×29

11. Critique Reasoning Is 2,750 a reasonable answer for 917 × 33? Explain.

12. A-Z **Vocabulary** What two partial products would you add to find 513 × 46?

13. How many kilometers could the red car travel in 12 hours? Write an equation to show your work.

14. Higher Order Thinking In 12 hours, how many more kilometers could the yellow car go than the red car? Show your work.

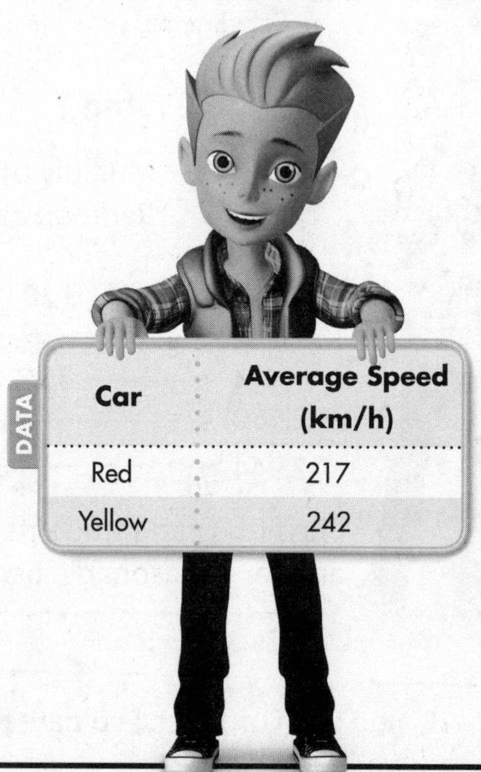

Car	Average Speed (km/h)
Red	217
Yellow	242

Assessment Practice

15. Katie is building a rectangular wall. The wall will be 332 bricks wide and 39 bricks tall. How many bricks does she need to build the wall?

16. What is the product?

311 × 42

Ⓐ 1,822

Ⓑ 1,866

Ⓒ 13,062

Ⓓ 13,082

Name ____________________

Practice Video Tools Games

Additional Practice 3-6
Multiply Whole Numbers with Zeros

Another Look!

Find the product of 304 × 23.

```
    1
   304
×   23
   912      Step 1: First, multiply 304 by 3 ones.
+ 6080      Step 2: Then, multiply 304 by 2 tens.
 6,992      Step 3: Finally, add to get the final product.
```

1. Use the place-value chart at the right to multiply 36 × 405. Record each step in the correct place in the chart.

A place-value chart can help keep the numbers in the right place!

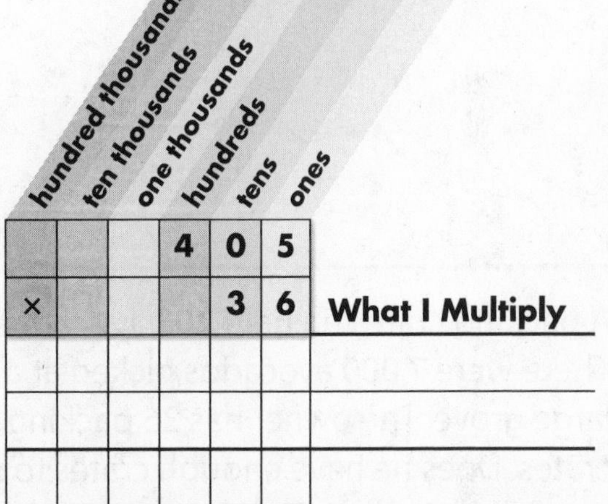

thousands period
ones period
hundred thousands
ten thousands
one thousands
hundreds
tens
ones
4 0 5
× 3 6
What I Multiply

In **2–9**, find each product. Estimate to check for reasonableness.

2. 203 × 12

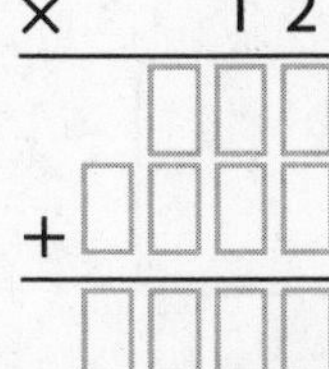

3. 306 × 21

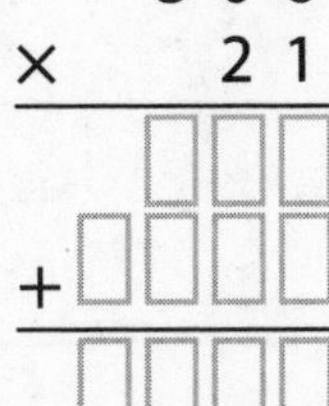

4. 109 × 73

5. 601 × 45

6. 708 × 34

7. 520 × 63

8. 405 × 70

9. 802 × 94

10. The Memorial Middle School Band has 108 members. They want to buy jackets with the name of the band on the back. What is the difference in the total price of the screen-print and the embroidered jackets?

DATA

Jackets	Price (in $)
Screen print name	35
Embroidered name	48

11. **Critique Reasoning** Wildlife protection groups build bat houses to help save bats. One bat house holds about 300 bats. Larry says that 12 bat houses can hold about 4,500 bats. Do you agree? Explain.

12. **Higher Order Thinking** Replace the *a*, *b*, *c*, and *d* with the digits 2, 4, 6, 8 to form the greatest product. Each digit can only be used once. Explain your substitutions.

$$\begin{array}{r} a\,0\,b \\ \times \quad c\,d \\ \hline \end{array}$$

13. A packing crate can hold 205 avocados. There were 7,000 avocados picked at a large grove. The owner has 36 packing crates. Does he have enough crates to ship out the avocados? Explain.

14. Sarah found that the product of 49 and 805 is 3,165. How would finding an estimate help her know that the answer is NOT reasonable?

Assessment Practice

15. What is the product?

$$\begin{array}{r} 990 \\ \times \quad 37 \\ \hline \end{array}$$

Name

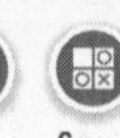
Practice Video Tools Games

Additional Practice 3-7
Multiply Multi-Digit Numbers

Another Look!

A sports store sells skateboards for $112. Last month the store sold 45 skateboards. How much money did the store bring in from selling them?

```
    1
  112
×  45
  560
+ 4480
 5,040
```

The store brought in $5,040 from selling skateboards.

The Standard Algorithm is always an effective method for multiplying two numbers.

For **1–12**, find each product.

1. 1 2 0 6 × 1 5

2. 2 4 0 × 2 2

3. 6 5 4 × 4 5

4. 3 3 9 × 5 0

5. 423 × 18

6. 914 × 12

7. 125 × 15

8. 425 × 82

9. 185 × 24

10. 1,288 × 33

11. 6,301 × 47

12. 3,440 × 75

13. Tomika plans to run 84 miles in 4 weeks. If she continues the pattern, how many miles will she run in 1 year? Explain.

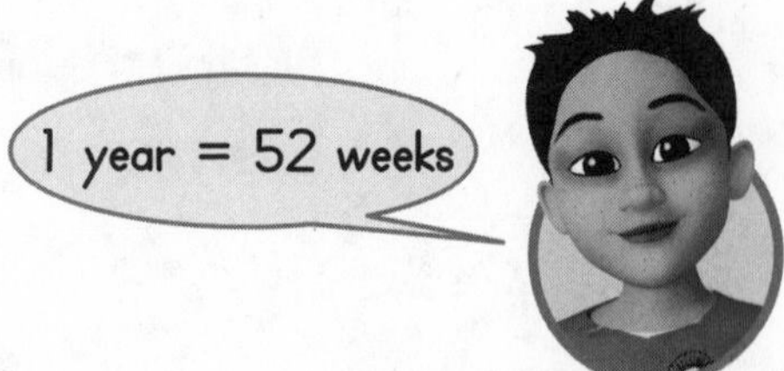

14. Pete owns several pizza restaurants. He sells cheese pizzas for $12 each. How much money was made in January at the Westland location?

DATA

Cheese Pizza Sales for January

Location	Number Sold
Downtown	1,356
Center City	998
Westland	1,824

15. How many more pizzas did the Downtown location sell than the Center City location? Write an equation to show your work.

16. Make Sense and Persevere How many more pizzas does the Westland location need to sell to equal the total number of pizzas sold by the Downtown and Center City locations? Explain your work.

17. Higher Order Thinking A farmer grows 128 red tomato plants and 102 yellow tomato plants. Each plant produces about 32 tomatoes. The farmer plans to sell each tomato for $2. Explain how to find a reasonable estimate for the total amount of money the farmer will earn if she sells all of the tomatoes.

Assessment Practice

18. The product of the following expression is 15,688.

$$\begin{array}{r} 212 \\ \times\ \square 4 \\ \hline \end{array}$$

What is the missing digit?

Ⓐ 0

Ⓑ 1

Ⓒ 4

Ⓓ 7

19. The product of the following expression is 22,718.

$$\begin{array}{r} \square 14 \\ \times\ 37 \\ \hline \end{array}$$

What is the missing digit?

Ⓐ 1

Ⓑ 4

Ⓒ 6

Ⓓ 7

Name

Practice Video Tools Games

Additional Practice 3-8
Solve Word Problems Using Multiplication

Another Look!

Hailey's family is saving money for a vacation. If they save \$525 each month for 12 months, how much will they save?

Draw a bar diagram.

s total amount saved

\$525	\$525	\$525	\$525	\$525	\$525	\$525	\$525	\$525	\$525	\$525	\$525

Write and solve an equation.

$12 \times 525 = s$

$s = 6{,}300$

Hailey's family will save \$6,300 over the 12 months.

The variable *s* represents the total amount saved. You can draw a bar diagram and write an equation to model the problem.

In **1–5**, draw a bar diagram and write an equation. Solve.

1. A stadium has 7,525 seats. What is the total attendance for 5 games if each game is sold out? Complete the bar diagram to help you.

n total number of people

2. An aquarium has display tanks that each contain 175 fish. How many fish are on display in 6 tanks?

? fish → ?

6 tanks →	175	175	175	175	175	175

3. Each elephant at the zoo eats 125 pounds of food per day. How many pounds of food will 18 elephants eat?

4. Joy travels a lot for her job. She flies 2,840 miles each week for 4 weeks. How many miles in all does she fly?

5. Jerry weighs 105 pounds. If a male brown bear weighs 11 times as much, what is the brown bear's weight?

6. Meg measured the length of some pieces of wire. What is the difference in length between the longest and shortest piece of wire?

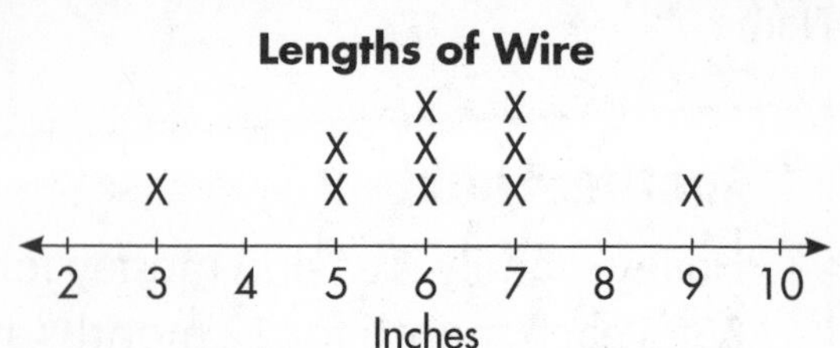

7. What is the combined length of all the pieces Meg measured? Write an equation using a variable to show your work.

8. **Higher Order Thinking** Daniel has 102 stamps. Manuel has twice as many stamps as Daniel. Kendra has twice as many stamps as Manuel. How many stamps do they have in all?

9. Caroline has enough pumpkin seeds to cover an area of 350 square feet. Her garden measures 18 feet by 22 feet. Does she have enough pumpkin seeds to fill the whole garden? Explain.

What do you need to find to solve this problem?

10. **Be Precise** The table shows the number of miles 3 runners ran last week. Order the numbers from least to greatest. Which runner ran the farthest? How do you know?

DATA

Name	Miles
Darla	15.2
Casey	15.25
Juan	15.03

Assessment Practice

11. Tia drives 127 miles a week. Mac drives 23 times as many miles as Tia a week. How many miles does Mac drive a week?

Ⓐ 635 miles

Ⓑ 1,801 miles

Ⓒ 2,921 miles

Ⓓ 3,021 miles

12. Kai sends 184 text messages a month. Bo sends 12 times as many text messages a month as Kai. How many text messages does Bo send a month?

Ⓐ 1,004 text messages

Ⓑ 1,840 text messages

Ⓒ 2,008 text messages

Ⓓ 2,208 text messages

Name ______________________

 Practice  Video  Tools   Games

Additional Practice 3-9
Critique Reasoning

Another Look!

Mr. Jansen needs to order picture frames for his paintings. He has $4,000 to buy 98 frames priced at $42 each. Mr. Jansen says he has enough money because $100 \times \$40 = \$4,000$.

Tell how you can critique Mr. Jansen's reasoning.

- I can decide if his strategy makes sense to me.
- I can look for flaws in his estimates.

When you critique reasoning, you explain why someone's thinking is correct or incorrect.

Critique Mr. Jansen's reasoning.

His reasoning does not make sense. He should find an overestimate or an exact amount to be sure he has enough money. An overestimate would be $100 \times \$42 = \$4,200$, and the exact amount is $98 \times \$42 = \$4,116$.

He does not have enough money.

Critique Reasoning

Jason has 75 feet of wallpaper border. He wants to put up a wallpaper border around his rectangular bedroom that measures 12 feet by 14 feet. He multiplies $12 \times 14 = 168$ to get an exact answer of how much border he needs. He concludes that he does not have enough border for the whole job.

1. Tell how you can critique Jason's reasoning.

2. Critique Jason's reasoning.

3. Jason uses an overestimate to decide how many rolls of wallpaper he needs for another room. Explain why his reasoning to use an overestimate does or does not make sense.

Performance Task

A Spool of Wire

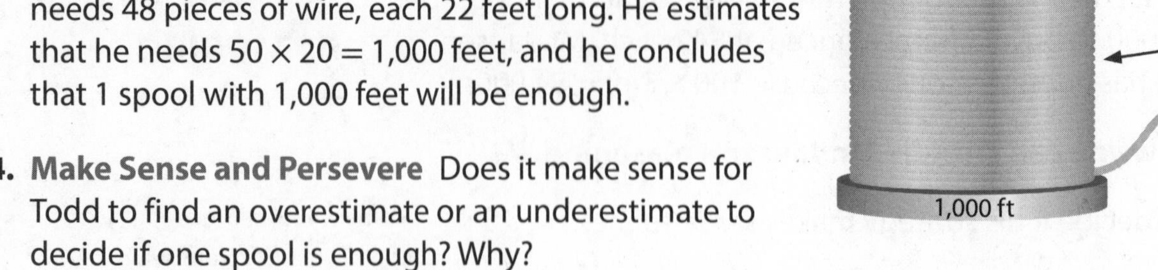

Todd has a new spool of wire like the one pictured. He needs 48 pieces of wire, each 22 feet long. He estimates that he needs $50 \times 20 = 1{,}000$ feet, and he concludes that 1 spool with 1,000 feet will be enough.

4. Make Sense and Persevere Does it make sense for Todd to find an overestimate or an underestimate to decide if one spool is enough? Why?

5. Reasoning Should Todd use multiplication to estimate the total amount of wire he needs? Explain your reasoning.

6. Be Precise Did Todd correctly calculate the appropriate estimate? Explain.

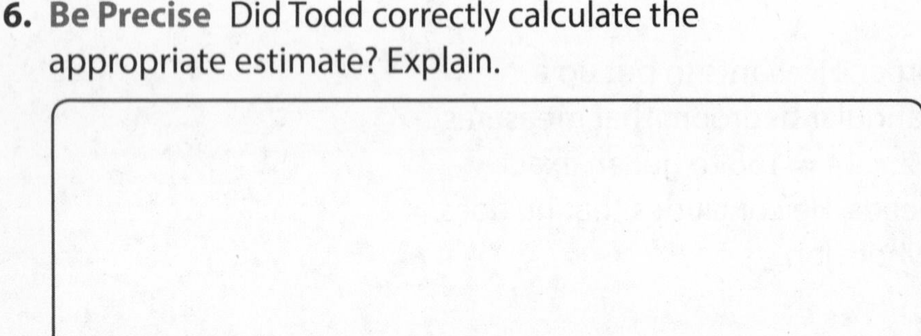

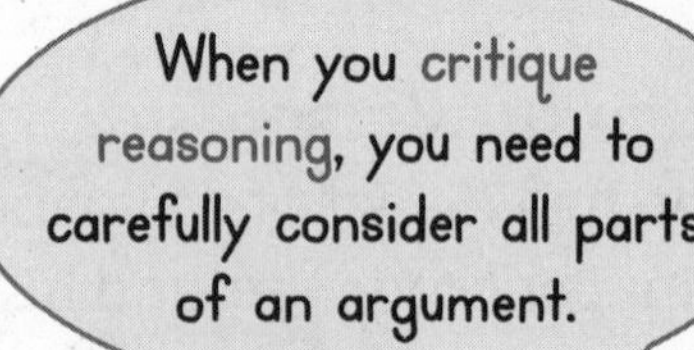

When you critique reasoning, you need to carefully consider all parts of an argument.

7. Critique Reasoning Explain if Todd's conclusion is logical. How did you decide? If it is not logical, what can you do to improve his reasoning?

Name ________________

Additional Practice 4-1

Multiply Decimals by Powers of 10

Another Look!

A builder is installing tiles at a restaurant. The area of each tile is 0.25 square meter. What is the area of 1,000 tiles?

$0.25 \times 10 = 0.25 \times 10^1 = 2.5$
$0.25 \times 100 = 0.25 \times 10^2 = 25$
$0.25 \times 1{,}000 = 0.25 \times 10^3 = 250$

So, the area of 1,000 tiles is 250 square meters.

Use patterns and place value to help you multiply a decimal by powers of 10.

In **1** and **2**, use patterns to find the products.

1. $0.057 \times 10 =$ ________

$0.057 \times 100 =$ ________

$0.057 \times 1{,}000 =$ ________

2. $2.148 \times 1 =$ ________

$2.148 \times 10 =$ ________

$2.148 \times 10^2 =$ ________

$2.148 \times 10^3 =$ ________

In **3–10**, find each product. Use place-value patterns to help you.

3. 0.62×10

4. 0.0063×100

Use the number of zeros or the exponent in the power of 10 to decide how to move the decimal point.

5. 19.212×10^2

6. $0.024 \times 1{,}000$

7. 92.3×10^4

8. 5.001×10^1

9. 1.675×1

10. 843.5×10^2

In **11–12**, find the missing exponent.

11. $0.936 \times 10^{\square} = 93.6$

12. $10^{\square} \times 12.35 = 12{,}350$

13. Jennifer planted a tree that was 0.17 meter tall. After 10 years, the tree was 100 times as tall as when she planted it. What is the height of the tree after 10 years?

14. Critique Reasoning Marco and Suzi each multiplied 0.721×10^2. Marco got 7.21 for his product. Suzi got 72.1 for her product. Which student multiplied correctly? How do you know?

15. The table shows the distance a small motor scooter can travel using one gallon of gasoline. Complete the table to find the number of miles the scooter can travel for other amounts of gasoline.

Gallons	Miles
0.1	
1	118
10	

What pattern do you see in the table?

16. Give an example of two numbers that both have six digits, but the greater number is determined by the hundreds place.

17. Higher Order Thinking A store has a contest to guess the mass of 10,000 peanuts. If a peanut has a mass of about 0.45 gram, what would be a reasonable guess for the mass of 10,000 peanuts?

Assessment Practice

18. Choose all equations that are **NOT** true.

- ☐ $360 \times 10^3 = 36{,}000$
- ☐ $0.36 \times 100 = 3{,}600$
- ☐ $360 \times 10^1 = 36.0$
- ☐ $0.036 \times 1{,}000 = 36$
- ☐ $3.6 \times 10^1 = 36$

19. Choose all equations that are true when 10^3 is placed in the box.

- ☐ $4.2 = \square \times 0.042$
- ☐ $420 = \square \times 0.42$
- ☐ $4{,}200 = \square \times 4.2$
- ☐ $0.042 = \square \times 42.0$
- ☐ $42 = \square \times 0.042$

Name ______________________

Additional Practice 4-2

Estimate the Product of a Decimal and a Whole Number

Another Look!

Zane needs to buy 27 party favors for the family reunion. The favors cost \$2.98 each. About how much will the party favors cost in all?

Is an overestimate or an underestimate better when estimating how much something will cost?

Here are two ways you can estimate.

Round both numbers.

$\$2.98 \times 27$

$\downarrow \quad \downarrow$

$\$3 \times 30 = \$90$

The favors will cost about \$90.

Replace the factors with compatible numbers and multiply mentally.

$\$2.98 \times 27$

$\downarrow \quad \downarrow$

$\$3 \times 25 = \$75$

The favors will cost about \$75.

Since 27 is between 25 and 30, the total cost will be between \$75 and \$90.

1. Round to the greatest place to estimate 23×1.75.

23×1.75

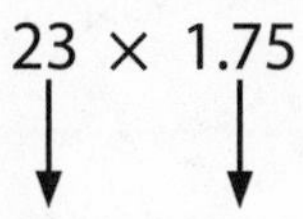

____ ____

So, 23×1.75 is about ____

2. Use compatible numbers to estimate 12×0.49.

12×0.49

$\downarrow \quad \downarrow$

____ ____

So, 12×0.49 is about ____

In **3–14**, estimate each product.

3. 19.3×6

4. 345×5.79

5. 9.66×0.46

6. 8.02×70

7. 1.56×48

8. 45.1×5

9. 0.13×11

10. 99.7×92

11. 147×10.4

12. 23.7×4.76

13. 3×0.85

14. 0.35×9

15. Can Mrs. Davis and her two sisters get their hair colored for less than $100 if they include a $10 tip? Explain.

DATA

Treatment	Cost
Shampoo	$7.95
Haircut	$14.95
Coloring	$28.95

16. If Mrs. Davis and her sisters also get haircuts, about how much will they pay in all?

17. Reasoning Mrs. Smith bought her three children new raincoats. Each raincoat cost $25.99. About how much did Mrs. Smith spend on the 3 raincoats? Is your estimate an overestimate or underestimate? Write an equation to show your work.

18. Higher Order Thinking Some Native American tribes made jewelry with Dentalia shells. Each Dentalia shell is about 1.5 inches long. About how much longer would a necklace made with 24 shells be than a necklace made with 18 shells? Use compatible numbers.

19. Algebra A youth hockey league is selling boxes of popcorn to raise money for new uniforms. Sidney sold 9 boxes for a total of $72 in sales. Use the bar diagram and write an equation to find the value of *c*, the cost of each box Sidney sold.

$72

c	c	c	c	c	c	c	c	c

Assessment Practice

20. Rounding to the nearest tenth, which of the following give an **overestimate**?

- ☐ 37.63×0.54
- ☐ 54.49×0.45
- ☐ 1.19×1.45
- ☐ 0.81×8.01
- ☐ 27.83×13.64

21. Rounding to the nearest whole number, which of the following give an **underestimate**?

- ☐ 2.7×13.5
- ☐ 4.51×8.7
- ☐ 9.19×8.48
- ☐ 7.49×11.4
- ☐ 3.6×6.5

Name

Practice Video Tools Games

Additional Practice 4-3

Use Models to Multiply a Decimal and a Whole Number

Another Look!

A nature preserve has two hiking trails. Trail 1 is 1.3 miles long. Trail 2 is twice as long as Trail 1. How long is Trail 2?

Use place-value blocks to find the product.

Show 2 groups of 1.3.

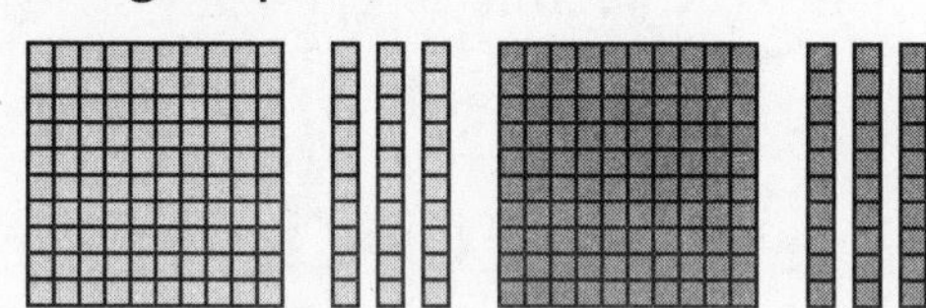

You can use estimation to check your work. $1 \times 2 = 2$, so your answer to 1.3×2 will be about 2.

Combine the blocks.

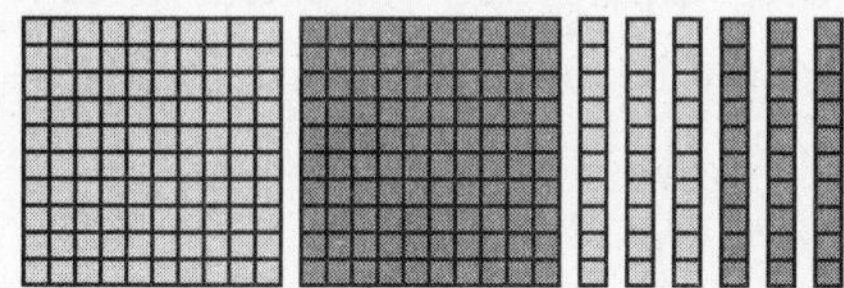

So, $1.3 \times 2 = 2.6$. Trail 2 is 2.6 miles long.

In **1** and **2**, find the product. Use place-value blocks for help.

1. $0.45 \times 3 =$

2. $0.08 \times 6 =$

In **3–10**, find the product. Use models to help, if needed.

3. 12×0.08

4. 1.75×4

5. 0.85×3

6. 6×0.12

7. 3×0.33

8. 0.45×10^2

9. 3×2.89

10. 7.6×2

11. Ryan measures the perimeter of his square painting so he can make a wood frame. Find the perimeter of the painting in centimeters. Remember, the formula for perimeter is $P = 4 \times s$.

30.5 centimeters

12. **Reasoning** Write a multiplication number sentence that matches the model.

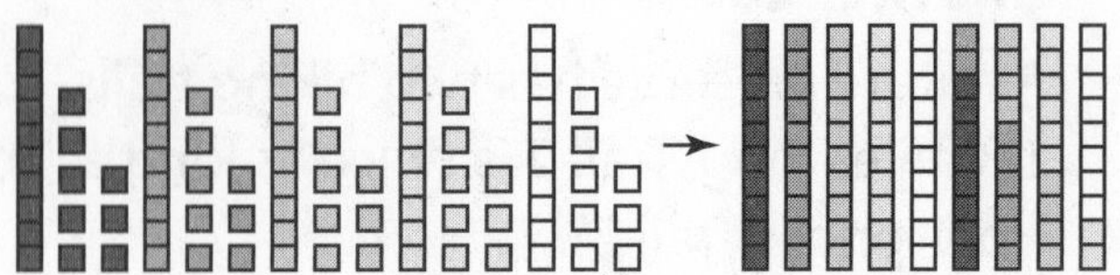

Remember, each small square is 1 hundredth.

13. Anthony bikes a 16.2-mile long trail. If he bikes it 4 times, how far will he have traveled? Draw a bar diagram to help you.

14. **enVision®** STEM If 7 giant solar power plants generate 1.3 gigawatts (GW) of energy to power 900,000 homes, how many gigawatts can 21 giant solar plants generate?

15. **Higher Order Thinking** If $0.36 \times 4 = 1.44$, how would your product be different if the factors were 0.36 and 0.4?

Assessment Practice

16. Doug's family buys 7 postcards while on vacation. Each postcard costs $0.25 including tax.

Part A

How can Doug use place-value blocks to find the total cost of the postcards? What is the total cost?

Part B

How can Doug use what he knows about whole-number multiplication to check his answer?

Name ______________________

 Practice  Video  Tools  Games

Additional Practice 4-4
Multiply a Decimal and a Whole Number

Another Look!

Travis can read a book chapter in 2.3 hours. The book has 18 chapters. How long will it take Travis to read the book?

Multiply as with whole numbers.

$$\begin{array}{r} \overset{2}{2}3 \\ \times\ 18 \\ \hline 184 \\ +\ 230 \\ \hline 414 \end{array}$$

So, $23 \times 18 = 414$. Now think about the number of decimal places to find 2.3×18.

Since $2 \times 18 = 36$ and $3 \times 18 = 54$, the product must be between 36 and 54.

41.4

It will take Travis 41.4 hours.

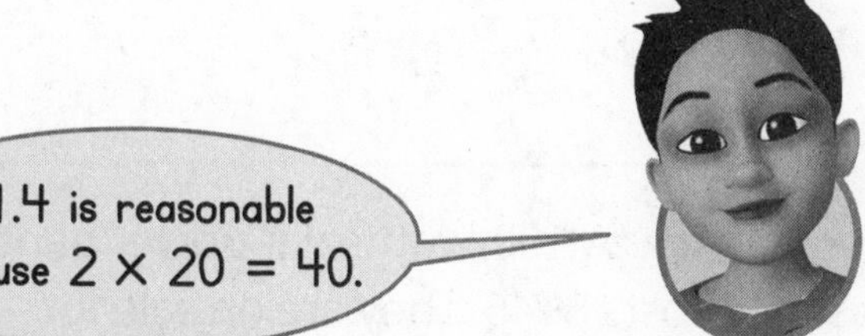

In **1** and **2**, use number sense to find the products.

1. $46 \times 3 = 38$

$4.6 \times 3 =$ ______

$0.46 \times 3 =$ ______

2. $17 \times 15 = 255$

$17 \times 1.5 =$ ______

$17 \times 0.15 =$ ______

In **3–14**, find each product.

3. $\begin{array}{r} 27.4 \\ \times\ \ 7 \\ \hline \end{array}$

4. $\begin{array}{r} 336 \\ \times\ 0.4 \\ \hline \end{array}$

5. $\begin{array}{r} 88 \\ \times\ 1.8 \\ \hline \end{array}$

6. $\begin{array}{r} 4.02 \\ \times\ \ 9 \\ \hline \end{array}$

7. 1.7×12

8. 105×0.4

9. 1.4×32

10. 0.89×21

11. 4.4×18

12. 0.3×279

13. 95×5.7

14. 46×0.46

15. If each month in Reno had the same average rainfall as in August, what would the total amount of rainfall be after 12 months?

16. List the deserts in order from greatest amount of rainfall in August to least amount of rainfall in August.

DATA

Desert Rainfall in August

Desert	Average Rainfall (mm)
Mojave	0.1
Reno	0.19
Sahara	0.17

17. Number Sense Write two numbers that are greater than 32.46 and less than 32.56. Then find the difference of your two numbers.

18. Each juice bottle contains 8.6 fluid ounces. How many fluid ounces of juice are in a carton with 12 bottles?

19. Be Precise A 100-watt solar power panel usually costs $146. They are on sale for 0.75 of the regular price. Multiply 146 by 0.75 to find the sale price.

20. Higher Order Thinking A family has a huge array of solar panels to make electricity. If each month they sell back 420 kWh for $0.07 per kWh, how much money could they make in a year?

21. Carla had a piece of rope that was $14\frac{7}{8}$ in. long. She used some of the rope for a crafts project. Now there is $14\frac{3}{8}$ in. left. How much rope did she use? Use the number line to help.

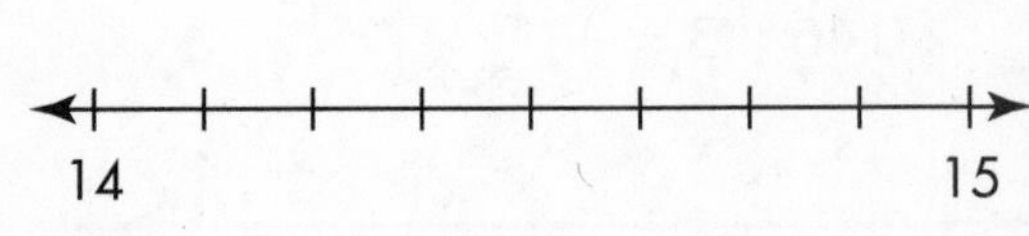

Assessment Practice

22. Which of the following equations is **NOT** true?

Ⓐ $225 \times 4 = 9{,}000$

Ⓑ $225 \times 0.04 = 9$

Ⓒ $22.5 \times 4 = 90$

Ⓓ $225 \times 0.4 = 90$

23. Which of the following equations is **NOT** true?

Ⓐ $80 \times 15 = 1{,}200$

Ⓑ $0.8 \times 15 = 12$

Ⓒ $80 \times 0.15 = 1.2$

Ⓓ $80 \times 1.5 = 120$

Name ____________________

 Practice  Video  Tools Games

Additional Practice 4-5

Use Models to Multiply a Decimal and a Decimal

Another Look!

Find 0.7×0.9. Use an area model to find the product.

Use each factor as a side of a rectangle on a hundredths grid.

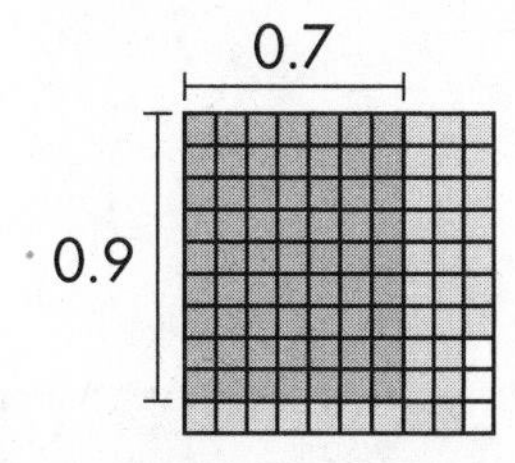

The squares in the double shaded area represent the product.

The double shaded area contains 63 hundredths squares, so $0.7 \times 0.9 = 0.63$.

Both factors are less than 1, so their product is also less than 1.

In **1–3**, shade the hundredths grids to find the product.

1. 0.8×0.8

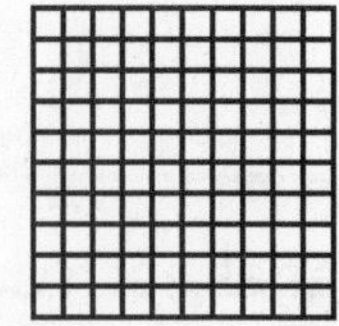

2. 0.5×0.6

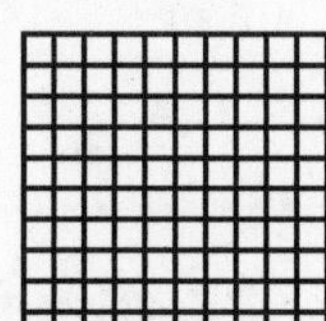

3. 0.7×1.6

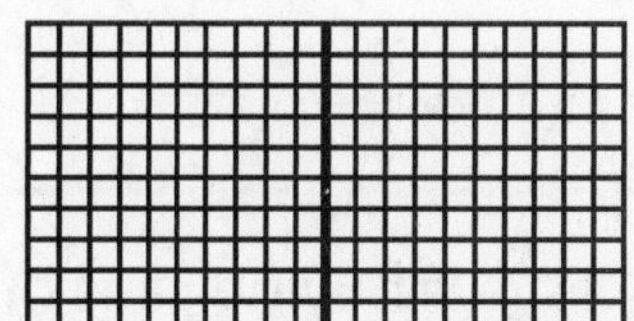

In **4–15**, find the product. You may use grids to help.

4. 1.9×0.4

5. 0.2×0.9

6. 2.8×0.6

7. 0.3×3.4

8. 5.6×0.8

9. 0.8×0.1

10. 0.9×4.1

11. 3.7×0.2

12. 4.4×0.7

13. 0.9×0.5

14. 0.2×6.8

15. 9.1×0.3

16. Phil uses the model below to help him multiply decimals. Write a multiplication equation to represent the decimal model.

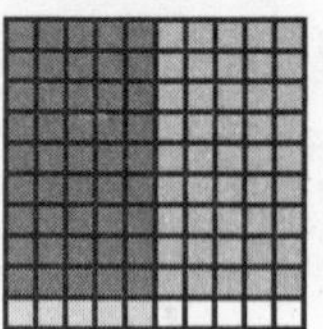

17. **Number Sense** Write a problem that requires multiplying two decimals to find the answer. The product must have two decimal places.

18. **Vocabulary** Describe the difference between an **underestimate** and an **overestimate**.

19. Raul hit a golf ball 26.4 yards. A.J. can hit a golf ball 10 times as far. How far can A.J. hit the ball?

20. **Be Precise** Marco wants to set up 12 small wind turbines with 3 blades each. If 4 wind turbine blades cost \$79.64, how much will all the blades cost? Show your work.

21. **Higher Order Thinking** Explain why multiplying 37.4×0.1 gives a product that is less than 37.4.

22. Leslie is buying cans of diced tomatoes that weigh 14.5 ounces each. If she buys 8 cans, how many total ounces does she buy?

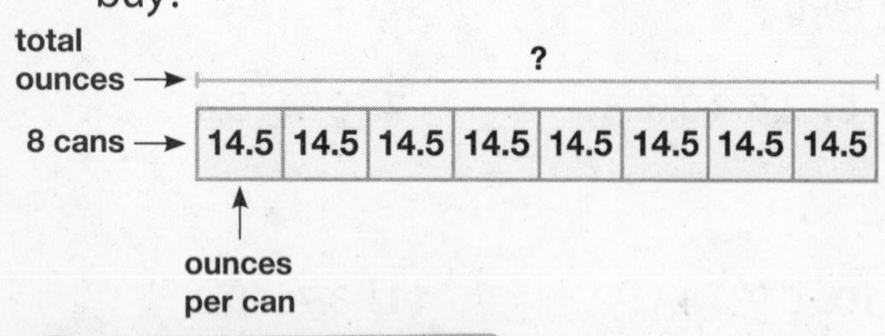

23. **Algebra** Jorge reads 15 pages each day for 7 days. Write and solve an algebraic equation to find *p*, the total number of pages he reads.

Assessment Practice

24. Find two numbers that you can multiply to get a product of 0.4. Write the numbers in the box.

Product = 0.4
0.9   0.5   8   0.1   0.8   9   5

Name ______________________

Additional Practice 4-6

Multiply Decimals Using Partial Products

Another Look!

If a truck travels 9.5 miles on 1 gallon of fuel, how many miles will the truck travel on 5.6 gallons of fuel?

Step 1

First, estimate your product so you can check for reasonableness.

9.5×5.6

$10 \times 6 = 60$

Since 53.2 is close to the estimate 60, the answer is reasonable.

Step 2

Add all the partial products to find the answer. Use an area model if you need help keeping track of them.

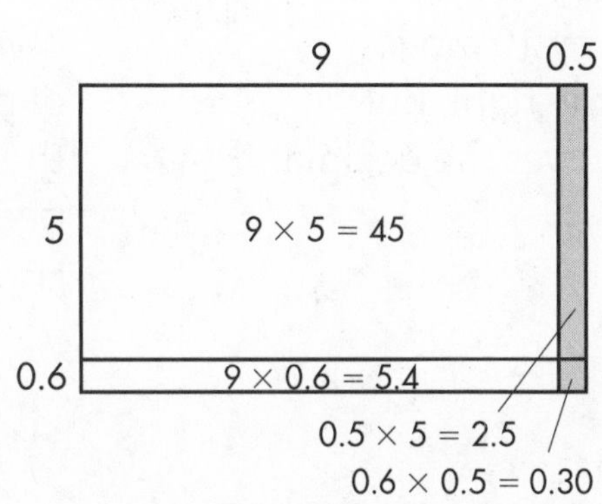

$$\begin{array}{lr} & 9.5 \\ & \times\ 5.6 \\ \hline .6 \times .5 = & .30 \\ .6 \times 9 = & 5.4 \\ 5 \times .5 = & 2.5 \\ 5 \times 9 = & 45 \\ \hline & 53.20 \end{array}$$

The truck will travel 53.2 miles on 5.6 gallons of fuel.

1. If a truck travels 8.6 miles on 1 gallon of fuel, how many miles will the truck travel on 9.2 gallons of fuel? Estimate. Then, find the product. Is your answer is reasonable? Explain.

Estimate:
8.6×9.2

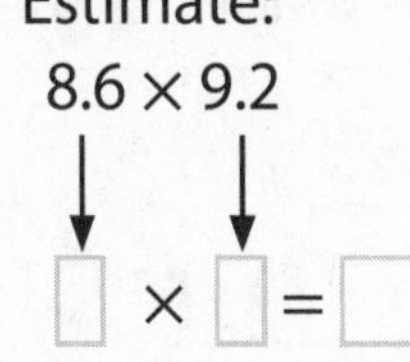

$$\begin{array}{r} 8.6 \\ \times\ \ 9.2 \\ \hline \end{array}$$

In **2–9**, estimate first. Then multiply using partial products. Check that your answer is reasonable.

2. $\begin{array}{r} 0.2 \\ \times\ 4.6 \\ \hline \end{array}$

3. $\begin{array}{r} 3.9 \\ \times\ 7.1 \\ \hline \end{array}$

4. $\begin{array}{r} 5.4 \\ \times\ 0.1 \\ \hline \end{array}$

5. $\begin{array}{r} 15.3 \\ \times\ 6.4 \\ \hline \end{array}$

6. 9.3×5.8

7. 23.7×4.4

8. 0.8×0.5

9. 13.2×0.3

10. Find the approximate length of each highway in kilometers.

One mile is about 1.6 kilometers.

DATA

Highway	Length (miles)
A	11.9
B	46.2
C	121

11. Higher Order Thinking Why does multiplying numbers by 10 move the decimal point to the right, but multiplying by 0.10 moves the decimal point to the left?

12. Make Sense and Persevere A pick-your-own pecan farm charges $1.35 per pound of pecans plus $0.40 per pound to crack the pecans. Amelia picks 20 pounds of pecans. The farm cracks 5 pounds for her. How much does Amelia pay all together?

13. Adrian bought fruit to make a salad for a picnic. He bought 0.89 pound of grapes, 2.45 pounds of oranges, and 1.49 pounds of apples. What is the weight of the fruit?

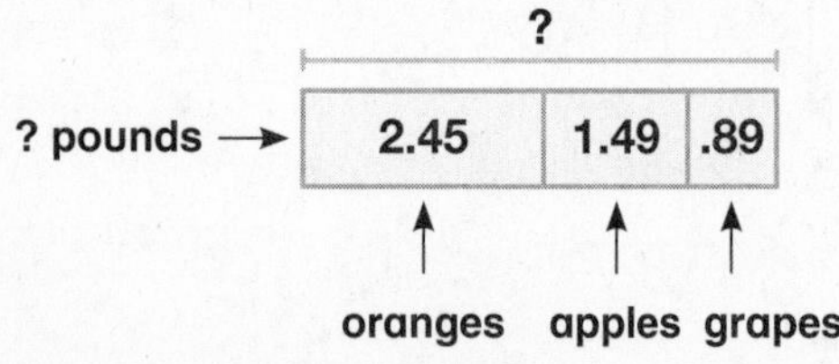

14. In exercise 13, suppose grapes cost $2.35 per pound, oranges cost $0.99 per pound, and apples cost $1.65 per pound. Rounding to the nearest whole number, about how much did Adrian pay for all the fruit?

Assessment Practice

15. Karly used 3.5 cans of tomato sauce to make lasagna. Each can contains 10.5 ounces. How many ounces of tomato sauce is in the lasagna?

Ⓐ 24.00

Ⓑ 36.75

Ⓒ 52.50

Ⓓ 63.00

16. A bag of grass seed weighs 5.8 pounds. How many pounds would 2.5 bags weigh?

Ⓐ 14.5 pounds

Ⓑ 13.8 pounds

Ⓒ 8.3 pounds

Ⓓ 3.3 pounds

Name ______________________

 Practice  Video  Tools  Games

Additional Practice 4-7
Use Properties to Multiply Decimals

Another Look!

Marco hiked 2.5 miles in an hour. If he continues at the same speed, how far will he hike in 3.25 hours?

$2.5 \times 3.25 =$

$= (25 \times 325) \times (0.1 \times 0.01)$

$= 8{,}125 \times 0.001$

$= 8.125$

Marco will hike 8.125 miles in 3.25 hours.

Remember, one tenth times one hundredth equals one thousandth.

1. To find 0.6×0.35, multiply the whole numbers ______ and ______ by the decimals ______ and ______. The product is ______.

In **2–16**, write each product.

2. 0.2×0.9

3. 0.58×0.3

4. 2.5×0.77

5. 3.1×0.4

6. 0.07×1.2

7. 14.3×0.8

8. 0.1×2.85

9. 1.18×0.6

10. 9.2×0.01

11. 0.45×5.5

12. 3.9×3.9

13. 0.16×0.5

14. 0.55×6.9

15. 0.1×7.25

16. 0.13×0.5

17. Helen uses 0.12 kilogram of nuts in each batch of granola that she makes. If she makes 2.5 batches, how many kilograms of nuts will she use?

18. The weight of an empty pickup truck is 2.1 times the weight of an empty car. If the empty car weighs 1.8 tons, how many tons does the pickup weigh carrying a 0.5-ton load?

19. Make Sense and Persevere Mr. Chaplin measured his sons' rectangular bedrooms for new carpeting. Whose bedroom has the greatest area?

George's bedroom	3.5 meters by 4.4 meters
Steven's bedroom	3.8 meters by 3.8 meters
Andy's bedroom	3.6 meters by 4.1 meters

20. Higher Order Thinking Hank has a board 1.75 meters long. He used 0.8 meter to build the walls of a birdhouse. He used 0.4 of what is left for the floor. He needs 0.6 meter for the roof. Does he have enough wood for the roof? Explain.

21. The times for five sprinters in a 50-meter dash were 6.72 seconds, 6.4 seconds, 6.08 seconds, 7.03 seconds, and 6.75 seconds. Write these times from fastest to slowest.

Assessment Practice

22. Which expression is equivalent to 1.18×0.6?

Ⓐ $(1.18 \times 0.01) \times (0.6 \times 0.1)$

Ⓑ $(118 \times 0.01) \times (6 \times 0.1)$

Ⓒ $(118 \times 100) \times (6 \times 10)$

Ⓓ $(118 \times 0.1) \times (6 \times 0.1)$

23. Which expression is equivalent to 0.4×8.7?

Ⓐ $(4 \times 87) \times (0.01 \times 0.1)$

Ⓑ $(4 \times 87) \times (100 \times 10)$

Ⓒ $(4 \times 87) \times (0.01 \times 0.01)$

Ⓓ $(4 \times 87) \times (0.1 \times 0.1)$

Name ______________________

 Practice  Video  Tools  Games

Additional Practice 4-8
Use Number Sense to Multiply Decimals

Another Look!

Amelia can walk 3.6 miles in one hour. How far can she walk in 2.1 hours?

$3.6 \times 2.1 = 756$

Use number sense to place the decimal in the product.

75.6 and 756 are not reasonable answers.

Estimate: $3 \times 2 = 6$ and $4 \times 2 = 8$.
So the answer is between 6 and 8.

Amelia will walk 7.56 miles in 2.1 hours.

Use estimation and number sense to help you place the decimal point.

In **1–4**, the product is shown without the decimal point. Use number sense to place the decimal point appropriately.

1. $6 \times 5.01 = 3006$

2. $12.8 \times 3.2 = 4096$

3. $4.06 \times 20.1 = 81606$

4. $24 \times 6.3 = 1512$

In **5–10**, tell whether or not the decimal point has been placed correctly in the product. If not, rewrite the product with the decimal point correctly placed.

5. $0.6 \times 0.7 = 0.042$

6. $1.1 \times 13.8 = 1.518$

7. $8.06 \times 3 = 241.8$

8. $19 \times 8.3 = 157.7$

9. $2.8 \times 345.1 = 966.28$

10. $56.2 \times 7.9 = 4{,}439.8$

11. Jordan enters 3.4×6.8 into his calculator. He writes the digits 2312 from the display and forgets the decimal point. Where should Jordan write the decimal point? Explain.

12. Mrs. Cooper has $20. Can she buy a museum ticket for her 10-year-old daughter, a ticket for herself, and a book that costs $3.99? Explain.

DATA

Science Museum	
Ticket	**Price**
Child	$5.75
Adult	$11.25

13. Estimate the product of 3.9 and 4.6 using mental math. Explain the method you used.

14. Reasoning Will the actual product of 7.69×5 be greater than or less than its estimate of 8×5? Explain your reasoning.

15. One serving of yogurt has 95 calories. What is a reasonable estimate for the number of calories in 2.5 servings of yogurt?

16. Higher Order Thinking Bruce jogs from his house to the library and back again to tutor students. The distance from his house to the library is 0.28 mile. If Bruce tutored at the library 328 days last year, about how many miles did he jog?

17. Alicia drew a pentagon with equal side lengths and equal angles. Then she added red lines of symmetry to her drawing. How many lines did she draw? Use the picture to show how you know.

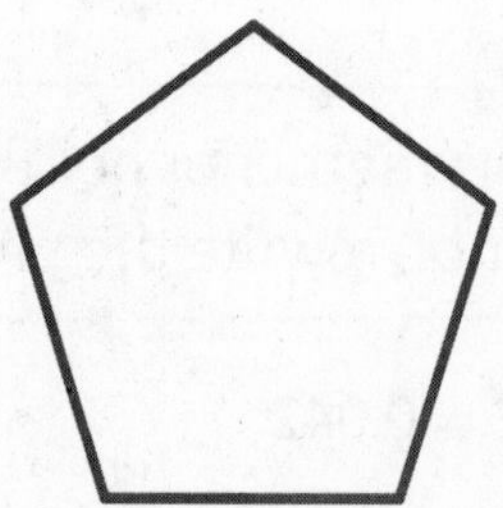

Assessment Practice

18. Which of the following is the missing factor?

$\_\_\_\_ \times 0.7 = 0.287$

Ⓐ 0.041

Ⓑ 0.41

Ⓒ 4.1

Ⓓ 41

19. Which two factors would give a product of 8.34?

Ⓐ 0.06 and 1.39

Ⓑ 0.06 and 13.9

Ⓒ 0.6 and 1.39

Ⓓ 0.6 and 13.9

Name ______________________________

 Practice  Video  Tools  Games

Additional Practice 4-9

Model with Math

Another Look!

The Franklin School library is made up of two rectangular regions, the Reading Room and the Computer Lab. What is the total area of the library?

Write an equation to represent this situation. Let A represent the total area.
$A = (24 \times 19.6) + (9.2 \times 8.5)$

Franklin School Library

Section	Dimensions
Reading room	24 meters by 19.6 meters
Computer lab	9.2 meters by 8.5 meters

Multiply to find the area of each room.

$$\begin{aligned}24 \times 19.6 &= 24 \times (196 \times 0.1)\\ &= (24 \times 196) \times 0.1\\ &= 4{,}704 \times 0.1\\ &= 470.4\end{aligned}$$

$$\begin{array}{r} 9.2 \\ \times\ 8.5 \\ \hline 0.10 \\ 4.5 \\ 1.6 \\ 72 \\ \hline 78.2 \end{array}$$

Add to find the total area.

$$\begin{array}{r} \overset{1}{4}70.4 \\ +\ 78.2 \\ \hline 548.6 \end{array}$$

The total area is 548.6 square meters.

You can use equations to apply the math you know to solve a problem.

Model with Math

Mrs. Gordon measured three rectangular rooms she wants to tile. What is the total area of the rooms?

Family room	24.5 ft by 16 ft
Kitchen	15 ft by 12.75 ft
Laundry room	10.5 ft by 10.5 ft

1. Describe the steps you would take to solve the problem.

2. Write an equation to represent the problem.

3. What is the solution to the problem?

Trail Mix Sales

The table shows the number of bags of trail mix sold last month at Patsy's Pantry and Mo's Munch-and-Crunch. Each small bag of trail mix sells for \$5.87 at Patsy's Pantry and \$4.59 at Mo's Munch-and-Crunch. Which store earned more money from the sales of small bags of trail mix? How much more?

DATA

Trail Mix Bag	Number of Bags Sold	
	Patsy's Pantry	Mo's Munch and Crunch
Small (1.5 lb)	31	40
Medium (3 lb)	14	68
Large (4.5 lb)	53	35

4. **Make Sense and Persevere** What are you asked to find?

5. **Model with Math** Write and solve an equation to represent the total amount earned from the sale of small bags at Patsy's. Then write and solve an equation to represent the total amount earned from the sales of small bags at Mo's.

You can model with math by using what you know about multiplying whole numbers to multiply decimals.

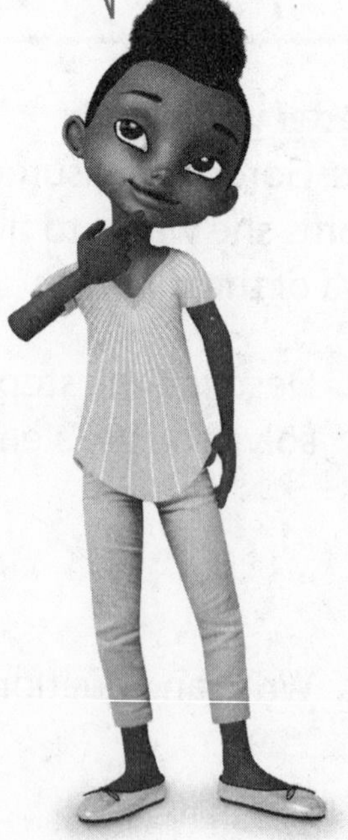

6. **Be Precise** Which store earned more money from the sales of small bags of trail mix? How much more? Show your work.

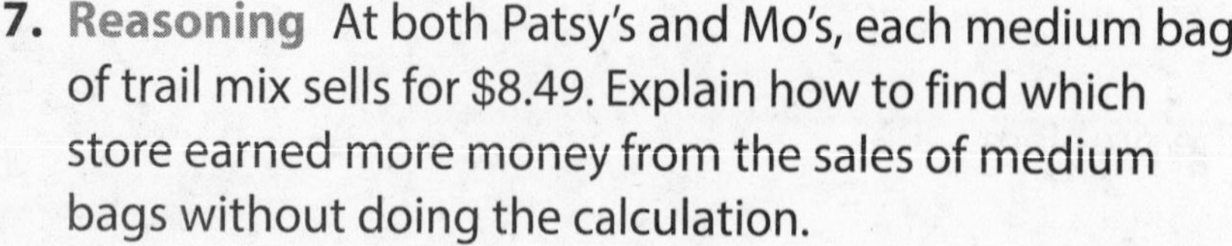

7. **Reasoning** At both Patsy's and Mo's, each medium bag of trail mix sells for \$8.49. Explain how to find which store earned more money from the sales of medium bags without doing the calculation.

Name ____________________

Practice Video Tools Games

Additional Practice 5-1

Use Patterns and Mental Math to Divide

Another Look!

A school spends $12,000 on 20 new computers. Each computer costs the same amount. How much does each computer cost?

Find a basic fact, and then use patterns.

A basic fact that can be used for 12,000 ÷ 20 is 12 ÷ 2 = 6.

120 ÷ 20 = 6
1,200 ÷ 20 = 60
12,000 ÷ 20 = 600

Multiply to check: 600 × 20 = 12,000

Each computer costs $600.

Use place-value patterns to help find the quotient.

Leveled Practice In **1–16**, use mental math to help solve.

1. 720 ÷ 90 = 72 tens ÷ 9 tens = ____

2. 4,800 ÷ 60 = 480 tens ÷ 6 tens = ____

3. 1,200 ÷ 30 = ____ tens ÷ ____ tens = ____

4. 25,000 ÷ 50 = ____ tens ÷ ____ tens = ____

5. 320 ÷ 40

6. 9,000 ÷ 30

7. 1,800 ÷ 90

8. 2,000 ÷ 40

9. 24,000 ÷ 80

10. 32,000 ÷ 40

11. 3,600 ÷ 90

12. 40,000 ÷ 50

13. 42,000 ÷ 60

14. 5,400 ÷ 60

15. 49,000 ÷ 70

16. 56,000 ÷ 80

17. A carton of staples has 50 packages. The carton contains 25,000 staples in all. Each package has an equal number of staples. How many staples are in each package? Explain how to use a basic fact to find the answer.

18. A club collected $3,472 to buy computers. If each computer costs $680, estimate the number of computers that the club can buy. Explain.

19. Higher Order Thinking A railroad car container can hold 42,000 pounds. Mr. Evans wants to ship 90 ovens and some freezers in the same container. If each freezer weighs 600 pounds, how many freezers could be shipped in the container? Explain.

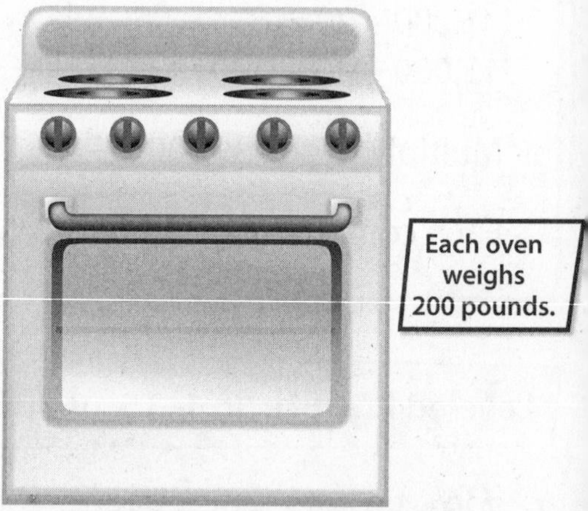

20. Critique Reasoning There are 50 communities in Kalb County. Each community has about the same number of people. Marty estimates there are about 300 people living in each community. Is his estimate reasonable? Justify your answer.

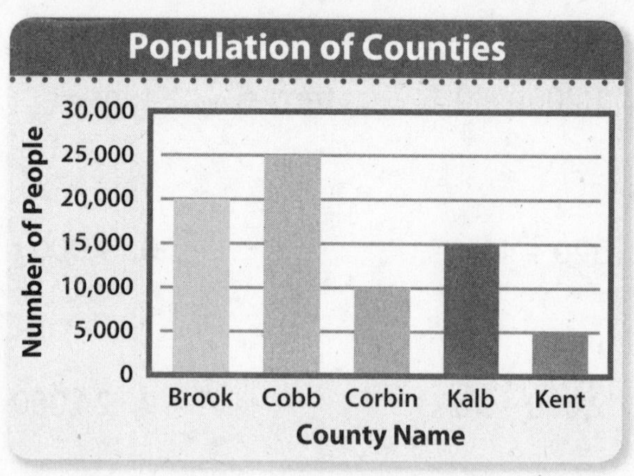

Assessment Practice

21. Which is 2,000 divided by 50?

Ⓐ 4
Ⓑ 40
Ⓒ 400
Ⓓ 4,000

22. Which expression has a quotient of 400?

Ⓐ 800 ÷ 2
Ⓑ 8,000 ÷ 2
Ⓒ 8,000 ÷ 20
Ⓓ 80,000 ÷ 20

Name ________________

Practice Video Tools Games

Additional Practice 5-2
Estimate Quotients with 2-Digit Divisors

Another Look!

Frog Trail is 1,976 meters long. Shondra walks 43 meters of the trail each minute. About how many minutes will it take Shondra to walk the trail?

Find compatible numbers. Think of a basic fact. Then use place-value patterns.

$1{,}976 \div 43$

$\downarrow \quad \downarrow$

$2{,}000 \div 40 = 50$

$2{,}000 \div 40 = 50$, so
$1{,}976 \div 43$ is about 50.

It would take Shondra about 50 minutes.

You can use a basic fact and place-value patterns.

Leveled Practice In **1–3**, fill in the blanks to find the estimates.

1. $1{,}769 \div 23$
$1{,}800 \div \square = \square$

2. $516 \div 48$
$500 \div \square = \square$

3. $891 \div 32$
$\square \div \square = \square$

In **4–15**, estimate using compatible numbers.

4. $241 \div 34$

5. $705 \div 11$

6. $7{,}968 \div 22$

7. $5{,}624 \div 72$

8. $1{,}043 \div 23$

9. $986 \div 12$

10. $642 \div 94$

11. $4{,}870 \div 58$

12. $5{,}721 \div 79$

13. $148 \div 51$

14. $9{,}073 \div 11$

15. $3{,}514 \div 58$

16. Critique Reasoning Meredith says "Since 1 times 1 equals 1, then 0.1 times 0.1 equals 0.1." Do you agree? Explain your reasoning.

17. enVision® STEM A gray whale traveled 152 kilometers in one day. The whale swam between 7 and 8 kilometers each hour. About how many hours did it take the whale to swim the distance? Show two different ways that you can use compatible numbers to find an answer. Then solve.

18. Meg wants to find about how many phones the company activated in one minute. Explain why Meg can use 15,000 ÷ 50 to find the answer.

DATA: Clear Connect Company
phones activated: 14,270 in 50 minutes
calls made: 59,835
text messages sent: 2,063

19. Higher Order Thinking Ester's choir wants to learn a new song for the school concert in 7 weeks. The song has 3,016 lines. The choir learns an equal number of lines each day. About how many lines do they need to learn each day to learn the song in time for the concert? Explain.

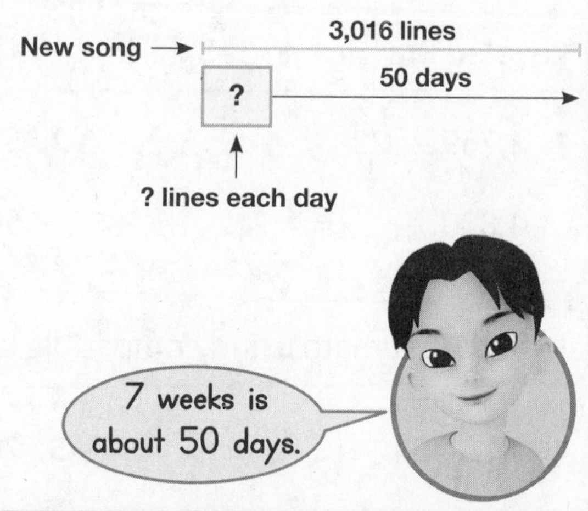

Assessment Practice

20. Mr. Crane's farm is 593 acres. He divides the farm into 32 equal parts. Which is the best estimate of the number of acres in each part?

Ⓐ 10 acres
Ⓑ 20 acres
Ⓒ 100 acres
Ⓓ 200 acres

21. A scientist counted 3,921 total eggs in 49 sea turtle nests. Each nest had about the same number of eggs. Which is the best estimate of the number of eggs she counted in each nest?

Ⓐ 800 eggs
Ⓑ 100 eggs
Ⓒ 80 eggs
Ⓓ 10 eggs

Name ______________________

Practice Video Tools Games

Additional Practice 5-3

Use Models to Divide with 2-Digit Divisors

Another Look!

Hal's store just got a shipment of 195 cans of soup. Hal wants to divide the cans equally on 13 shelves. How many cans should he put on each shelf?

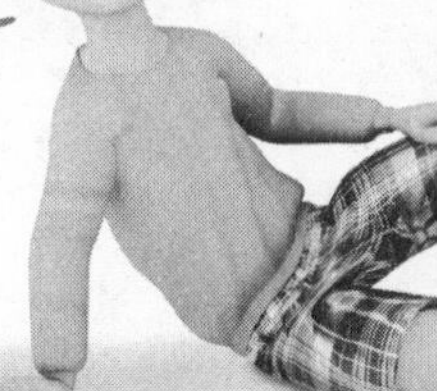

Are there enough cans for 10 in each group? For 20 in each group?

Step 1

Divide the tens. Record.

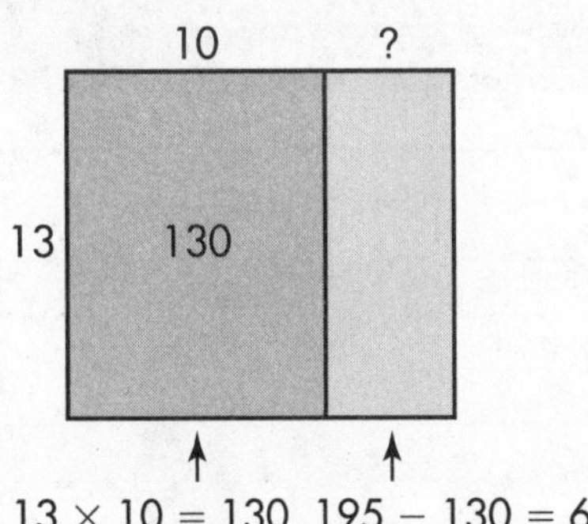

$13 \times 10 = 130$ $195 - 130 = 65$

Step 2

Divide the ones. Record.

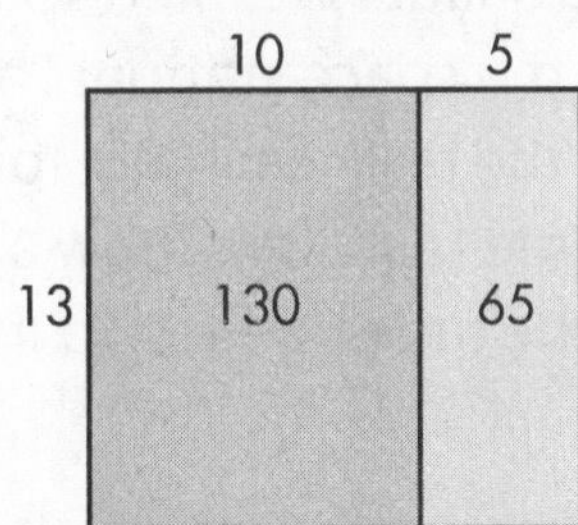

Multiply to check:

$13 \times 15 = 13 \times (10 + 5) = 130 + 65 = 195$

So $195 \div 13 = 15$

He should put 15 cans on each shelf.

In **1** and **2**, use the diagram to find each quotient.

1. $12\overline{)168}$

___ + ___

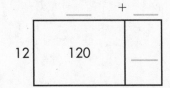

12 | 120 | ___

2. $16\overline{)208}$

___ + ___

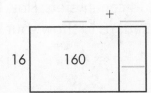

16 | 160 | ___

In **3–8**, use grid paper or draw a picture to find each quotient.

3. $420 \div 14$

4. $385 \div 11$

5. $744 \div 24$

6. $675 \div 27$

7. $558 \div 18$

8. $228 \div 19$

9. Anna has 10^2 quarters. Jazmin has 10^2 dimes. Who has more money, Anna or Jazmin? How much more? Explain your reasoning.

10. Make Sense and Persevere A 208-yard-long road is divided into 16 parts of equal length. Mr. Ward paints a 4-yard-long strip in each part. How long is the unpainted strip of each part of the road?

What steps do you need to solve to find the answer?

11. Use the bar graph. Astronauts installed 15 new tiles on the outside of the space station. They spent 390 minutes on the task. Each tile took the same amount of time to install. Draw a bar in the graph to show the time needed to install a tile. Explain.

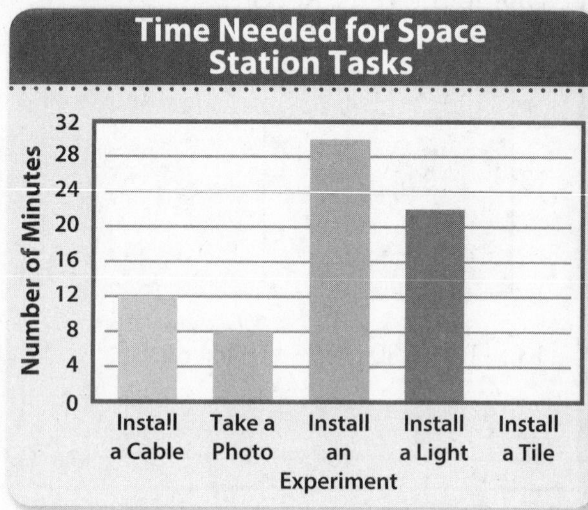

12. How much longer does an astronaut take to install a light than to install a cable?

13. Higher Order Thinking A rectangular poster has an area of 504 square centimeters. The width of the poster is 14 centimeters. How long is the poster? Write equations to show your work.

Assessment Practice

14. Which is 540 divided by 30?

Ⓐ 17
Ⓑ 18
Ⓒ 170
Ⓓ 180

15. Which is 391 divided by 17?

Ⓐ 23
Ⓑ 24
Ⓒ 230
Ⓓ 240

Name ____________

Practice Video Tools Games

Additional Practice 5-4

Use Partial Quotients to Divide

Another Look!

A baker made 312 bagels in one day. If he puts 12 bagels in each package, how many packages did he make that day?

```
    6
   20
12)312
 - 240   20 groups of 12 = 240
    72
 -  72   6 groups of 12 = 72
     0   0 left over
```

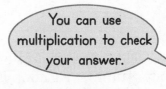

Add the partial quotients: 20 + 6 = 26.

So, the baker made 26 packages of bagels.

You can use multiplication to check your answer.

Leveled Practice In **1–13**, use partial quotients to divide. Show your work.

1.

```
   [ ]
   [ ]
21)714
 - 630   [ ] groups of 21 = 630
    84
 -  84   [ ] groups of 21 = 84
     0   [ ] left over
```

Add the partial quotients: [ ] + [ ] = [ ].

So, 714 ÷ 21 = ____.

2. 41)533 **3.** 15)344 **4.** 39)780 **5.** 50)700

6. 11)801 **7.** 24)648 **8.** 33)396 **9.** 17)763

10. 23)920 **11.** 30)810 **12.** 16)469 **13.** 53)954

14. Use the table. What is the total amount of electricity a computer, a television, and a heater use in 1 hour? Show your work.

15. Number Sense How many hours does it take for a light bulb to use as much electricity as a heater uses in 1 hour?

DATA

Electricity Used	
Appliance	**Kilowatts Per Hour**
Computer	0.09
Heater	1.5
Light bulb	0.1
Television	0.3

16. The cost of each plane ticket for the Baltazar family's summer vacation is $329. If there are 7 family members, what is the total cost of the plane tickets?

17. Make Sense and Persevere Shannon biked in an endurance cycling race. She traveled 2,912 miles and biked about 95 miles each day. About how many days did it take her to complete the race?

18. Algebra Twelve buses bring a total of 420 people to The Alhambra in Granada, Spain. Each bus carries the same number of people. How many people are on each bus? Write and solve an equation to find *p*, the number of people on each bus.

19. Higher Order Thinking How can you use partial quotients to find 684 ÷ 57? Explain.

Use an estimate to see if your answer makes sense.

Assessment Practice

20. Which expressions are equivalent to 28?

- ☐ 980 ÷ 35
- ☐ 480 ÷ 16
- ☐ 1,400 ÷ 50
- ☐ 625 ÷ 25
- ☐ 1,680 ÷ 60

21. Which expressions are equivalent to 53?

- ☐ 1,680 ÷ 40
- ☐ 2,385 ÷ 45
- ☐ 1,612 ÷ 62
- ☐ 3,127 ÷ 59
- ☐ 3,763 ÷ 71

Name ______________________

Practice Video Tools Games

Additional Practice 5-5
Use Sharing to Divide: Two-Digit Divisors

Another Look!

Bo has 215 baseball cards to divide equally among 15 friends. How many cards will each friend get? Will there be any cards left?

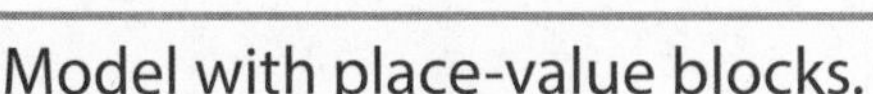
Model with place-value blocks.

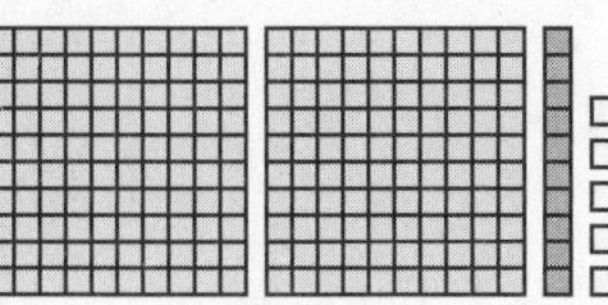

Regroup the blocks.

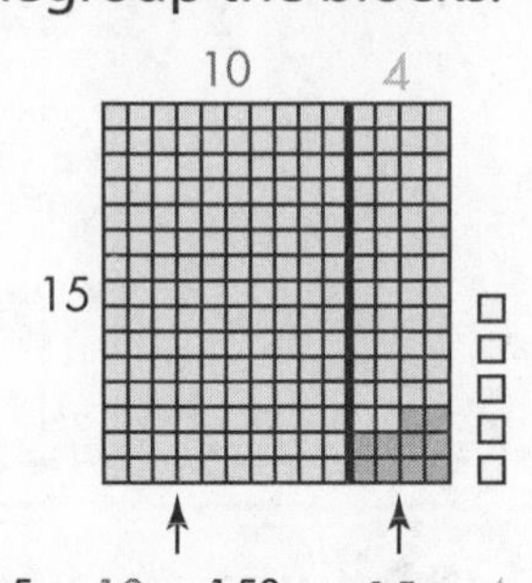

$15 \times 10 = 150$ $\quad$ $15 \times 4 = 60$

$215 - 150 = 65$ $\quad$ $65 - 60 = 5$ left over

$$\begin{array}{r} 14 \\ 15\overline{)215} \\ -\,150 \\ \hline 65 \\ -\,60 \\ \hline 5 \end{array}$$

21 tens ÷ 15 equal groups = 1 ten in each group

15 groups of 10 = 150

65 ones ÷ 15 equal groups = 4 ones in each group

15 groups of 4 = 60

5 cards left over

$215 \div 15 = 14$ R5 because $15 \times 14 + 5 = 215$.

Each friend will get 14 cards, with 5 cards left over.

Leveled Practice In **1–8**, find the quotient.

1. $19\overline{)3\ 5\ 9}$ = ☐☐ R ☐

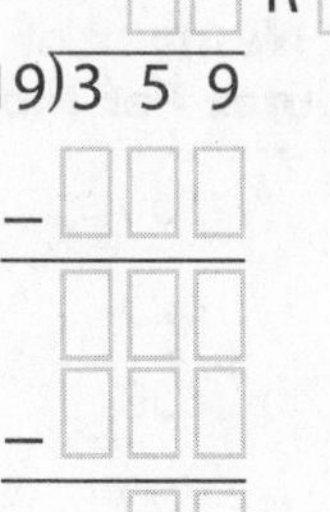

2. $32\overline{)5\ 1\ 2}$ = ☐☐

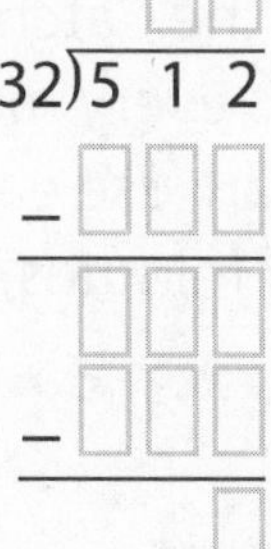

Remember to compare the remainder to the divisor.

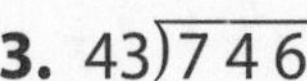

3. $43\overline{)746}$ **4.** $22\overline{)800}$ **5.** $70\overline{)632}$

6. $62\overline{)779}$ **7.** $40\overline{)920}$ **8.** $29\overline{)332}$

9. Why can the calculations on the side be thought of as simpler problems? Describe the simpler problems.

```
     1 2 R13
80)9 7 3   ←— 97 tens ÷ 80 groups
  −8 0 0   ←— 80 × 1 ten
   1 7 3   ←— 173 ones ÷ 80 groups
  −1 6 0   ←— 80 × 2 ones
     1 3
```

10. Construct Arguments A county has 88 schools. The county received 992 new computers. Are there enough computers so that each school can get 11 new computers? Explain.

11. Twin Oaks Soccer Field is a rectangle. The longer side of the field is 108 yards long. What is the perimeter of the field?

12. Higher Order Thinking Liza makes 20 minutes of phone calls each day. Which plan will give Liza enough minutes for June, with between 30 and 50 minutes left? Show your work.

13. Mark and his brother signed up for the Catch Up phone plan. They share the minutes every month equally. How many minutes can Mark use each day without going over his share of minutes?

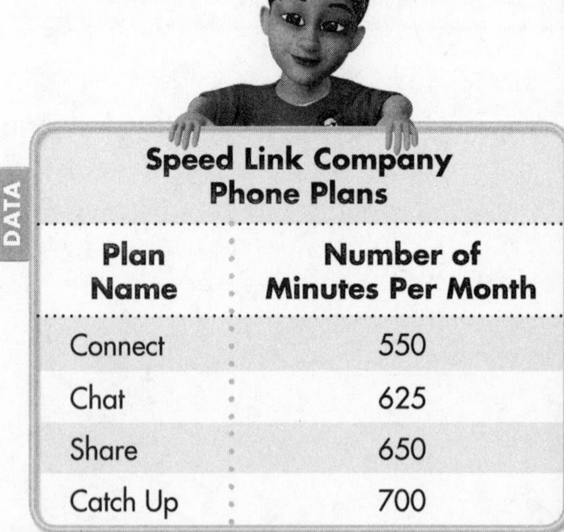

DATA

Speed Link Company Phone Plans

Plan Name	Number of Minutes Per Month
Connect	550
Chat	625
Share	650
Catch Up	700

Assessment Practice

14. Find an expression that gives a quotient of 16. Write the expression in the box.

Quotient: 16		
600 ÷ 40	620 ÷ 40	640 ÷ 40
644 ÷ 40	660 ÷ 40	680 ÷ 40

Name

Practice Video Tools Games

Additional Practice 5-6
Use Sharing to Divide: Greater Dividends

Another Look!

Find 5,890 ÷ 65.

$$\begin{array}{r} 90 \\ 65\overline{)5{,}890} \\ -\,5{,}850 \\ \hline 40 \end{array}$$

589 tens divided into 65 equal groups is 9 tens in each group

65 groups of 90 = 5,850

40 left over

5,890 ÷ 65 = 90 R40 because 65 × 90 + 40 = 5,890.

You can use place-value blocks to model the division if you need help.

In **1–12**, find the quotient. Use place-value blocks or an area model if you need help.

1. $11\overline{)2{,}014}$

2. $34\overline{)7{,}006}$

3. $70\overline{)5{,}591}$

4. 1,620 ÷ 18

5. 4,400 ÷ 30

6. 8,899 ÷ 61

7. $40\overline{)8{,}175}$

8. $28\overline{)770}$

9. $14\overline{)1{,}726}$

10. $75\overline{)688}$

11. $29\overline{)5{,}123}$

12. $17\overline{)1{,}699}$

13. **Number Sense** Will the quotient 7,818 ÷ 25 be greater than 100 or less than 100? How do you know?

14. **Reasoning** Choose the best estimate for 2,819 ÷ 13 from the following:

100 200 500

How did you decide?

15. Jordan bought 1.8 pounds of ham, 2.15 pounds of onions, and 8 cans of soup. What was the total cost before sales tax? Round your answer to the nearest cent.

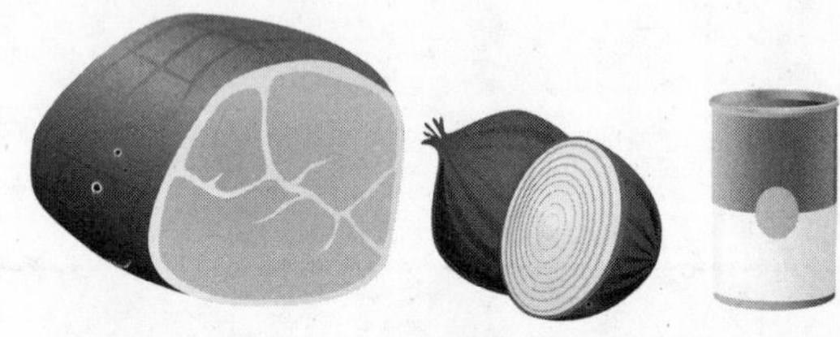

16. The sales tax for the food Jordan bought is $0.87. He has a coupon for $1.75 off any purchase. Use your answer for Exercise 15 to find the final amount Jordan needs to pay.

Ham $3.95 per pound	Onions $0.89 per pound	Soup $1.05 per can

17. Which quotient will be larger? Explain how you can tell without dividing.

3,444 ÷ 42
4,368 ÷ 42

18. There are 347 students going on a field trip. Each bus holds 44 students. If each bus costs $95, is the total cost of the buses more than $1,000? Estimate, then find the exact answer.

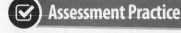

Assessment Practice

19. Find 3,384 ÷ 47. How can you check the reasonableness of your answer?

Name ______________________

Practice

Video

Tools

Games

Additional Practice 5-7
Choose a Strategy to Divide

Another Look!

At the driving range, golfers can rent buckets of 32 golf balls. The range has a supply of 2,650 golf balls. How many buckets are needed for the balls?

Use compatible numbers to estimate 2,650 ÷ 32. You can use 2,700 ÷ 30 = 90.

82 32)2,650 − 2,560 80 groups of 32 = 2,560. 90 − 64 2 groups of 32 = 64. 26 26 balls left over	They can fill 82 buckets with golf balls. They need 1 more bucket for the 26 balls that are left. So the range needs 83 buckets. 83 is close to 90, so the answer is reasonable.

Leveled Practice In **1–4**, fill in the boxes.

1. 42)926   2☐ R☐

2. 38)1,558   ☐☐

3. 77)693   ☐

4. 21)2,567   ☐☐☐ R☐

In **5–16**, estimate, and then find the quotient. Use your estimate to check reasonableness.

5. 462 ÷ 77

6. 44)817

7. 21)777

8. 35)280

9. 2,465 ÷ 29

10. 203 ÷ 29

11. 8,114 ÷ 46

12. 13)1,748

13. 6,264 ÷ 87

14. 5,578 ÷ 68

15. 9,855 ÷ 45

16. 7,308 ÷ 12

17. Make Sense and Persevere A farmer has 4,700 carrots to put in bunches of 15 carrots. He plans to sell the carrots for $5 per bunch at his farm stand. About how many bunches will the farmer make?

Is there information you don't need?

18. Higher Order Thinking You are dividing 3,972 by 41. Explain why the first digit in the quotient should be placed over the tens place of the dividend.

19. Ⓐ-Ⓩ **Vocabulary** Write a division story problem with 53 as the divisor and 2,491 as the dividend. Solve.

20. Reasoning How can estimating the quotient help you check that your answer to a division problem is reasonable?

21. Number Sense Maya has 462 pennies. Use mental math to find how many pennies are left if she puts them in stacks of 50 pennies. Explain your reasoning.

22. A caravan crossed 1,378 miles of desert in 85 days. It traveled 22 miles on the first day and 28 miles on the second day. If the caravan traveled the same number of miles on each of the remaining days, how many miles did it travel on each of those days? Complete the bar diagram to show how you found the answer.

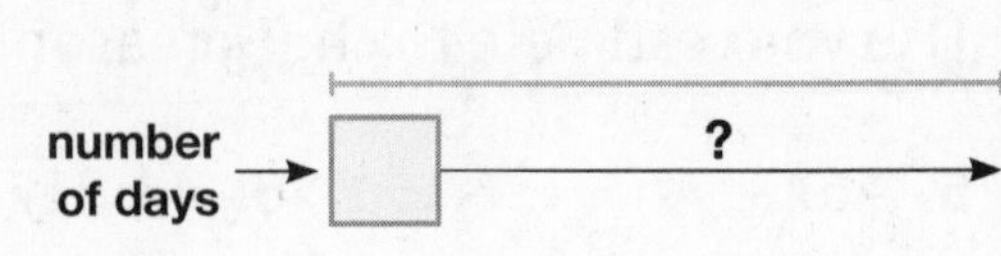
number of days
?

Assessment Practice

23. For which division problems is 54 the quotient? Write those division problems in the box.

Quotient = 54
$45\overline{)2{,}430}$ $12\overline{)660}$ $81\overline{)3{,}645}$ $11\overline{)594}$ $19\overline{)950}$

Name ______________________

Additional Practice 5-8

Make Sense and Persevere

Another Look!

Dex works at a dog adoption shelter. He has 4 large boxes of dog treats with 34 treats in each box and 3 small boxes with 28 treats in each box. How many bags of 20 treats can Dex make from all the treats?

You can use bar diagrams to model the steps you need to solve.

What Do You Know? There are 4 large boxes with 34 treats each and 3 small boxes with 28 treats each.

What Are You Trying to Find? The number of bags of 20 treats that Dex can make.

Use bar diagrams and equations to find the number of treats in the large and small boxes.

ℓ total treats in large boxes

34	34	34	34

$4 \times 34 = \ell, \ell = 136$ treats

***s* total treats in small boxes**

28	28	28

$3 \times 28 = s,\ s = 84$ treats

Add to find the number of treats in all. $136 + 81 = 220$

Divide to find the number of bags Dex can make with 220 treats. $220 \div 20 = b, b = 11$

Dex can make 11 bags of treats.

In **1** and **2**, solve the multi-step problems.

1. A tropical storm has been moving at 15 miles per hour for the past two days. Bess recorded that the storm moved 135 miles yesterday and 75 miles today. For how many hours has Bess been keeping track of the storm? Draw a bar diagram and write equations to help you solve.

2. A parking garage has 6 levels. Each level has 15 rows. Each row has the same number of parking spaces. There are 2,250 parking spaces in all. How many parking spaces are in each row? Write an equation or equations to show your work.

Performance Task

Fruit Punch
Ana's fifth-grade class is making a large batch of punch for the all-day science fair. There are 25 students in Ana's class. The ingredients they will mix together to make the punch are listed on the recipe card. The class is going to pour 12-ounce servings. How many full servings can they make?

Fruit Punch Recipe

Ingredient	Number of Ounces
Grape Juice	240
Apple Juice	480
Orange Juice	640
Ginger Ale	150

3. **Make Sense and Persevere** What do you know? What are you trying to find?

4. **Reasoning** How are the quantities in the problem related? What steps are needed to solve the problem?

5. **Model with Math** Write equations with variables to represent the steps needed to solve the problem.

6. **Be Precise** Solve the equations and answer the problem.

7. **Critique Reasoning** Alejandro says that the division has remainder 10, so one more serving can be poured. Do you agree? Explain.

Think about the steps needed to solve the problem!

Name ______

Practice Video Tools Games

Additional Practice 6-1
Patterns for Dividing with Decimals

Another Look!

Sanjai has 275 pounds of clay. He uses the clay to make 100 identical bowls. How much clay does he use for each bowl?

To divide by 10, or 10^1, move the decimal point 1 place to the left.

To divide by 100, or 10^2, move the decimal point 2 places to the left.

$275 \div 100 = \mathbf{2.75} = 2.75$

Sanjai uses 2.75 pounds of clay for each bowl.

Leveled Practice In **1–18**, use mental math and patterns to complete each problem.

1. $2{,}500 \div 10 =$ ____
$250 \div$ ____ $= 25$
____ $\div 10 = 2.5$
$2.5 \div 10 =$ ____

2. $20 \div$ ____ $= 2$
$20 \div 10^2 =$ ____
$20 \div 10^3 =$ ____
$20 \div 10^4 =$ ____

3. ____ $\div 10 = \$675$
$\$675 \div$ ____ $= \$67.50$
$\$6{,}750 \div 10^2 =$ ____
$\$6{,}750 \div 10^3 =$ ____

4. $9{,}600 \div 10^1 =$ ____
$960 \div 10^1 =$ ____
$96 \div 10^1 =$ ____
$9.6 \div 10^1 =$ ____

5. $\$800 \div$ ____ $= \$80$
____ $\div 10 = \$8$
$\$8 \div 10 =$ ____
$\$0.80 \div 10 =$ ____

6. $1{,}200 \div 10^3 =$ ____
$120 \div$ ____ $= 12$
____ $\div 10^1 = 1.2$
$1.2 \div 10^2 =$ ____

7. $4 \div 100$

8. $15 \div 10^0$

9. $450 \div 10$

10. $60 \div 100$

11. $55 \div 10$

12. $30.9 \div 100$

13. $8{,}020 \div 10^2$

14. $150 \div 10^3$

15. $16 \div 10^3$

16. $1.8 \div 10^1$

17. $720 \div 100$

18. $3{,}500 \div 10^4$

Remember that you may need to insert zeros when you move the decimal point to the left.

19. The city has a section of land that is 3,694.7 feet long. The city wants to partition this length to form 10 equal-sized garden plots. How long will each garden plot be?

20. Higher Order Thinking A stack of 10^2 pennies is 6.1 inches tall. A stack of 10^2 dimes is 5.3 inches tall. How much taller is a stack of 10 pennies than a stack of 10 dimes?

21. For a party, 10 friends are buying 100 cups, 100 plates, a punchbowl, and 200 balloons. If the friends share the cost equally, how much should each friend contribute?

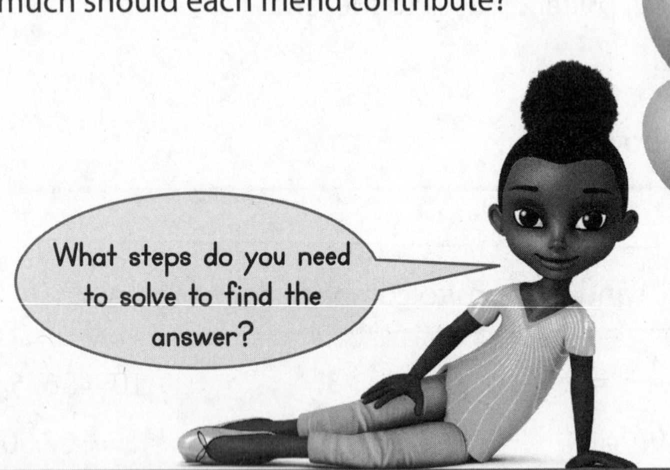

What steps do you need to solve to find the answer?

DATA

Party Supplies	
100 balloons	$7.80
100 plates	$4.75
100 cups	$5.45
100 napkins	$2.09
10 invitations	$1.60
plastic punchbowl	$11.50

22. Critique Reasoning Lance says that $2{,}376 \div 10^2$ is the same as $2{,}376 \times 0.1$. Is he correct? Why or why not?

23. On a large map, the distance from Austin, Texas, to Milwaukee, Wisconsin, is 13.7 inches. The actual distance is about 1,000 miles. What is the distance on the same map from Indianapolis, Indiana, to Louisville, Kentucky, if the actual distance is about 100 miles? Round your answer to the nearest tenth.

Assessment Practice

24. Choose the equations in which $n = 100$ will make the equation true.

- ☐ $12.4 \div n = 0.124$
- ☐ $3.8 \div n = 0.038$
- ☐ $52{,}350 \div n = 52.35$
- ☐ $850.4 \div n = 85.04$
- ☐ $0.41 \div n = 0.0041$

25. Choose the equations in which $d = 10^3$ will make the equation true.

- ☐ $37{,}162 \div d = 3.7162$
- ☐ $1{,}041.6 \div d = 1{,}041.6$
- ☐ $2.7 \div d = 0.0027$
- ☐ $168.2 \div d = 1.682$
- ☐ $80.7 \div d = 0.0807$

Name ______________________

Practice Video Tools Games

Additional Practice 6-2
Estimate Decimal Quotients

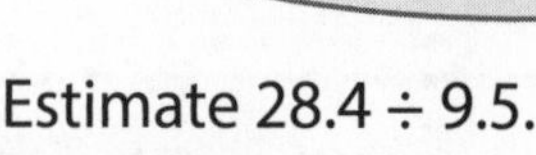

To estimate with decimal division, you can use rounding or compatible numbers.

Estimate 28.4 ÷ 9.5.

One Way

Use rounding. Round to the nearest whole number.

28.4 ÷ 9.5 — Write the original problem.

↓ ↓

28 ÷ 10 = 2.8 — Round 28.4 to 28. Round 9.5 to 10.

Another Way

Use compatible numbers.

28.4 ÷ 9.5 — Write the original problem.

↓ ↓

27 ÷ 9 = 3 — Use compatible numbers.

Leveled Practice In **1** and **2**, complete the work to estimate each quotient.

1. Estimate 52.3 ÷ 11.4 using rounding.

52.3 ÷ 11.4

↓ ↓

52 ÷ 10 = ______

2. Estimate 52.3 ÷ 11.4 using compatible numbers.

52.3 ÷ 11.4

↓ ↓

55 ÷ 11 = ______

In **3–11**, estimate each quotient.

3. 25.1 ÷ 8

4. 59.67 ÷ 11.1

5. 82.77 ÷ 7.5

6. 496.3 ÷ 98

7. 1.76 ÷ 0.91

8. 13.07 ÷ 7.41

9. 41.3 ÷ 6.76

10. 81.4 ÷ 10.03

11. 384.4 ÷ 88.1

12. Ms. Barton and three neighbors purchased a snowblower to share. The snowblower cost $439.20. Describe how you can estimate each person's share of the cost.

13. Is 100 a reasonable estimate for 915.25 ÷ 88.22? Explain.

14. **Make Sense and Persevere** Hodi is building a birdhouse. Each of the four walls of the birdhouse needs to be 5.5 inches long. Hodi has a piece of board that is 24.5 inches long. Is the board long enough to be cut into the four walls of the birdhouse? Estimate using compatible numbers.

15. On Monday, 3.11 inches of rain fell and on Tuesday, 0.81 inch of rain fell. On Wednesday, twice as much rain fell as on Tuesday. How much rain fell during the 3-day period?

16. **Number Sense** A veterinarian weighs three cats. The American Shorthair weighs 13.65 pounds. The Persian weighs 13.07 pounds, and the Maine Coon weighs 13.6 pounds. List the cats in order from least to greatest weight.

17. **Higher Order Thinking** Use estimation to decide which is the better value: 12 pairs of socks for $35.75 or 8 pairs of socks for $31.15. Explain your answer.

Assessment Practice

18. Elena wants to estimate 197.6 ÷ 5.48. Which number sentence shows the best way to estimate this quotient?

Ⓐ 100 ÷ 5 = 20

Ⓑ 100 ÷ 10 = 10

Ⓒ 200 ÷ 5 = 40

Ⓓ 200 ÷ 10 = 20

19. Connor cuts a board with a length of 78.5 centimeters into four equal pieces. Which is the best estimate for the length of each piece?

Ⓐ 2 cm

Ⓑ 5 cm

Ⓒ 20 cm

Ⓓ 25 cm

Name ______________________

Additional Practice 6-3
Use Models to Divide by a 1-Digit Whole Number

Another Look!

Draw a model to help you find 3.25 ÷ 5.

Think about how you can exchange place-value blocks to make 5 equal shares.

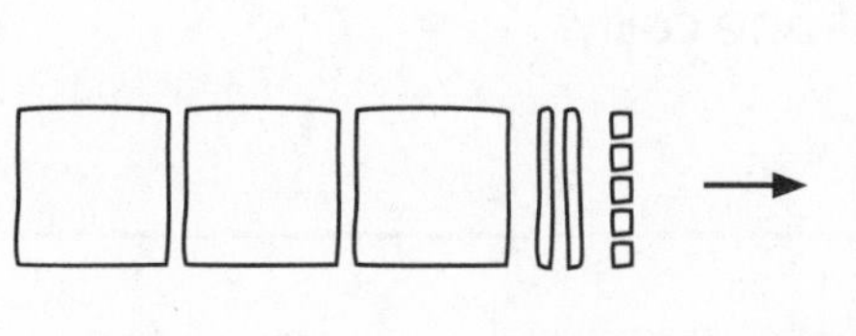

3 ones, 2 tenths, and 5 hundredths

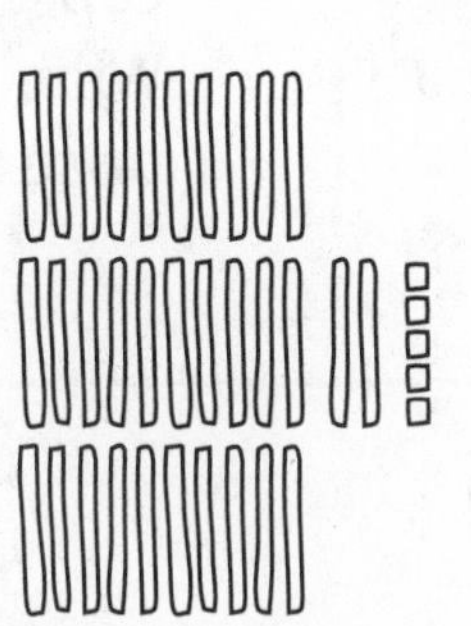

32 tenths and 5 hundredths

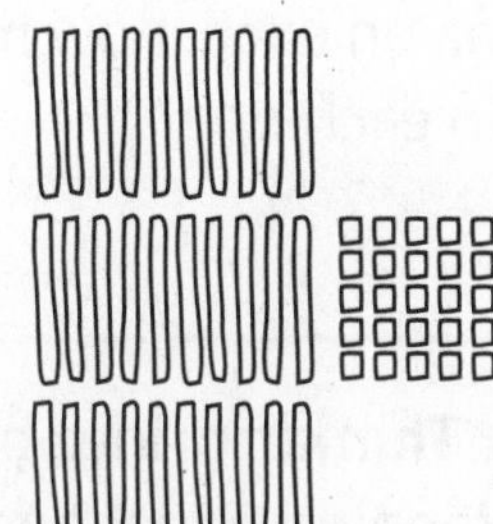

30 tenths and 25 hundredths

What You Show

What You Write

```
   0.6 5
5)3.2 5
 - 3.0 0
     .2 5
   - .2 5
        0
```

Think: Each equal share has 6 tenths and 5 hundredths.

Leveled Practice In **1–6**, divide. Use models to help.

1.
```
   0.☐☐
4)3. 4 8
 - ☐.☐☐
     .2 ☐
   - .☐☐
        0
```

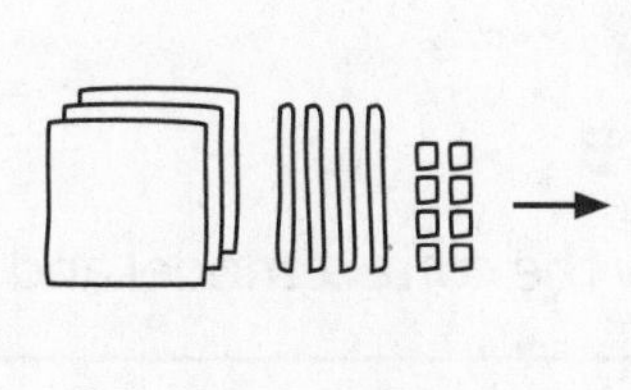

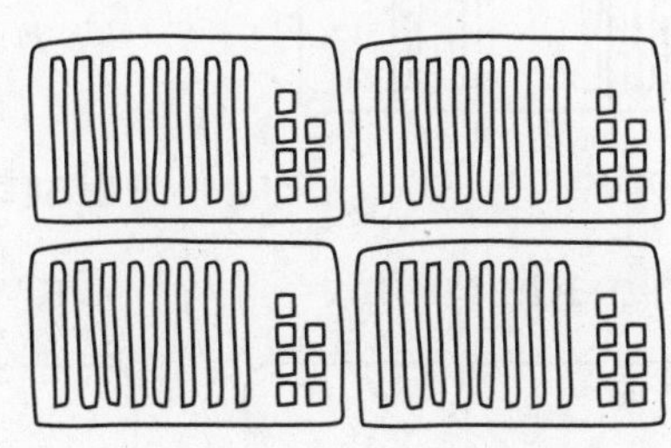

2.
```
   1.☐☐
8)9. 6 8
 - ☐.☐☐
    1.☐☐
  - ☐.☐☐
     .☐☐
   - .☐☐
        ☐
```

3. 3)2.91

4. 4)6.52

5. 7.02 ÷ 6

6. 4.75 ÷ 5

7. Critique Reasoning Janice is dividing 1.92 ÷ 6. Why does she exchange the place-value blocks shown for 18 tenths and 12 hundredths?

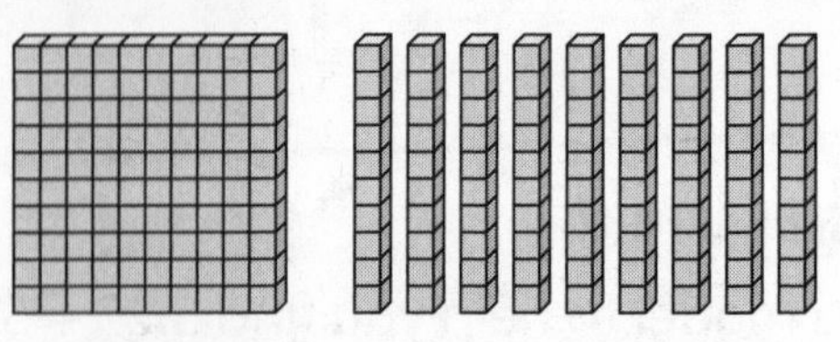

8. Keith has 7.8 ounces of tuna salad. If he makes 3 sandwiches with an equal amount of tuna on each, how much tuna does he put on each one?

9. Algebra A newspaper stand sold 1,000 copies of the city newspaper for $1,600. Write and solve an equation to find the price of one copy.

10. Higher Order Thinking Inez bought a package of wrapping paper and 4 bows. If she wrapped 4 identical gifts with the paper and bows, how much did it cost to wrap each gift?

11. Number Sense Without dividing, how can you decide whether the quotient 7.16 ÷ 4 will be less than or greater than 2?

12. Tina buys 5 pounds of potatoes for $4.35 and 3 pounds of carrots for $3.57. How much does one pound of potatoes cost?

Assessment Practice

13. Glen drew the model shown below for 1.95 ÷ 5.

Part A

Explain the mistake Glen made.

Part B

Draw the correct model and find the quotient.

Name ______________________

Practice Video Tools Games

Additional Practice 6-4

Divide by a 2-Digit Whole Number

Another Look!

The area of a sketch pad is 93.5 square inches. The length of the sketch pad is 11 inches. What is the width of the sketch pad?

First, estimate the width: 93.5 ÷ 11 is about 90 ÷ 10 = 9.

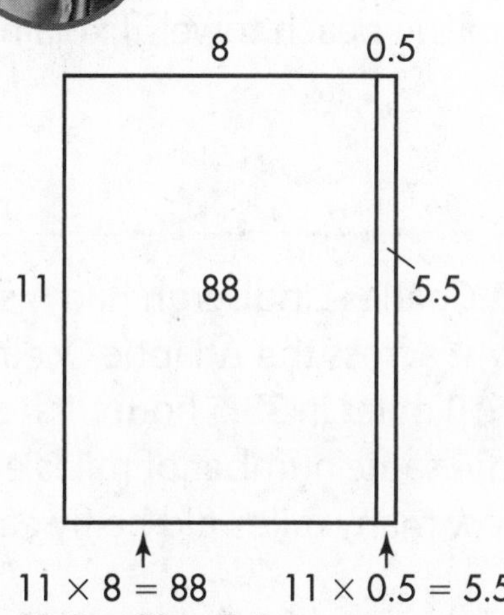

Divide 93.5 by 11.

$$\begin{array}{r} 8.5 \\ 11\overline{)93.5} \\ -\,88.0 \\ \hline 5.5 \\ -\,5.5 \\ \hline 0 \end{array}$$

8.5 is close to the estimate of 9, so the answer is reasonable.

The width of the sketch pad is 8.5 inches.

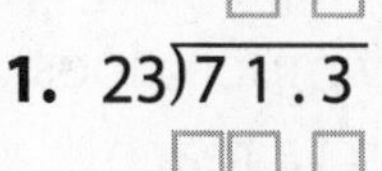

Leveled Practice In **1–12**, find each quotient.

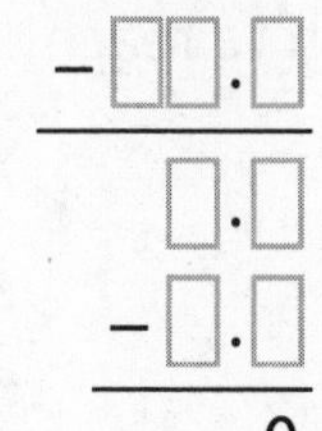

1. 23)71.3

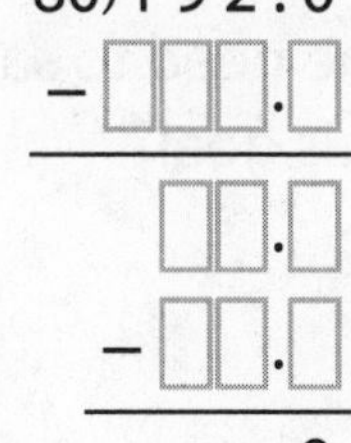

2. 80)192.0

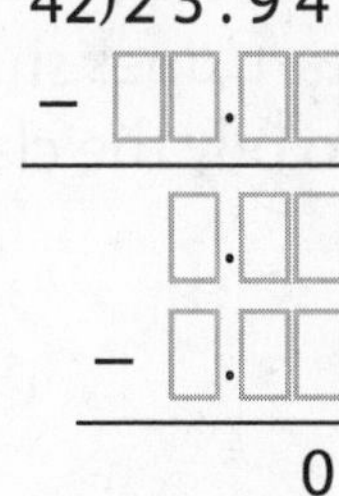

3. 42)23.94

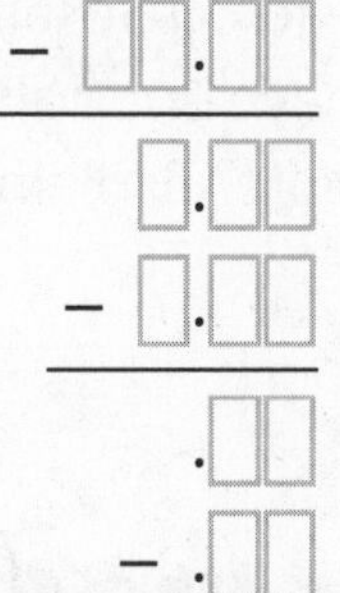

4. 18)40.50

5. 26)98.8

6. 17)14.62

7. 25)157.5

8. 13)113.1

9. 83.2 ÷ 26

10. 25.6 ÷ 4

11. 90.54 ÷ 18

12. 2.25 ÷ 15

13. The longest spin of a basketball on one finger is 255 minutes. About how many hours is that?

14. Kara paid $24.64 to ship 11 packages. Each package was the same size and weight. How much did it cost to ship 1 package?

15. Higher Order Thinking Liza needs a total of 22.23 square feet of terry cloth to make a beach towel and a beach bag. The beach bag requires 5.13 square feet of cloth. What is the length of the beach towel? Explain.

3 feet

16. In 1927, Charles Lindbergh had his first solo flight across the Atlantic Ocean. He flew 3,610 miles in 33.5 hours. If he flew about the same number of miles each hour, how many miles did he fly each hour?

17. Tiffany deposited the following amounts in her savings account last month: $6.74, $5.21, $5.53, and $3.52. Divide the sum by 30 to find the average amount she saved per day for the month. Show your work.

18. Make Sense and Persevere Susan bought 3 plants that cost $2.75 each. She wants to buy 3 clay pots that cost $4.15 each. If Susan had $20 to start, does she have enough money to also buy the clay pots? Explain.

19. Todd is saving for a vacation. The cost of his vacation is $1,089. Todd has a year to save the money. About how much does he need to save each month to reach his goal?

Assessment Practice

20. Which is equal to 78.2 divided by 17?

Ⓐ 0.46

Ⓑ 4.06

Ⓒ 4.6

Ⓓ 46

21. Which is equal to 12.74 divided by 13?

Ⓐ 0.09

Ⓑ 0.98

Ⓒ 9.08

Ⓓ 9.8

Name ____________________

Additional Practice 6-5
Divide by a Decimal

Another Look!

Find $1.35 \div 0.15$.

One Way

$1.35 \div 0.15$

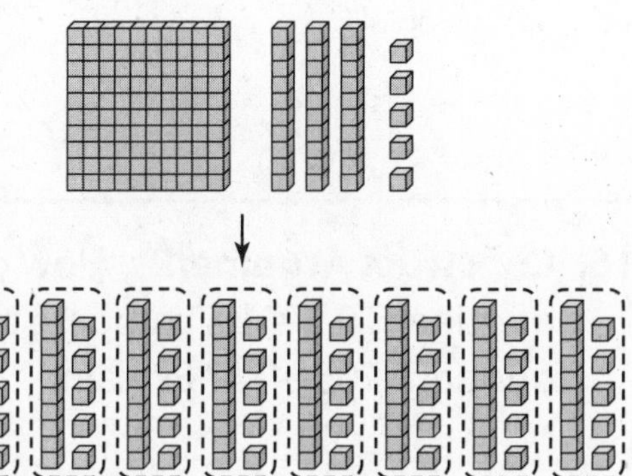

1.35 shown in place-value blocks can be divided into 9 groups of blocks each showing 0.15.

So, $1.35 \div 0.15 = 9$.

Another Way

Think multiplication:

To find $1.35 \div 0.15$, use the relationship between multiplication and division.

$0.15 \times ? = 1.35$

15 hundredths × ? = 135 hundredths

$? = 9$

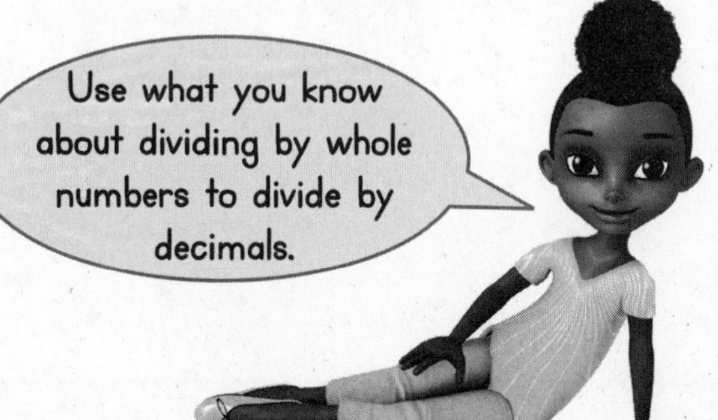

Use what you know about dividing by whole numbers to divide by decimals.

In **1–4**, use what you know about multiplication and division, place value, and partial quotients to divide.

1. $4.55 \div 0.35$

2. $45.5 \div 3.5$

3. $455 \div 35$

4. Describe the relationship among Problems 1, 2, and 3.

In **5–11**, find each quotient.

5. $0.32\overline{)1.92}$

6. $3.2\overline{)19.2}$

7. $0.01\overline{)8.64}$

8. $0.1\overline{)86.4}$

9. $0.22\overline{)8.8}$

10. $2.2\overline{)8.8}$

11. $0.22\overline{)88.0}$

12. Three friends paid \$26.25 to see a movie. How much did each ticket cost?

	\$26.25		
? cost per ticket →	?	?	?

13. In a timed typing test, Lara typed 63 words per minute. Estimate the number of words she should be able to type in half an hour. Show your work.

14. A stack of sheets of tissue paper is about 2.5 inches high. Each sheet is about 0.01 inch thick. How many sheets are in the stack? Show your work.

15. Is the quotient for $41 \div 0.8$ greater or less than 41? Explain.

16. **Construct Arguments** How does the quotient $10.5 \div 1.5$ compare to the quotient $105 \div 15$? Explain.

17. **Number Sense** The fence next to the creek near Adam's house leans a little more each year because the bank of the creek is eroding. If the fence leans about 3.7 degrees more each year, estimate how many more degrees the fence will lean after 5 years.

18. **Higher Order Thinking** The Clark family must pay \$2,820 in property tax on their home this year. Their house payment is \$752 per month. What is their payment each month with the tax? Assume that the tax is paid in equal monthly installments.

Assessment Practice

19. Select the expressions that have a quotient of 8.

- ☐ $0.56 \div 0.07$
- ☐ $0.56 \div 0.7$
- ☐ $5.6 \div 0.07$
- ☐ $5.6 \div 0.7$

20. Select the expressions that have a quotient of 4.

- ☐ $4.8 \div 0.12$
- ☐ $4.8 \div 1.2$
- ☐ $0.48 \div 1.2$
- ☐ $0.48 \div 0.12$

Name ______________________

Practice Video Tools Games

Additional Practice 6-6
Reasoning

Another Look!

Kim bought granola bars for the soccer team. Each granola bar cost \$0.89. She paid \$38.13, including \$0.75 for sales tax. How many granola bars did she buy?

Tell how you can use reasoning to solve the problem.

- I can write an equation to show relationships.
- I can give the answer using the correct unit.

Write an equation to find the total cost of the granola bars before tax.

$\$38.13 - \$0.75 = \$37.38$

Divide to find the number of granola bars.

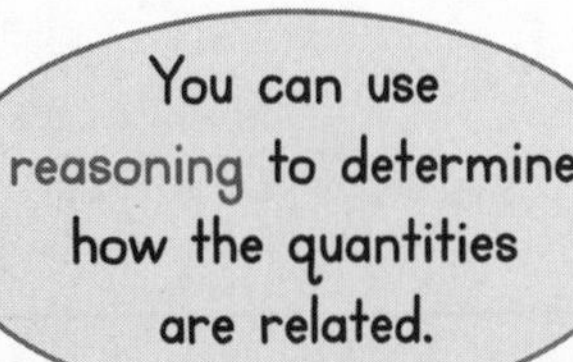

$\$37.38 \div \$0.89$

$\$0.89 \times ? = \$37.38$

$89 \text{ cents} \times ? = 3{,}738 \text{ cents}$

$? = 42$

So, Kim bought 42 granola bars for the soccer team.

Reasoning

Over the summer, Mr. Patel refilled a bird feeder 24 times using 6 cups of seed each time. A bag of seed holds 32 cups. How many bags of seed did Mr. Patel use?

1. Describe one way to solve the problem.

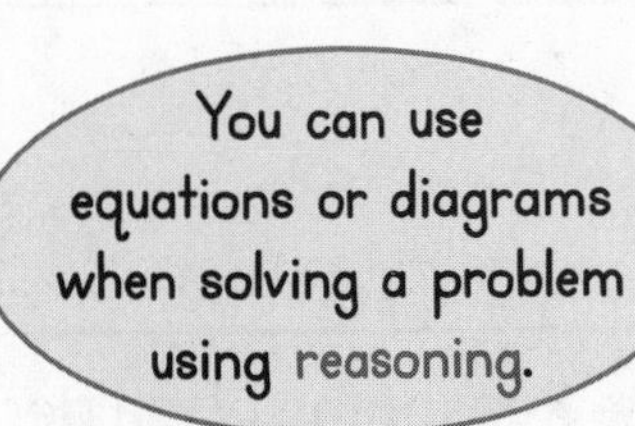

You can use equations or diagrams when solving a problem using reasoning.

2. Write an equation or draw bar diagrams to represent the problem.

3. What is the solution to the problem? Explain.

Performance Task

Greeting Cards

Jana is making greeting cards that are 4 inches long and 3.5 inches wide to sell at a craft fair. She decorates each card by putting a strip of red ribbon along the border all the way around the card. The table shows the amount of ribbon she has on hand.

DATA

Ribbon	Length (inches)
Gold	144
Red	96
Orange	152

4. **Make Sense and Persevere** Explain what each of the quantities means. Are all of the quantities given in the same units?

5. **Model with Math** Draw a diagram of the card and show how it is decorated. Label the width and length of the card.

6. **Reasoning** How could you determine the amount of red ribbon needed for one card?

7. **Be Precise** How many greeting cards can Jana decorate with the red ribbon? Show your work.

8. **Critique Reasoning** Jana decides to make some additional cards that are 7.5 inches long and 5 inches wide. She glues a strip of gold ribbon along each of the longer sides. She says that since $144 \div 7.5 = 19.2$, she can decorate 19 cards with gold ribbon. Do you agree? Explain.

Remember, you can use reasoning to find the amount of ribbon needed for each card.

Name ______________________________

 Practice  Video  Tools  Games

Additional Practice 7-1

Estimate Sums and Differences of Fractions

Another Look!

Estimate $\frac{10}{12} - \frac{4}{9}$.

You can use halfway numbers to help decide if each fraction is closest to 0, to $\frac{1}{2}$, or to 1.

Step 1

Is $\frac{10}{12}$ closest to 0, $\frac{1}{2}$, or 1?

Find the halfway number between 0 and the denominator.

6 is halfway between 0 and 12.

Decide if the numerator is about the same as the halfway number, closer to 0, or closer to 12.

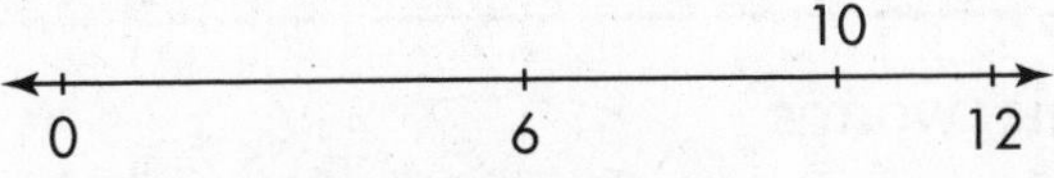

10 is closest to 12.

So, $\frac{10}{12}$ is closest to 1.

Step 2

Is $\frac{4}{9}$ closest to 0, $\frac{1}{2}$, or 1?

If the numerator is closest to the halfway number, the fraction is closest to $\frac{1}{2}$.

$4\frac{1}{2}$ is halfway between 0 and 9.

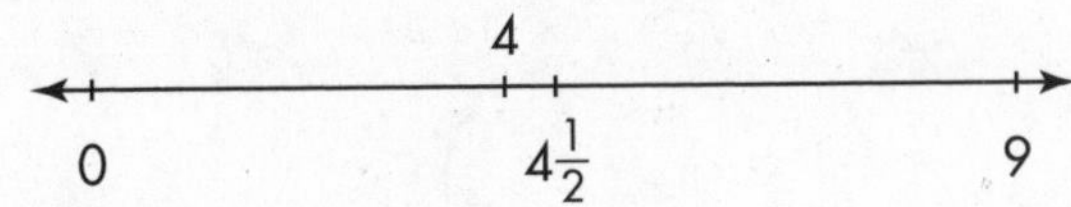

4 is closest to $4\frac{1}{2}$.

So, $\frac{4}{9}$ is closest to $\frac{1}{2}$.

$\frac{10}{12} - \frac{4}{9}$ is about $1 - \frac{1}{2} = \frac{1}{2}$.

Leveled Practice In **1–7**, estimate each sum or difference by replacing each fraction with 0, $\frac{1}{2}$, or 1.

1. (number line: 0, $\frac{1}{2}$, 1)

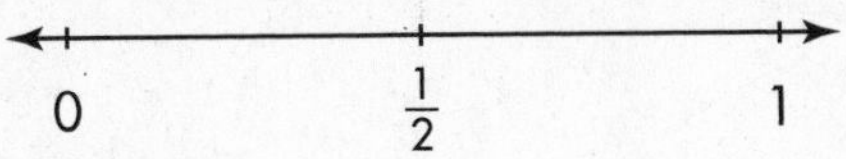

$\frac{4}{18} + \frac{3}{7}$

$\frac{4}{18}$ **Closest to:** ______

$\frac{3}{7}$ **Closest to:** ______

Estimate:

______ + ______ = ______

2. $\frac{8}{15} + \frac{2}{5}$

3. $\frac{17}{21} - \frac{2}{10}$

4. $\frac{8}{10} + \frac{4}{9}$

5. $\frac{12}{15} - \frac{3}{7}$

6. $\frac{15}{20} + \frac{7}{8}$

7. $\frac{8}{14} - \frac{4}{10}$

8. Sam and Lou need a total of 1 foot of wire for a science project. Sam's wire measured $\frac{8}{12}$-foot long. Lou's wire measured $\frac{7}{8}$-foot long. Do they have enough wire for the science project? Explain your reasoning.

9. Construct Arguments Katya measured the growth of a plant seedling. The seedling grew $\frac{1}{3}$ inch by the end of the first week and another $\frac{5}{6}$ inch by the end of the second week. About how much did the seedling grow in the first 2 weeks? Explain how you made your estimate.

10. A scientist measured the amount of rain that fell in a town during one month. How much more rainfall was there in Week 4 than in Week 1?

DATA

March Rainfall

Week	Millimeters
1	2.6
2	3.32
3	4.06
4	4.07

11. Higher Order Thinking Jack is growing Red Wiggler worms to help make compost. He measured the lengths of two young worms. The 10-day old worm is $\frac{10}{12}$ inch long. The 20-day old worm is $1\frac{4}{6}$ inches long. About how much longer is the 20-day old worm than the 10-day old worm? Explain how you found your estimate.

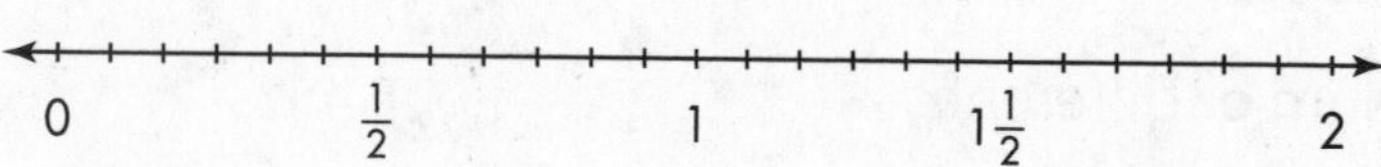

Assessment Practice

12. Julia has to mow two yards. She will need $\frac{13}{16}$ gallon of gas to mow the first yard and $\frac{2}{5}$ gallon to mow the second yard. She has $1\frac{1}{2}$ gallons of gas in her can. Does she have enough to mow both yards? Explain.

Name ______________________

Practice Video Tools Games

Additional Practice 7-2

Find Common Denominators

Another Look!

Rename $\frac{4}{10}$ and $\frac{3}{8}$ using a common denominator.

Remember: A multiple is a product of the number and any nonzero whole number.

Step 1

Find a common denominator for $\frac{4}{10}$ and $\frac{3}{8}$.

List multiples of the denominators 10 and 8. Then look for a common multiple.

10: 10, 20, 30, 40
8: 8, 16, 24, 32, 40

The number 40 can be used as the common denominator.

Step 2

Rename $\frac{4}{10}$ and $\frac{3}{8}$ using 40 as the common denominator.

Multiply the numerator and denominator by the same nonzero number.

$\frac{4}{10}$ $\quad \frac{4 \times 4}{10 \times 4} = \frac{16}{40}$ $\qquad \frac{3}{8}$ $\quad \frac{3 \times 5}{8 \times 5} = \frac{15}{40}$

So, $\frac{16}{40}$ and $\frac{15}{40}$ is one way to rename $\frac{4}{10}$ and $\frac{3}{8}$ using a common denominator.

In **1–9**, find a common denominator for each pair of fractions. Then write equivalent fractions with the common denominator.

1. $\frac{1}{3}$ and $\frac{4}{9}$

$\frac{1}{3}$ **Multiples of the denominator:** ______________ **Rename $\frac{1}{3}$:** ______

$\frac{4}{9}$ **Multiples of the denominator:** ______________ **Rename $\frac{4}{9}$:** ______

Common Denominator: ______ **Rename.** $\frac{1 \times \square}{3 \times \square} = \frac{\square}{\square}$ $\quad \frac{4 \times \square}{9 \times \square} = \frac{\square}{\square}$

2. $\frac{3}{4}$ and $\frac{2}{5}$ **3.** $\frac{4}{7}$ and $\frac{2}{3}$ **4.** $\frac{1}{2}$ and $\frac{7}{11}$ **5.** $\frac{5}{12}$ and $\frac{3}{5}$

6. $\frac{5}{4}$ and $\frac{11}{16}$ **7.** $\frac{6}{7}$ and $\frac{1}{5}$ **8.** $\frac{9}{15}$ and $\frac{4}{9}$ **9.** $\frac{5}{6}$ and $\frac{8}{21}$

10. On the Dell River, a boat will pass the Colby drawbridge and then the Wave drawbridge. Rename each of the two drawbridge opening times. There are 60 minutes in an hour, so use 60 as a common denominator. Then, rename each opening time using another common denominator. Explain how you found your answers.

DATA **Dell River Drawbridge Openings**

Bridge Name	Time of Opening
Asher Cross	On the hour
Colby	On the $\frac{3}{4}$ hour
Rainbow	On the $\frac{2}{3}$ hour
Red Bank	On the $\frac{1}{4}$ hour
Wave	On the $\frac{1}{6}$ hour

11. Higher Order Thinking Phil baked two kinds of pies. Each pie pan was the same size. He served $\frac{1}{2}$ of the blueberry pie. He served $\frac{1}{4}$ of the apple pie. If each pie had 8 pieces to start, what fraction in eighths of the apple pie did he serve? How many more pieces of the blueberry pie than the apple pie did he serve?

12. Look for Relationships Shelly is trying to improve her running time for a track race. She ran the first race in 43.13 seconds. Her time was 43.1 seconds in the second race and 43.07 seconds in the third race. If this pattern continues, what will Shelly's time be in the fourth race?

13. Alicia measured $\frac{1}{4}$ yard of the Blue Diamonds fabric and $\frac{5}{6}$ yard of the Yellow Bonnets fabric to make a quilt. Rename each length of fabric. Use the number of inches in a yard as a common denominator.
HINT: 1 yard = 3 feet; 1 foot = 12 inches

How many inches equal 1 yard?

Assessment Practice

14. Choose all the numbers that could be common denominators for $\frac{2}{3}$ and $\frac{7}{9}$.

- ☐ 6
- ☐ 9
- ☐ 18
- ☐ 27
- ☐ 30

15. Choose all the numbers that could be common denominators for $\frac{1}{9}$ and $\frac{1}{2}$.

- ☐ 11
- ☐ 16
- ☐ 18
- ☐ 36
- ☐ 45

Name ______________________________

Practice Video Tools Games

Additional Practice 7-3
Add Fractions with Unlike Denominators

Another Look!

Find $\frac{1}{6} + \frac{5}{8}$.

Remember: A multiple is a product of the number and any nonzero whole number.

Step 1	**Step 2**	**Step 3**
List multiples of the denominators. Look for a multiple that is the same in both lists. Choose the least one. 6: 6, 12, 18, 24, 30, 36, 42, 48 8: 8, 16, 24, 32, 40, 48 24 and 48 are common multiples of 6 and 8. 24 is the lesser of the two.	Write equivalent fractions using the common multiple as the denominator. $\frac{1}{6} \quad \frac{1 \times 4}{6 \times 4} = \frac{4}{24}$ $\frac{5}{8} \quad \frac{5 \times 3}{8 \times 3} = \frac{15}{24}$	Add the fractions to find the total number of twenty-fourths. $\frac{4}{24} + \frac{15}{24} =$ $\frac{4 + 15}{24} = \frac{19}{24}$ So, $\frac{1}{6} + \frac{5}{8} = \frac{19}{24}$.

In **1–4**, find each sum.

1. $\frac{1}{2} + \frac{1}{6}$

Least multiple that is the same: ____

Add using renamed fractions:

____ + ____ = ____ or $\frac{\square}{\square}$

2. $\frac{1}{9} + \frac{5}{6}$

Least multiple that is the same: ____

Add using renamed fractions:

____ + ____ = ____

3. $\frac{4}{5} + \frac{1}{15}$

Least multiple that is the same: ____

Add using renamed fractions:

____ + ____ = ____

4. $\frac{2}{8} + \frac{1}{2}$

Least multiple that is the same: ____

Add using renamed fractions:

____ + ____ = ____ or $\frac{\square}{\square}$

5. Model with Math Before school, Janine spends $\frac{1}{10}$ hour making the bed, $\frac{1}{5}$ hour getting dressed, and $\frac{1}{2}$ hour eating breakfast. What fraction of an hour does she spend doing these activities? Complete the drawing of fraction strips to show the solution.

1		
$\frac{1}{10}$	$\frac{1}{5}$	$\frac{1}{2}$

6. enVision® STEM Hair color is an inherited trait. In Marci's family, her mother has brown hair. Her father has blond hair. The family has 6 children in all. Of the 6 children, $\frac{1}{3}$ of them have blond hair, $\frac{1}{6}$ of them have red hair, and $\frac{1}{2}$ of them have brown hair. What fraction of the children have red or brown hair?

7. Abdul bought a loaf of bread for $1.59 and a package of cheese for $2.69. How much did Abdul spend? Complete the diagram below.

?

8. Higher Order Thinking Robert wants to walk one mile for exercise each day. He made a table to show the distance from his home to each of four different places. What is the total distance from home to the store and back home, and from home to the library and back home? If Robert walks this total distance, will he walk one mile? Explain how you found your answer.

DATA

Walking Distances from Home to Each Place

Place	Distance
Bank	$\frac{1}{5}$ mile
Library	$\frac{1}{10}$ mile
Park	$\frac{1}{2}$ mile
Store	$\frac{1}{4}$ mile

Assessment Practice

9. Which equations are true when $\frac{2}{3}$ is placed in the box?

- ☐ $\frac{1}{3} + \frac{1}{3} = \square$
- ☐ $\frac{1}{6} + \frac{1}{6} = \square$
- ☐ $\square + \frac{6}{9} = \frac{4}{3}$
- ☐ $\frac{2}{5} + \square = \frac{14}{15}$

10. Which equations are true when $\frac{4}{5}$ is placed in the box?

- ☐ $\frac{1}{5} + \square = 1$
- ☐ $\frac{1}{2} + \frac{3}{10} = \square$
- ☐ $\frac{7}{10} + \frac{1}{10} = \square$
- ☐ $\square + \frac{1}{15} = \frac{14}{15}$

Name

Additional Practice 7-4

Subtract Fractions with Unlike Denominators

Another Look!

Beth wants to exercise for $\frac{4}{5}$ hour. So far, she has exercised for $\frac{2}{3}$ hour. What fraction of an hour does she have left to exercise?

Step 1

Find a common multiple.

Multiples of 5:
5, 10, 15, 20

Multiples of 3:
3, 6, 9, 12, 15

Since 15 is a multiple of both 5 and 3, use 15 as a common denominator.

Step 2

Write equivalent fractions.

$\frac{4}{5} \times \frac{3}{3} = \frac{12}{15}$

$\frac{4}{5} = \frac{12}{15}$

$\frac{2}{3} \times \frac{5}{5} = \frac{10}{15}$

$\frac{2}{3} = \frac{10}{15}$

Step 3

Subtract the numerators.

$\frac{12}{15} - \frac{10}{15} = \frac{2}{15}$

Beth has $\frac{2}{15}$ hour left.

In **1–8**, find each difference.

1. $\frac{1}{3} = \frac{2}{6}$; $-\frac{1}{6} = \frac{1}{6}$; $\frac{1}{6}$

2. $\frac{2}{3} = \frac{8}{12}$; $-\frac{5}{12} = \frac{5}{12}$; $\frac{3}{12} = \frac{1}{4}$

3. $\frac{3}{5} = \frac{9}{15}$; $-\frac{1}{3} = \frac{5}{15}$; $\frac{4}{15}$

4. $\frac{2}{9} = \frac{16}{72}$; $-\frac{1}{8} = \frac{9}{72}$; $\frac{7}{72}$

5. $\frac{3}{4} - \frac{2}{5}$; $\frac{7}{20}$

6. $\frac{4}{3} - \frac{2}{5}$; $\frac{14}{15}$

7. $\frac{8}{8} - \frac{4}{9}$; $\frac{40}{72} = \frac{5}{9}$

8. $\frac{17}{18} - \frac{2}{3}$; $\frac{5}{18}$

Use the table for **9** and **10**. The trail around Mirror Lake in Yosemite National Park is 5 miles long.

Hiker	Fraction of Trail Hiked
Andrea	$\frac{2}{5}$
Jon	$\frac{1}{2}$
Callie	$\frac{4}{5}$

DATA

9. What fraction describes how much more of the trail Jon hiked than Andrea hiked?

10. What fraction describes how much more of the trail Callie hiked than Jon hiked?

11. Critique Reasoning Amy said that the perimeter of the triangle below is less than 10 yards. Do you agree with her? Why or why not?

2.45 yd 3.6 yd 4.5 yd

12. Eva had $\frac{7}{8}$ gallon of paint. Her brother Ivan used $\frac{1}{4}$ gallon to paint his model boat. Eva needs at least $\frac{1}{2}$ gallon to paint her bookshelf. Did Ivan leave her enough paint? Write an equation and fill in the bar diagram to solve.

?

13. Paul's dad made a turkey pot pie for dinner on Wednesday. The family ate $\frac{4}{8}$ of the pie. On Thursday after school, Paul ate $\frac{2}{16}$ of the pie for a snack. What fraction of the pie remained?

14. Higher Order Thinking Write a real-world problem in which you would subtract fractions with unlike denominators. Then, solve your problem.

Assessment Practice

15. Choose the correct numbers from the box below to complete the subtraction sentence that follows.

$\frac{1}{2}$ $\frac{5}{14}$ $\frac{3}{7}$ $\frac{1}{7}$ $\frac{1}{14}$

$\square - \frac{3}{7} = \square$

16. Choose the correct numbers from the box below to complete the subtraction sentence that follows.

$\frac{3}{20}$ $\frac{3}{5}$ $\frac{1}{20}$ $\frac{4}{5}$ $\frac{7}{9}$

$\square - \frac{3}{4} = \square$

Name ______________________________

Additional Practice 7-5

Add and Subtract Fractions

Another Look!

Carla wants to make a Veggie Toss using eggplant, green peppers, spring onions, and mushrooms. She already has eggplant at home. How many pounds of the other ingredients does she need in all? Use data from the recipe.

Use what you know about adding and subtracting fractions to solve problems.

Veggie Toss Recipe

Eggplant	$\frac{3}{4}$ pound (lb)
Green peppers	$\frac{1}{3}$ pound (lb)
Spring onions	$\frac{1}{4}$ pound (lb)
Mushrooms	$\frac{3}{8}$ pound (lb)

Step 1

List the amounts of green peppers, spring onions, and mushrooms. Then, find a common denominator and rename each fraction.

$$\left(\frac{1}{3}+\frac{1}{4}\right)+\frac{3}{8}=\left(\frac{8}{24}+\frac{6}{24}\right)+\frac{9}{24}$$

Step 2

Add the renamed fraction amounts.

$$\frac{14}{24}+\frac{9}{24}=\frac{23}{24}$$

Carla needs $\frac{23}{24}$ pound of the other veggies in all.

In **1–12**, find the sum or difference.

1. $\frac{1}{12} + \frac{7}{9}$

2. $\frac{4}{18} + \frac{2}{9}$

3. $\frac{1}{3} + \frac{1}{5}$

4. $\frac{5}{15} + \frac{3}{5}$

5. $\frac{1}{2}-\left(\frac{1}{8}+\frac{1}{8}\right)$

6. $\frac{3}{4}+\left(\frac{1}{4}-\frac{1}{6}\right)$

7. $\left(\frac{1}{2}+\frac{3}{20}\right)-\frac{2}{20}$

8. $\left(\frac{2}{5}+\frac{1}{5}\right)-\frac{3}{10}$

9. $\frac{5}{4}-\frac{5}{8}$

10. $\frac{2}{3}-\frac{2}{7}$

11. $\frac{12}{15}-\frac{1}{6}$

12. $\frac{5}{9}-\frac{3}{8}$

13. The table shows the amounts of two ingredients Tara used to make a snack mix. She ate $\frac{5}{8}$ cup of the snack mix for lunch. How much of the mix is left? Show how you solved.

DATA

Ingredient	Amount
Rice Crackers	$\frac{3}{4}$ c
Pretzels	$\frac{2}{3}$ c

14. Samantha is making soup. To make the broth, she combines $\frac{2}{5}$ cup of vegetable stock and $\frac{2}{3}$ cup of chicken stock. Boiling the broth causes $\frac{1}{4}$ cup of the liquid to evaporate. How much broth is left after it is boiled? Show how you solved.

15. Number Sense Mary has three lengths of cable, $\frac{3}{6}$ yard long, $\frac{1}{4}$ yard long, and $\frac{1}{3}$ yard long. Which two pieces together make a length of $\frac{20}{24}$ yard?

16. A kitten's heartbeat can be as fast as 240 beats per minute. To find the number of times a kitten's heart beats in 30 seconds, Aiden says divide 240 by 30. Do you agree with him? Why or why not?

17. Use Structure Explain how you know the quotients 540 ÷ 90 and 5,400 ÷ 900 are equal without doing any computation.

18. Higher Order Thinking Write an addition and subtraction problem and equation for the diagram. Then find the missing value.

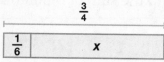

$\frac{3}{4}$

$\frac{1}{6}$	x

Assessment Practice

19. What fraction is missing from the following equation?

$$\frac{5}{6} - \square = \frac{3}{12}$$

Ⓐ $\frac{1}{3}$

Ⓑ $\frac{4}{9}$

Ⓒ $\frac{7}{12}$

Ⓓ $\frac{13}{12}$

20. What number is missing from the following equation?

$$\square - \frac{3}{4} = \frac{2}{12}$$

Ⓐ $\frac{11}{12}$

Ⓑ $\frac{8}{16}$

Ⓒ $\frac{2}{12}$

Ⓓ 1

Name ______________________

Practice Video Tools Games

Additional Practice 7-6

Estimate Sums and Differences of Mixed Numbers

Another Look!

Kyra has $4\frac{1}{8}$ yards of red ribbon and $7\frac{2}{3}$ yards of blue ribbon. About how many yards of ribbon does she have?

Round both numbers to the nearest whole number. Then add or subtract.

Estimate $4\frac{1}{8} + 7\frac{2}{3}$.

$4\frac{1}{8}$ rounds to 4.

$7\frac{2}{3}$ rounds to 8.

$4 + 8 = 12$

So, $4\frac{1}{8} + 7\frac{2}{3}$ is about 12.

Kyra has about 12 yards of ribbon.

If the fractional part of a mixed number is greater than or equal to $\frac{1}{2}$, round to the next greater whole number. If it is less than $\frac{1}{2}$, use only the whole number.

In **1–8**, round to the nearest whole number.

1. $8\frac{5}{6}$ **2.** $13\frac{8}{9}$ **3.** $43\frac{1}{3}$ **4.** $6\frac{6}{7}$

5. $7\frac{40}{81}$ **6.** $29\frac{4}{5}$ **7.** $88\frac{2}{4}$ **8.** $20\frac{3}{10}$

In **9–17**, estimate each sum or difference.

9. $7\frac{1}{9} + 8\frac{2}{5}$ **10.** $14\frac{5}{8} - 3\frac{7}{10}$ **11.** $2\frac{1}{4} + 5\frac{1}{2} + 10\frac{3}{4}$

12. $11\frac{3}{5} - 4\frac{1}{12}$ **13.** $9 + 3\frac{11}{14} + 5\frac{1}{9}$ **14.** $15\frac{6}{7} - 12\frac{2}{10}$

15. $3\frac{2}{5} + 6\frac{5}{7}$ **16.** $20\frac{1}{3} - 9\frac{1}{2}$ **17.** $25\frac{7}{8} + 8\frac{7}{12}$

Use the table for **18–20**.

18. **Critique Reasoning** Robert says his better long jump was about 1 foot farther than May's better long jump. Is he correct? Explain.

DATA

Participant	Event	Distance
Robert	Long Jump	**1.** $6\frac{1}{12}$ ft **2.** $5\frac{2}{3}$ ft
	Softball Throw	$62\frac{1}{5}$ ft
May	Long Jump	**1.** $4\frac{2}{3}$ ft **2.** $4\frac{3}{4}$ ft
	Softball Throw	$71\frac{7}{8}$ ft

19. If the school record for the softball throw is 78 feet, about how much farther must Robert throw the ball to match the record?

20. About how much farther is May's softball throw than Robert's softball throw?

21. **Higher Order Thinking** Use the problem $\frac{3}{5} + \frac{3}{4}$. First, round each fraction and estimate the sum. Then, add the two fractions using a common denominator and round the result. Which is closer to the actual sum?

22. To make one batch of granola, Linda mixes 1 pound of oat flakes, 6 ounces of walnuts, 5 ounces of raisins, and 4 ounces of sunflower seeds. How many pounds of granola does one batch make?

Remember:
1 pound = 16 ounces.

Assessment Practice

23. Clay's hair is $10\frac{2}{7}$ inches long. The barber trims off $\frac{1}{4}$ inch. About how long is his hair now?

Ⓐ 9 in.

Ⓑ 10 in.

Ⓒ 11 in.

Ⓓ 12 in.

24. Tom and Sami have two painting jobs but can only stop at the store once. The first job needs $1\frac{4}{5}$ gallons of paint. The second needs $12\frac{1}{3}$ gallons. How many gallon cans of paint should they buy?

Ⓐ 11 cans

Ⓑ 13 cans

Ⓒ 14 cans

Ⓓ 15 cans

Name ________________

Practice Video Tools Games

Additional Practice 7-7
Use Models to Add Mixed Numbers

Another Look!

Draw a model to add $1\frac{7}{8} + 2\frac{1}{4}$.

Remember that you can use what you know about adding fractions to help you add mixed numbers.

Step 1

Model each addend using fraction strips.

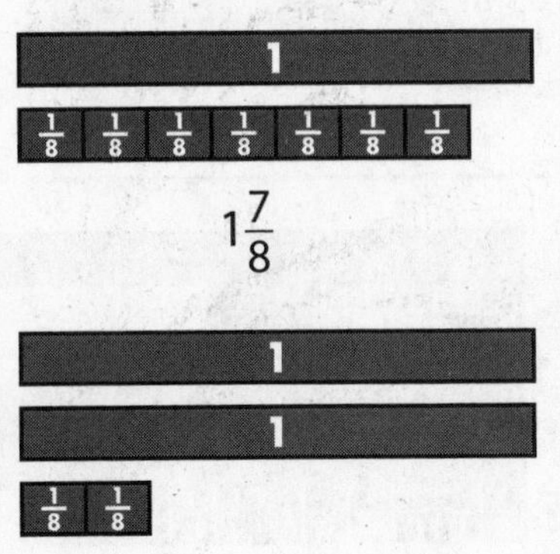

Step 2

Add the fractions. Regroup if possible.

$$\frac{7}{8} + \frac{2}{8} = \frac{9}{8} = 1\frac{1}{8}$$

$\frac{8}{8} = 1$

$\frac{1}{8}$ left

Step 3

Add the whole numbers to the regrouped fractions. Write the sum.

So, $1\frac{7}{8} + 2\frac{1}{4} = 3\frac{9}{8} = 4\frac{1}{8}$.

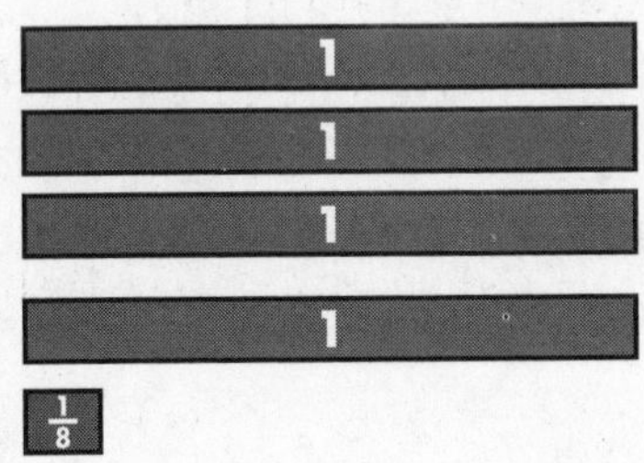

In **1–12**, use fraction strips to find each sum.

1. $3\frac{1}{2} + 1\frac{4}{8}$

2. $2\frac{5}{12} + 4\frac{1}{4}$

3. $3\frac{3}{4} + 3\frac{1}{2}$

4. $2\frac{5}{8} + 4\frac{3}{4}$

5. $5\frac{1}{3} + 3\frac{5}{6}$

6. $2\frac{1}{2} + 6\frac{3}{4}$

7. $3\frac{1}{4} + 4\frac{7}{8}$

8. $4\frac{5}{6} + 5\frac{7}{12}$

9. $2\frac{1}{4} + 4\frac{5}{8}$

10. $6\frac{1}{2} + 7\frac{3}{4}$

11. $4\frac{5}{8} + 6\frac{1}{2}$

12. $2\frac{1}{3} + 4\frac{5}{12}$

13. Ken used $1\frac{3}{8}$ cups of walnuts and $1\frac{3}{4}$ cups of raisins to make trail mix. How many total cups of trail mix did he make?

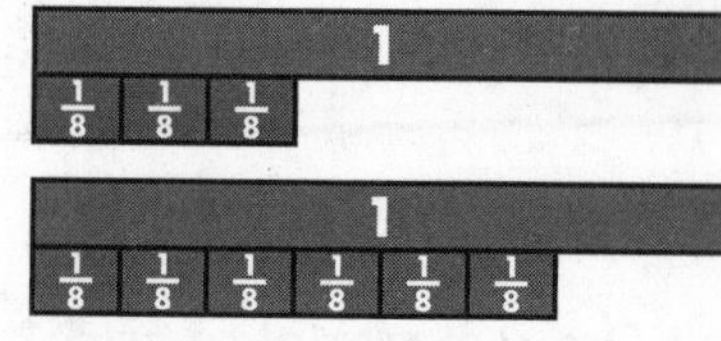

14. Ken added $\frac{5}{8}$ cup more walnuts to the trail mix. How many cups of trail mix does he have?

---

15. **Higher Order Thinking** Kayla walked $1\frac{1}{4}$ miles from home to school. Then, she walked $1\frac{3}{4}$ miles from school to the store and $2\frac{1}{2}$ miles from the store to the library. How many miles did Kayla walk from school to the library?

16. A painter mixes $\frac{1}{4}$ gallon of red paint, 3 quarts of yellow paint, and 2 quarts of white paint. How many quarts of paint are in the mixture?

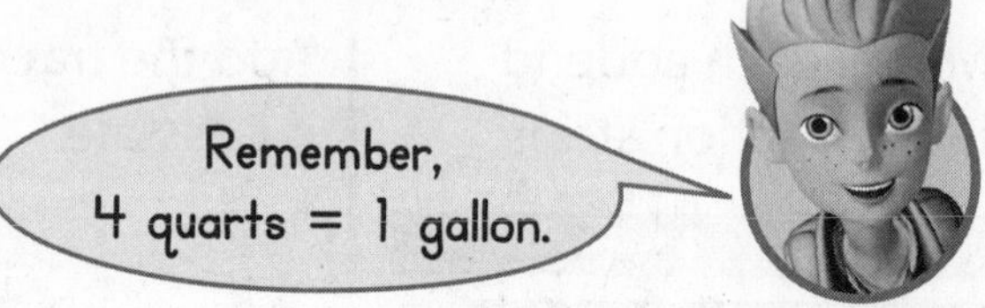

---

17. **Model with Math** Rachel has a board that is $1\frac{7}{12}$ feet long and another board that is $2\frac{11}{12}$ feet long. Write an expression Rachel can use to find the total length in feet of the two boards.

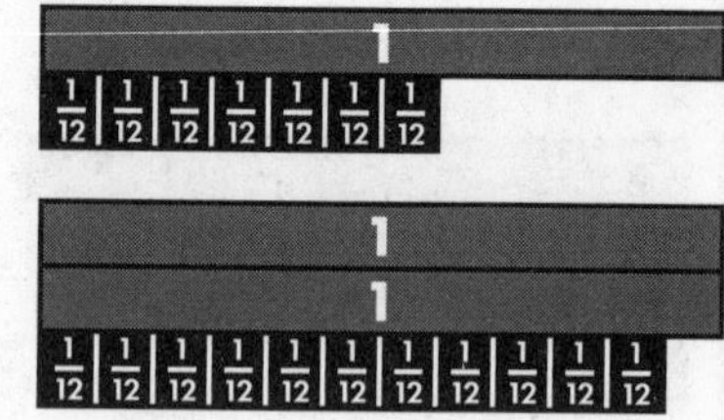

---

18. Lori went to the movies. She spent \$9.50 for a movie ticket, \$5.50 for a box of popcorn, and \$2.25 for a drink. How much did Lori spend in all? Show your work.

19. **Construct Arguments** Jane is adding $3\frac{1}{4} + 2\frac{7}{8}$ using fraction strips. How can she rename the sum of the fraction parts of the problem? Explain your thinking.

Assessment Practice

20. McKenna spends $1\frac{3}{4}$ hours mopping the floors and $3\frac{3}{8}$ hours mowing and weeding the yard. How many hours does she spend on her chores?

Ⓐ 4 hours
Ⓑ $4\frac{1}{8}$ hours
Ⓒ 5 hours
Ⓓ $5\frac{1}{8}$ hours

21. Jackie's rain gauge showed $2\frac{2}{5}$ inches on April 15 and $5\frac{2}{10}$ inches on April 30. How many inches of rain fell on those two days?

Ⓐ 7 in.
Ⓑ $7\frac{6}{10}$ in.
Ⓒ $7\frac{4}{5}$ in.
Ⓓ 8 in.

Name ______________________

Practice Video Tools Games

Additional Practice 7-8
Add Mixed Numbers

Another Look!

Randy did homework for $2\frac{5}{6}$ hours. Then he played soccer for $1\frac{3}{4}$ hours. How many hours did he spend on the two activities?

Before you add, you need to write equivalent fractions.

Step 1

Write equivalent fractions with a common denominator. You can use fraction strips to show the equivalent fractions.

$2\frac{5}{6} = 2\frac{10}{12}$

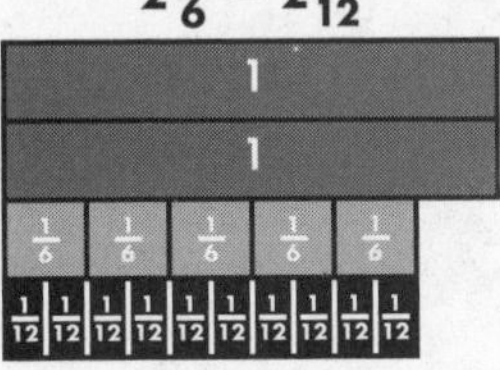

$1\frac{3}{4} = 1\frac{9}{12}$

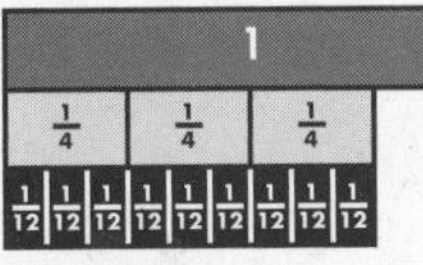

Step 2

Add the fraction part of the mixed numbers first. Then add the whole numbers.

$\frac{9}{12} + \frac{10}{12} = \frac{19}{12}$

$1 + 2 = 3$

$\frac{19}{12} + 3 = 3\frac{19}{12}$

Step 3

Regroup $\frac{19}{12}$ as $1\frac{7}{12}$. Find the sum.

$3\frac{19}{12} = 3 + 1\frac{7}{12} = 4\frac{7}{12}$

Randy spent $4\frac{7}{12}$ hours on the two activities.

In **1–12**, find each sum.

Remember to use an estimate to check that your answer is reasonable.

1. $2\frac{5}{6} = 2\frac{\square}{12}$
$+\ 3\frac{1}{4} = 3\frac{\square}{12}$

2. $5\frac{2}{5} = 5\frac{\square}{10}$
$+\ 4\frac{1}{2} = 4\frac{\square}{10}$

3. $1\frac{3}{8}$
$+\ 6\frac{3}{4}$

4. $10\frac{1}{3} + \frac{7}{9}$

5. $3\frac{1}{4} + 6\frac{2}{3}$

6. $2\frac{1}{2} + 2\frac{1}{6}$

7. $3\frac{7}{8} + 5\frac{2}{3}$

8. $4\frac{5}{6} + 9\frac{5}{9}$

9. $15\frac{1}{3} + 1\frac{5}{12}$

10. $12\frac{3}{4} + 6\frac{3}{8}$

11. $14\frac{7}{10} + 3\frac{3}{5}$

12. $8\frac{5}{8} + 7\frac{7}{16}$

13. Tirzah wants to put a fence around her garden. She has 22 yards of fence material. Does she have enough to go all the way around the garden? Explain why or why not.

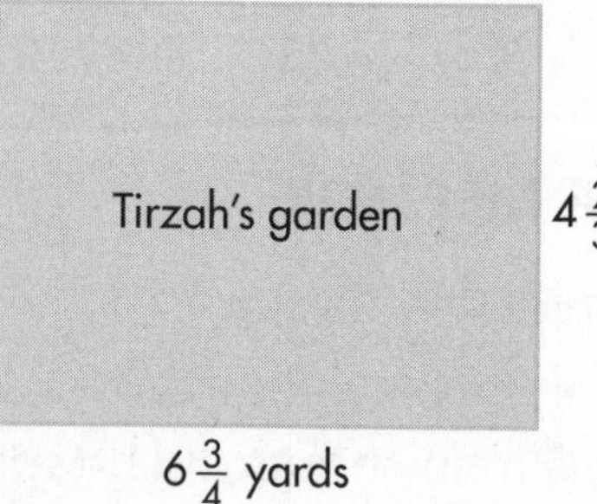

14. Higher Order Thinking Lake Trail is $4\frac{3}{5}$ miles long. Outlook Trail is $5\frac{5}{6}$ miles long. Pinewoods Trail is $1\frac{3}{10}$ miles longer than Lake Trail. Which trail is longer, Pinewoods Trail or Outlook Trail? Explain.

15. Reasoning Can the sum of two mixed numbers be equal to 2? Explain.

Use the data table for **16–18**.

16. Joan reads that the mass of an average elephant's brain is $3\frac{4}{10}$ kilograms greater than an average man's brain. How many kilograms is an average elephant's brain?

Vital Organ Measures

DATA		
Average woman's brain	$1\frac{3}{10}$ kg	$2\frac{4}{5}$ lb
Average man's brain	$1\frac{2}{5}$ kg	3 lb
Average human heart	$\frac{3}{10}$ kg	$\frac{7}{10}$ lb

17. What is the total mass of an average man's brain and heart in kilograms (kg)?

18. What is the total weight of an average woman's brain and heart in pounds (lb)?

19. What is the missing number in the following equation?

$$1\frac{4}{9} + \frac{1}{\square} = 1\frac{7}{9}$$

20. Trish drove $18\frac{1}{8}$ miles yesterday. She drove $13\frac{2}{3}$ miles today. Write an addition sentence to show how many miles Trish drove in all.

Name ______________________

Practice Video Tools Games

Additional Practice 7-9

Use Models to Subtract Mixed Numbers

Another Look!

Draw a model to find $2\frac{1}{5} - 1\frac{3}{10}$.

Remember to check that your answer makes sense.

Step 1

Rename the fractions with a common denominator. Use the common denominator to model the number you are subtracting from, $2\frac{1}{5}$ or $2\frac{2}{10}$.

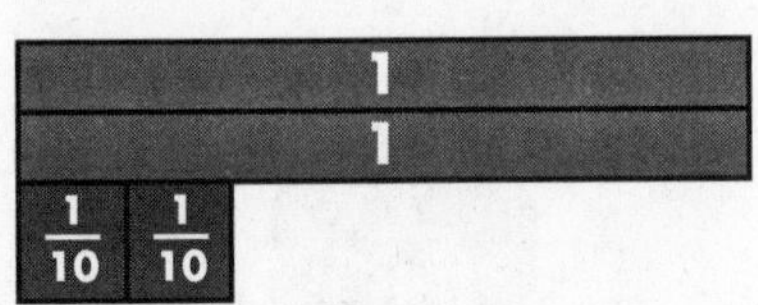

Step 2

Rename $2\frac{2}{10}$ as $1\frac{12}{10}$. Cross out one whole and $\frac{3}{10}$ to show subtracting $1\frac{3}{10}$.

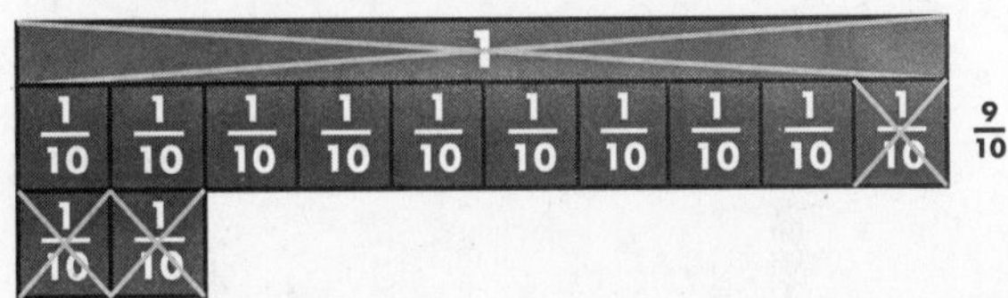

Write the parts of the model that are left as a fraction or mixed number.

So, $2\frac{1}{5} - 1\frac{3}{10} = \frac{9}{10}$.

In **1–12**, find each difference.

Use fraction strips to help.

1. $6\frac{1}{4} - 3\frac{5}{8}$

2. $4 - 1\frac{1}{2}$

3. $5\frac{1}{3} - 3\frac{1}{6}$

4. $7\frac{2}{5} - 4\frac{7}{10}$

5. $12\frac{3}{4} - 11\frac{7}{8}$

6. $9\frac{3}{10} - 2\frac{2}{5}$

7. $8\frac{1}{4} - 2\frac{5}{12}$

8. $12\frac{1}{3} - 5\frac{4}{6}$

9. $9\frac{1}{2} - 6\frac{9}{10}$

10. $3\frac{4}{5} - 1\frac{4}{10}$

11. $7\frac{1}{4} - 3\frac{5}{8}$

12. $10\frac{1}{3} - 7\frac{5}{9}$

13. Use the model to find the difference.
$3\frac{1}{5} - 1\frac{4}{5}$

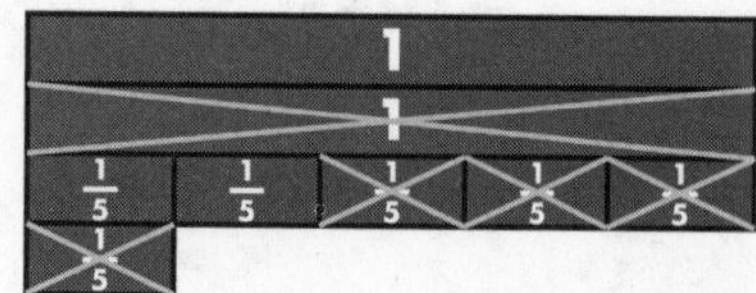

14. Micah's rain gauge showed that $9\frac{1}{2}$ centimeters of rain fell last month. This month, the rain gauge measured $10\frac{3}{10}$ centimeters. How many more centimeters of rain fell this month?

15. Higher Order Thinking Suppose you are finding $8\frac{3}{10} - 6\frac{4}{5}$. Do you need to rename $8\frac{3}{10}$? If so, explain how you rename it to subtract. Then find the difference.

16. Critique Reasoning Danny said 12.309 rounded to the nearest tenth is 12.4. Is Danny correct? Explain.

17. enVision® STEM Fossils show that insects were much larger around 300 million years ago than they are today. The table at the right shows some of the wing lengths found in fossils. How much longer was the wing length of the dragonfly than the wing length of the fly?

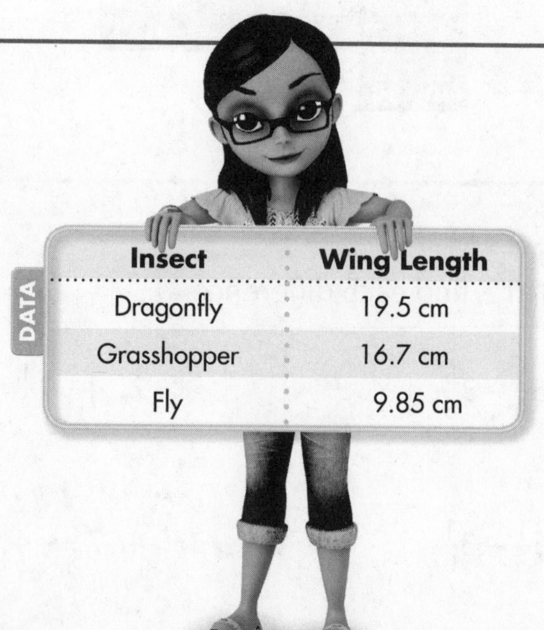

DATA

Insect	Wing Length
Dragonfly	19.5 cm
Grasshopper	16.7 cm
Fly	9.85 cm

Assessment Practice

18. What is the missing fraction in the following equation?

$1\frac{1}{2} - \square = \frac{3}{4}$

19. What is the missing number in the following equation?

$15\frac{3}{\square} - 13\frac{7}{8} = 1\frac{7}{8}$

Name ____________________

Practice Video Tools Games

Additional Practice 7-10
Subtract Mixed Numbers

Another Look!

The Plainville Zoo has had elephants for $2\frac{2}{3}$ years. The zoo has had zebras for $1\frac{1}{2}$ years. How many more years has the zoo had elephants?

Remember: You need a common denominator to subtract fractions.

Step 1

Write equivalent fractions with a common denominator. You can use fraction strips.

$2\frac{2}{3} = 2\frac{4}{6}$

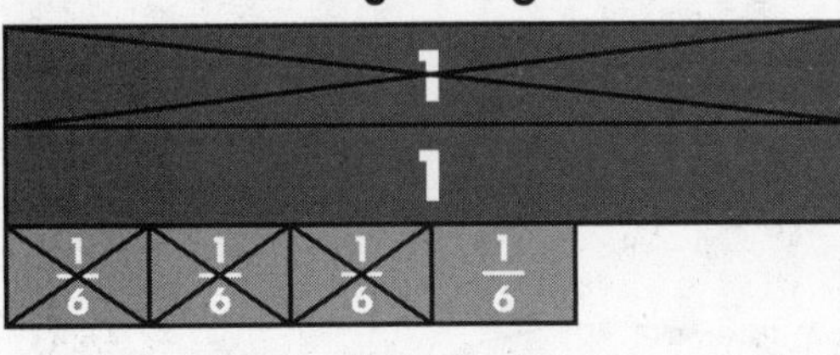

$1\frac{1}{2} = 1\frac{3}{6}$

Step 2

Find the difference $2\frac{4}{6} - 1\frac{3}{6}$. Subtract the fractions. Then subtract the whole numbers.

$\frac{4}{6} - \frac{3}{6} = \frac{1}{6}$ $\qquad$ $2 - 1 = 1$

So, $2\frac{2}{3} - 1\frac{1}{2} = 1\frac{1}{6}$.

The zoo has had the elephants $1\frac{1}{6}$ years longer.

In **1–9**, find each difference.

1. $4\frac{3}{5} = 4\frac{\square}{15}$
$- 2\frac{1}{3} = 2\frac{\square}{15}$

2. $5 - 3\frac{5}{6}$

3. $10\frac{5}{8} - 5\frac{3}{4}$

4. $5\frac{6}{7} - 1\frac{1}{2}$

5. $3 - 1\frac{3}{4}$

6. $6\frac{5}{6} - 5\frac{1}{2}$

7. $7\frac{3}{10} - 2\frac{1}{5}$

8. $9\frac{2}{3} - 6\frac{1}{2}$

9. $8\frac{1}{4} - \frac{7}{8}$

10. To find the difference of $7 - 3\frac{5}{12}$, how do you rename the 7?

11. Higher Order Thinking Is it necessary to rename $4\frac{1}{4}$ to subtract $\frac{3}{4}$? Explain.

Use the table for **12–15**. The table shows the length and width of different bird eggs.

DATA

Egg Sizes in Inches (in.)

Bird	Length	Width
Canada goose	$3\frac{2}{5}$	$2\frac{3}{10}$
Robin	$\frac{3}{4}$	$\frac{3}{5}$
Turtle dove	$1\frac{1}{5}$	$\frac{9}{10}$
Raven	$1\frac{9}{10}$	$1\frac{3}{10}$

12. How much longer is the Canada goose egg than the raven egg?

13. How much wider is the turtle-dove egg than the robin egg?

14. Write the birds in order from the shortest egg to the longest egg.

How can you compare fractions with unlike denominators?

15. Model with Math Write and solve an equation to find the difference between the length and width of a turtle-dove egg.

Assessment Practice

16. Choose the correct number from the box below to complete the subtraction sentence that follows.

1 2 6 8 12 18

$1\frac{5}{6} - \frac{4}{9} = 1\frac{7}{\square}$

17. Choose the correct number from the box below to complete the subtraction sentence that follows.

1 2 3 4 5 6

$9\frac{5}{12} - 3\frac{2}{3} = 5\frac{\square}{4}$

Name

Practice
Video
Tools
Games

Additional Practice 7-11

Add and Subtract Mixed Numbers

Another Look!

A park ranger had $4\frac{1}{8}$ cups of birdseed. He bought $6\frac{1}{4}$ more cups of birdseed. Then he filled the park's bird feeders, using $2\frac{1}{2}$ cups of birdseed. How much birdseed is left?

You can write an expression to help solve the problem: $\left(4\frac{1}{8} + 6\frac{1}{4}\right) - 2\frac{1}{2}$

Always perform operations in parentheses first.

Step 1 Add the mixed numbers in parentheses first. Find a common denominator.

$4\frac{1}{8} + 6\frac{1}{4}$

$4\frac{1}{8} + 6\frac{2}{8} = 10\frac{3}{8}$

Step 2 Subtract $2\frac{1}{2}$ from the sum you found. Find a common denominator.

$10\frac{3}{8} - 2\frac{1}{2}$

$10\frac{3}{8} - 2\frac{4}{8}$

You can't subtract $\frac{4}{8}$ from $\frac{3}{8}$. Regroup $10\frac{3}{8}$ as $9\frac{11}{8}$.

Step 3 Find the difference.

$9\frac{11}{8} - 2\frac{4}{8} = 7\frac{7}{8}$

So, there are $7\frac{7}{8}$ cups of birdseed left.

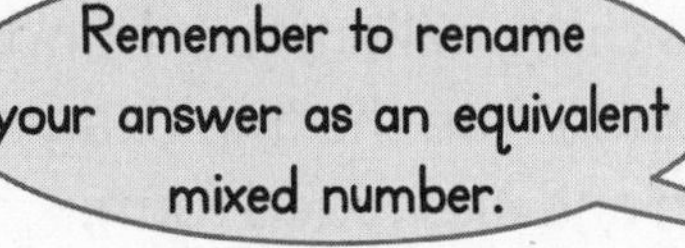

Remember to rename your answer as an equivalent mixed number.

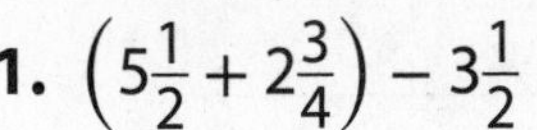

In **1–9**, solve. Do the operation in parentheses first.

1. $\left(5\frac{1}{2} + 2\frac{3}{4}\right) - 3\frac{1}{2}$

2. $10\frac{5}{16} - \left(5\frac{1}{4} + 2\frac{9}{16}\right)$

3. $5\frac{3}{8} + \left(6\frac{3}{4} - 4\frac{1}{8}\right)$

4. $\frac{6}{9} + \frac{5}{18} + 1\frac{3}{6}$

5. $1\frac{4}{10} + 1\frac{3}{20} + 1\frac{1}{5}$

6. $\left(4\frac{2}{3} + 1\frac{1}{6}\right) - 1\frac{5}{6}$

7. $\left(3\frac{3}{8} - 1\frac{1}{5}\right) + 1\frac{7}{8}$

8. $1\frac{6}{7} + \left(4\frac{13}{14} - 3\frac{1}{2}\right)$

9. $10\frac{5}{8} - \left(4\frac{3}{4} + 2\frac{5}{8}\right)$

10. Joel is $2\frac{1}{2}$ inches shorter than Carlos. Carlos is $1\frac{1}{4}$ inches taller than Dan. If Dan is $58\frac{1}{4}$ inches tall, how many inches tall is Joel?

11. Suzy spent $6\frac{7}{8}$ days working on her English paper, $3\frac{1}{6}$ days doing her science project, and $1\frac{1}{2}$ days studying for her math test. How many more days did Suzy spend on her English paper and math test combined than on her science project?

12. **Higher Order Thinking** Veronica needs to buy $1\frac{3}{4}$ pounds of cheese. When the clerk places some cheese in a container and weighs it, the scale shows $1\frac{1}{4}$ pounds. The container weighs $\frac{1}{16}$ pound. How many more pounds of cheese should be added to the scale to get the amount that Veronica needs? Explain how you solved the problem.

Be sure to find all of the questions you need to answer.

13. At a museum, Jenny learned about a fossil that was three billion, four hundred million years old. Write the fossil's age in standard form and expanded form.

14. **Model with Math** Four students raised \$264 for a charity by washing cars. The students received \$8 for each car they washed. How many cars did they wash?

$264

$8	?

Assessment Practice

15. Which equations are true when $1\frac{3}{4}$ is placed in the box?

- ☐ $2\frac{1}{4} - \frac{6}{7} = \square$
- ☐ $2\frac{5}{12} - \square = \frac{2}{3}$
- ☐ $7\frac{1}{12} - 5\frac{3}{8} = \square$
- ☐ $\square + \frac{7}{10} = 2\frac{9}{20}$

16. Which equations are true when $2\frac{1}{2}$ is placed in the box?

- ☐ $9\frac{1}{8} - 6\frac{3}{4} = \square$
- ☐ $\square - 1\frac{1}{2} = 1$
- ☐ $\square + 1\frac{1}{8} = 3\frac{5}{8}$
- ☐ $1\frac{1}{2} + \frac{5}{8} + \frac{4}{7} = \square$

Name ______________________

Practice Video Tools Games

Additional Practice 7-12
Model with Math

Another Look!

Each Monday in science class, students measure the height of their plants. In week 3, Andrew's plant was $4\frac{3}{4}$ inches tall. In week 4, his plant was $5\frac{3}{8}$ inches tall. How much had the plant grown from week 3 to week 4?

Tell how you can use math to model the problem.

- I can use math I know to help solve the problem.
- I can use bar diagrams and equations to represent and solve this problem.

Draw a bar diagram and write an equation to solve.

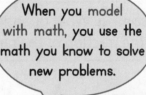

$5\frac{3}{8}$ inches

$4\frac{3}{4}$	g

$4\frac{3}{4} + g = 5\frac{3}{8}$

$$\begin{array}{r} 5\frac{3}{8} = 4\frac{11}{8} \\ -\,4\frac{3}{4} = 4\frac{6}{8} \\ \hline \frac{5}{8} \end{array}$$

The plant grew $\frac{5}{8}$ inch.

When you model with math, you use the math you know to solve new problems.

Model with Math

Mrs. Lohens made curtains for her children's bedrooms. She used $4\frac{3}{4}$ yards of fabric for Nicky's room and $6\frac{5}{8}$ yards for Linda's room. How much fabric did she use in all?

1. Draw a diagram and write an equation to represent the problem.

2. Solve the equation. What fraction computations did you do?

3. How much fabric did Mrs. Lohens use for the curtains?

Performance Task

Fans in the Bleachers

In the bleachers at the basketball game, $\frac{1}{4}$ of the fans are adult men, and $\frac{5}{12}$ are adult women. What fraction of the fans are adults? What fraction of the fans are children?

4. **Make Sense and Persevere** What do you know and what do you need to find?

5. **Reasoning** What quantities and operations will you use to find the fraction of the fans that are adults? that are children?

When you model with math, you decide what steps need to be completed to find the final answer.

6. **Critique Reasoning** Phyllis says you have to know the number of fans in order to determine the fraction of the fans that are children. Is she right? Explain.

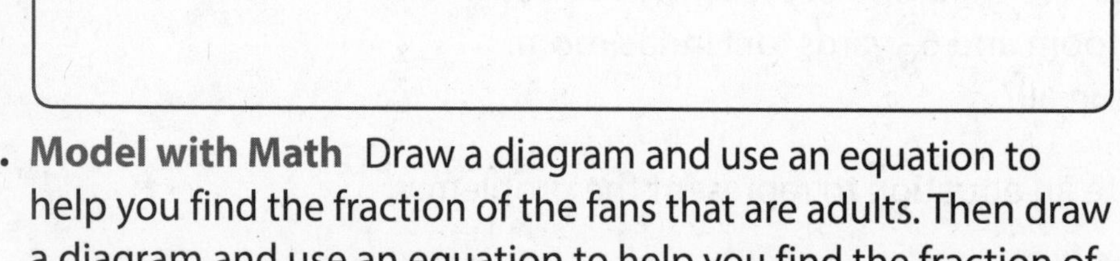

7. **Model with Math** Draw a diagram and use an equation to help you find the fraction of the fans that are adults. Then draw a diagram and use an equation to help you find the fraction of the fans that are children.

Name ______________________

Practice Video Tools Games

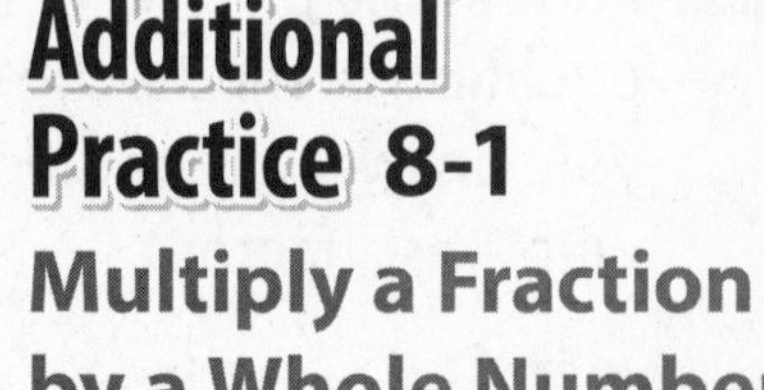

Additional Practice 8-1

Multiply a Fraction by a Whole Number

Another Look!

Juan needs $\frac{3}{4}$ yard of fabric to make a pillowcase. How many yards of fabric will Juan need to sew 5 pillowcases?

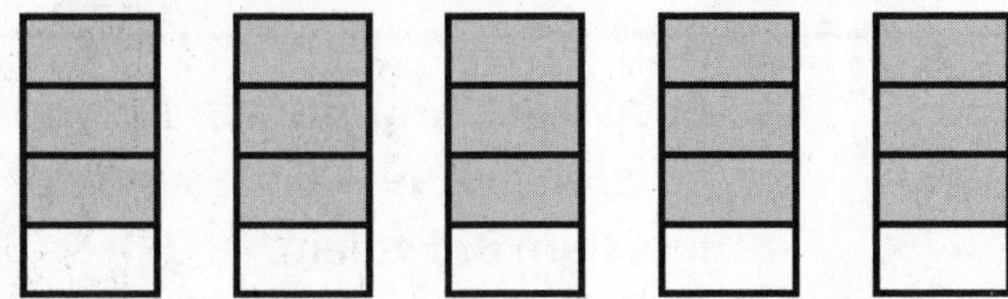

Multiply the whole number by the numerator.

$5 \times 3 = 15$

Write the product over the denominator.

$\frac{15}{4} = 3\frac{3}{4}$

Juan will need $3\frac{3}{4}$ yards of fabric.

Remember: You can check your answer using repeated addition.

Leveled Practice In **1–11**, find each product. Use models to help.

1. $72 \times \frac{5}{12} = \square \times 5 \times \frac{1}{12} = \frac{\square \times 1}{12} = \frac{360}{\square} = \square$

2. $35 \times \frac{2}{5} = \square \times 2 \times \frac{1}{\square} = \frac{\square \times 1}{5} = \frac{\square}{\square} = \square$

3. $12 \times \frac{3}{4} = \frac{\square}{\square} + \frac{\square}{\square} + \frac{\square}{\square} + \frac{\square}{\square} + \frac{\square}{\square} + \frac{\square}{\square} + \frac{\square}{\square} + \frac{\square}{\square} + \frac{\square}{\square} + \frac{\square}{\square} + \frac{\square}{\square} + \frac{\square}{\square} = \frac{\square}{4} = \square$

4. $13 \times \frac{2}{3}$

5. $70 \times \frac{9}{10}$

6. $81 \times \frac{2}{9}$

7. $57 \times \frac{2}{3}$

8. $600 \times \frac{3}{10}$

9. $16 \times \frac{3}{5}$

10. $400 \times \frac{1}{4}$

11. $48 \times \frac{5}{6}$

12. Look at the picture. Write and solve an equation to model the picture. Show your answer as a multiplication equation with $\frac{1}{2}$ as a factor.

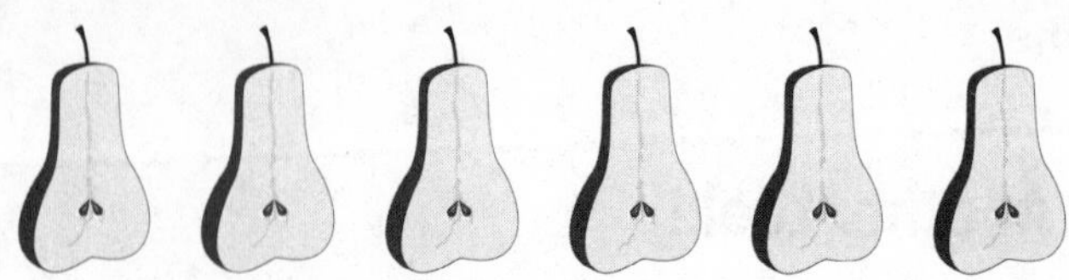

13. Higher Order Thinking Explain how you would find $45 \times \frac{7}{9}$ mentally.

14. Construct Arguments Do you think the difference $2.99 - 0.01$ is greater than 3 or less than 3? Explain.

15. Ben runs $\frac{3}{4}$ mile each day. How many miles does Ben run in 12 days?

16. Write a multiplication expression that shows 10^5.

17. Algebra Tina had \$145. She spent \$40 on fruit at the farmer's market. Solve the equation $40 + c = 145$ to find the amount Tina has left.

\$145	
\$40	*c*

18. Hippos eat a lot of food. How much food do 28 hippos eat in a week?

Hippos eat about $\frac{1}{2}$ ton of food in a week.

Assessment Practice

19. Select all equations that would be made true with the number 34.

- ☐ $\square \times \frac{1}{2} = 17$
- ☐ $51 \times \frac{2}{3} = \square$
- ☐ $\square \times \frac{3}{8} = 12$
- ☐ $300 \times \frac{1}{9} = \square$

20. Select all equations that would be made true with the fraction $\frac{2}{9}$.

- ☐ $81 \times \square = 18$
- ☐ $900 \times \square = 200$
- ☐ $72 \times \square = 16$
- ☐ $450 \times \square = 100$

Name ______________________

Practice Video Tools Games

Additional Practice 8-2

Multiply a Whole Number by a Fraction

Another Look!

Tyler used $\frac{2}{3}$ of a 9-yard-long piece of fabric to make a jacket. What was the length of fabric, in yards, that he used?

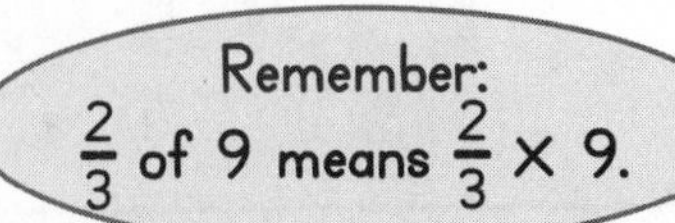

Step 1

Draw 9 pieces each representing 1 yard and separate them into 3 equal groups.

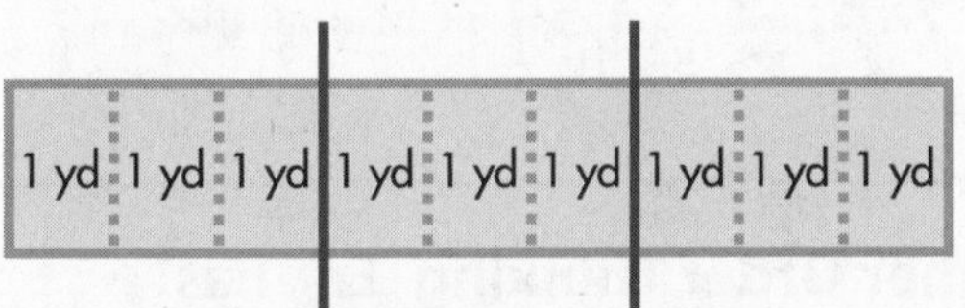

Step 2

Circle 2 of the groups.

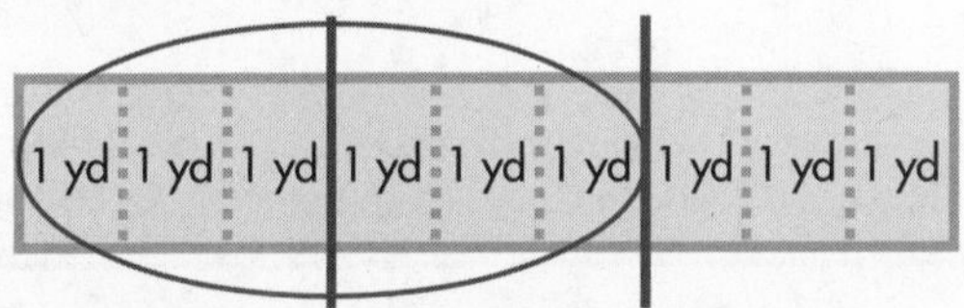

So, Tyler used 6 yards of fabric.

Leveled Practice In **1–8**, find each product. Use models to help.

1. $\frac{5}{10} \times 5$

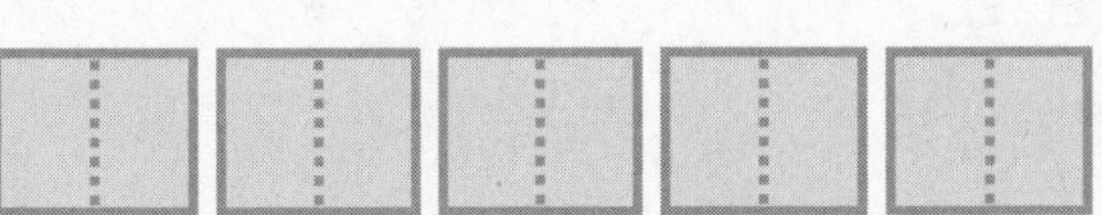

2. $\frac{3}{5} \times 10$

3. $\frac{5}{6} \times 3$

4. $\frac{5}{6}$ of 12

5. $\frac{3}{5}$ of 20

6. $\frac{2}{3}$ of 8

7. $\frac{2}{9} \times 3$

8. $\frac{4}{7} \times 10$

9. Critique Reasoning Find the error in the work below. Then show the correct calculation.

$\frac{8}{12} \times 6 = 8 \times \frac{1}{12} \times 6 = 8 \times \frac{1}{72} = \frac{8}{72} = \frac{1}{9}$

10. A scientist measured the amount of rainfall during the afternoon. It rained 0.43 inch each hour. What was the total amount of rainfall in 3 hours?

11. A giraffe can run at a speed of 32 miles per hour. Which animal listed in the chart has a speed that is $\frac{15}{16}$ of the speed of a giraffe? Explain how you found your answer.

DATA

Animal	Speed (in miles per hour)
Cat	30
Cheetah	70
Jackal	35

12. If a frilled lizard is 90 centimeters long, how long is the tail?

The frilled lizard's tail is $\frac{2}{3}$ of its length.

13. Higher Order Thinking Eric has 240 coins in his collection. $\frac{11}{20}$ of the coins are pennies. $\frac{4}{20}$ of the coins are nickels. The rest of the coins are quarters. How many of the coins are quarters? Explain how you found your answer.

Assessment Practice

14. Select all of the equations that would be made true with the fraction $\frac{2}{3}$.

- ☐ $\square \times 4 = \frac{8}{3}$
- ☐ $\square \times 15 = 12$
- ☐ $\square \times 21 = 14$
- ☐ $\frac{1}{6} \times 4 = \square$

15. Select all of the equations that would be made true with the number 14.

- ☐ $\frac{11}{12} \times 12 = \square$
- ☐ $\frac{7}{9} \times 18 = \square$
- ☐ $\frac{3}{8} \times 16 = \square$
- ☐ $\frac{3}{4} \times 12 = \square$

Name ______________________

Practice Video Tools Games

Additional Practice 8-3
Multiply Fractions and Whole Numbers

Another Look!

Lorena has a 16-inch long scarf, and $\frac{2}{3}$ of its length is red. How many inches long is the red section of the scarf?

Since you are multiplying 16 by a fraction less than 1, the answer will be less than 16.

Step 1	Step 2	Step 3
Multiply. $\frac{2}{3} \times 16 = \frac{2 \times 16}{3} = \frac{32}{3}$	Rewrite as a mixed number. $\frac{32}{3} = 10\frac{2}{3}$	Answer the question. The red section of the scarf is $10\frac{2}{3}$ inches long.

Leveled Practice In **1–16**, find each product. Write each product as a mixed number.

1. $26 \times \frac{3}{4} = \frac{\square \times \square}{\square} = \frac{\square}{\square} = \square\frac{\square}{\square}$

2. $9 \times \frac{7}{10} = \frac{\square \times \square}{\square} = \frac{\square}{\square} = \square\frac{\square}{\square}$

3. $\frac{2}{5} \times 32 = \frac{\square \times \square}{\square} = \frac{\square}{\square} = \square\frac{\square}{\square}$

4. $\frac{1}{8} \times 400 = \frac{\square \times \square}{\square} = \frac{\square}{\square} = \square$

5. $15 \times \frac{4}{5}$

6. $\frac{3}{11} \times 66$

7. $45 \times \frac{3}{8}$

8. $\frac{3}{10} \times 12$

9. $55 \times \frac{2}{5}$

10. $\frac{5}{6} \times 40$

11. $\frac{7}{9} \times 54$

12. $600 \times \frac{5}{12}$

13. $\frac{2}{3} \times 21$

14. $500 \times \frac{3}{5}$

15. $72 \times \frac{5}{8}$

16. $\frac{2}{9} \times 35$

17. Find $6 \times \frac{3}{5}$. Use the model at the right to find the product.

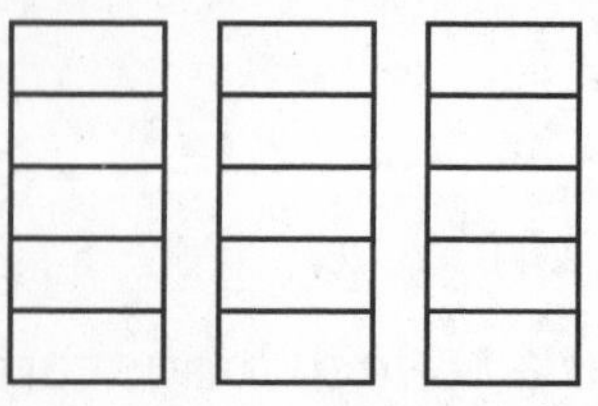

18. What mixed number represents the part of the model you did **NOT** shade for Exercise 17?

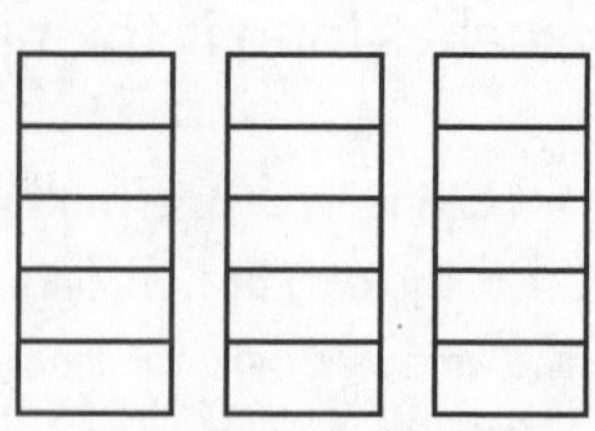

19. Without multiplying, tell which is greater: 0.75×81 or 0.9×81. Explain.

20. Use Structure Without multiplying, tell which is greater: $\frac{4}{5} \times 45$ or $\frac{2}{3} \times 45$. Explain.

21. Higher Order Thinking The school library has 2,469 books. Two-thirds of the books are paperbacks. How many books are paperbacks?

How can you use estimation to check that your answer is reasonable?

22. The table shows the amount of apple sauce made from one apple of each size. Patrice has 17 medium apples and 23 large apples. What is the total amount of applesauce that she can make with these apples?

DATA

Apple Size	Amount of Applesauce
Small	$\frac{1}{3}$ cup
Medium	$\frac{1}{2}$ cup
Large	$\frac{3}{4}$ cup

Assessment Practice

23. Select all that are true.

- ☐ $\frac{4}{9} \times 3 = \frac{4}{27}$
- ☐ $72 \times \frac{4}{9} = 32$
- ☐ $14 \times \frac{2}{7} = \frac{1}{49}$
- ☐ $15 \times \frac{3}{5} = 9$

24. Select all that are true.

- ☐ $6 \times \frac{3}{5} = \frac{1}{10}$
- ☐ $\frac{7}{8} \times 13 = \frac{7}{104}$
- ☐ $\frac{7}{8} \times 28 = 24\frac{1}{2}$
- ☐ $56 \times \frac{5}{9} = 31\frac{1}{9}$

Name

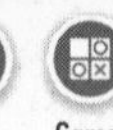
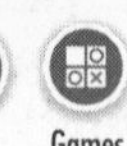

Practice Video Tools Games

Additional Practice 8-4
Use Models to Multiply Two Fractions

Another Look!

Graeme reserved $\frac{1}{2}$ of the seats in a restaurant for a dinner party. $\frac{1}{8}$ of those seats will be needed for family and the rest for his friends. What fraction of the restaurant's seats will be used by the family?

Find $\frac{1}{2} \times \frac{1}{8}$.

Step 1

Draw a picture to represent $\frac{1}{8}$. Draw a rectangle that has lines dividing it into 8 equal parts. Shade 1 of the 8 parts.

Step 2

Then draw a horizontal line to show $\frac{1}{2}$. Shade $\frac{1}{2}$ of the whole rectangle. The purple overlap is the answer.

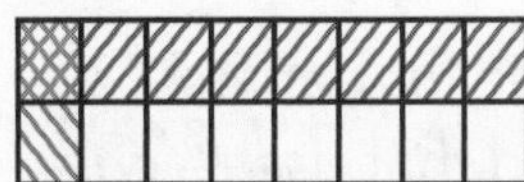

The two shadings overlap on $\frac{1}{16}$ of the whole rectangle.

$\frac{1}{16}$ of the restaurant's seats will be used by Graeme's family.

In **1–3**, find each product. Shade the model to help solve.

1. $\frac{4}{7} \times \frac{2}{3}$

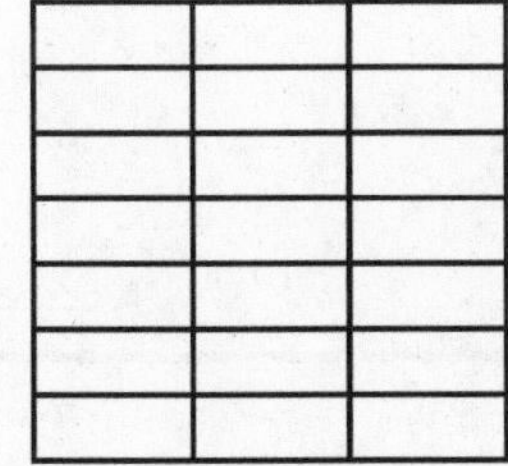

2. $\frac{1}{2} \times \frac{11}{12}$

3. $\frac{2}{5}$ of $\frac{1}{4}$

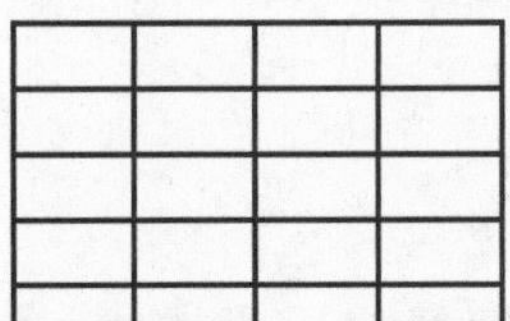

In **4–11**, find each product. Use models to help you.

4. $\frac{3}{4} \times \frac{1}{8}$

5. $\frac{8}{9}$ of $\frac{9}{10}$

6. $\frac{3}{7} \times \frac{2}{3}$

7. $\frac{1}{5} \times \frac{5}{6}$

8. $\frac{1}{6}$ of $\frac{3}{4}$

9. $\frac{7}{8} \times \frac{1}{2}$

10. $\frac{1}{12} \times \frac{3}{5}$

11. $\frac{1}{2}$ of $\frac{5}{9}$

12. Algebra What value of n makes the equation $n \times \frac{3}{4} = \frac{3}{16}$ true?

13. Use Structure $\frac{4}{9} \times \frac{7}{8} = \frac{7}{18}$. What is $\frac{7}{8} \times \frac{4}{9}$? How do you know without multiplying?

14. The stained glass shown here is a hexagon. How can you use multiplication to find its perimeter?

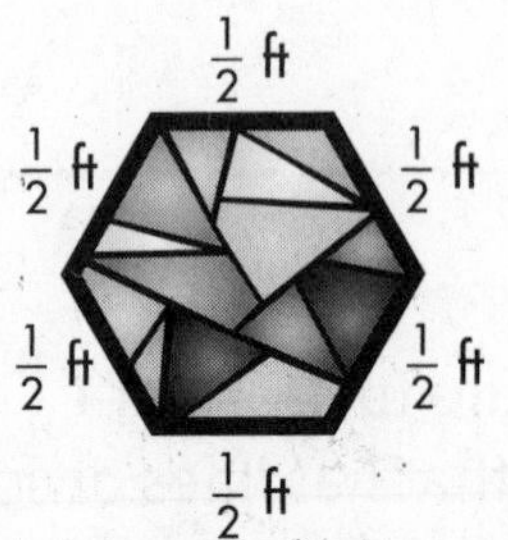

15. Vincent found a recipe for banana macadamia nut bread that uses $\frac{3}{4}$ cup of macadamia nuts. If he only wants to make half the recipe, how many cups of macadamia nuts should he use?

16. Higher Order Thinking If $\frac{1}{2}$ is multiplied by $\frac{1}{2}$, will the product be greater than $\frac{1}{2}$? Explain.

17. In gym class, Matthew runs $\frac{3}{4}$ mile. His gym teacher runs 3 times that distance. How far does Matthew's gym teacher run?

18. Titus had $\frac{1}{2}$ of a can of paint. He used $\frac{2}{3}$ of the paint to cover a tabletop. What fraction of a full can of paint did Titus use?

Assessment Practice

19. Nola made the model to show multiplying a fraction by a fraction. Which multiplication sentence does the model show?

Ⓐ $\frac{1}{2} \times \frac{1}{2} = \frac{1}{4}$

Ⓑ $\frac{1}{3} \times \frac{4}{5} = \frac{4}{15}$

Ⓒ $\frac{1}{3} \times \frac{1}{5} = \frac{1}{15}$

Ⓓ $\frac{4}{9} \times \frac{4}{5} = \frac{16}{45}$

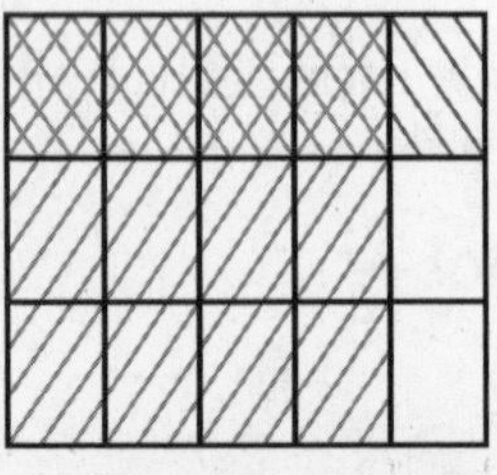

Name ________________________

Additional Practice 8-5

Multiply Two Fractions

Another Look!

Find $\frac{3}{4} \times \frac{2}{3}$.

You can multiply the numerators and denominators to find the product.

Step 1

Multiply the numerators, and then multiply the denominators.

$\frac{3 \times 2}{4 \times 3} = \frac{6}{12} = \frac{1}{2}$

Step 2

Check that the answer is reasonable.

Since $\frac{1}{2}$ is less than 1, the answer is reasonable.

Leveled Practice In **1–24**, find each product.

1. $\frac{7}{8} \times \frac{2}{3} = \frac{\square \times 2}{8 \times \square} = \frac{\square}{24} = \frac{\square}{\square}$

2. $\frac{3}{4} \times \frac{5}{9} = \frac{\square \times 5}{4 \times \square} = \frac{15}{\square} = \frac{\square}{\square}$

3. $\frac{4}{5} \times \frac{1}{8} = \frac{\square \times 1}{5 \times \square} = \frac{\square}{\square} = \frac{\square}{\square}$

4. $\frac{4}{7} \times \frac{1}{2} = \frac{\square \times \square}{\square \times \square} = \frac{\square}{\square} = \frac{\square}{\square}$

5. $\frac{3}{5} \times \frac{3}{7} = \frac{\square \times \square}{\square \times \square} = \frac{\square}{\square}$

6. $\frac{4}{9} \times \frac{2}{3} = \frac{\square \times \square}{\square \times \square} = \frac{\square}{\square}$

7. $\frac{11}{12} \times \frac{2}{5}$

8. $\frac{2}{3} \times \frac{4}{5}$

9. $\frac{1}{6} \times \frac{2}{3}$

10. $\frac{3}{4}$ of $\frac{1}{2}$

11. $\frac{6}{7} \times \frac{1}{5}$

12. $\frac{2}{3} \times \frac{5}{9}$

13. $\frac{1}{3}$ of $\frac{3}{10}$

14. $\frac{4}{5}$ of $\frac{5}{6}$

15. $\frac{3}{7} \times \frac{2}{7}$

16. $\frac{1}{2}$ of $\frac{2}{3}$

17. $\frac{4}{5} \times \frac{2}{3}$

18. $\frac{3}{10} \times \frac{3}{10}$

19. $\left(\frac{1}{2} + \frac{1}{3}\right) \times \frac{8}{9}$

20. $\left(\frac{2}{3} - \frac{1}{6}\right) \times \frac{11}{12}$

21. $\left(\frac{3}{5} + \frac{1}{4}\right) \times \frac{2}{3}$

22. $\frac{7}{8} \times \left(\frac{1}{3} + \frac{1}{3}\right)$

23. $\left(\frac{11}{12} - \frac{5}{6}\right) \times \frac{3}{4}$

24. $\frac{1}{3} \times \left(\frac{9}{10} - \frac{3}{5}\right)$

25. A full bottle holds $\frac{1}{4}$ gallon of juice. If $\frac{3}{5}$ of the juice has been poured out, how much juice is left in the bottle?

26. Natasha has 3 pounds of apples and $2\frac{1}{2}$ pounds of grapes. If she gives $\frac{1}{3}$ of her apples to Silvie, how many pounds of apples does she have left?

27. Keyshia is riding her bike on Bay View bike path. Keyshia's bike got a flat tire $\frac{2}{3}$ of the way down the path and she had to stop. How far did Keyshia ride?

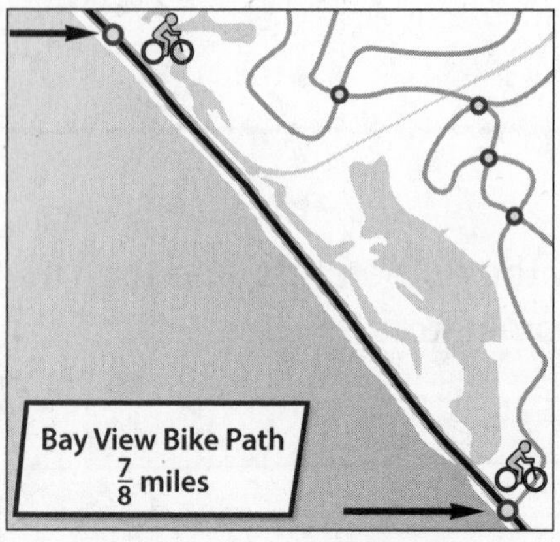

28. Of the apps on Juan's tablet, $\frac{3}{4}$ are gaming apps, and $\frac{5}{7}$ of the gaming apps are action games. What fraction of the apps on Juan's tablet are action games?

29. **Higher Order Thinking** In Mrs. Hu's classroom, $\frac{4}{5}$ of the students have a dog as a pet. Of the students who have a dog as a pet, $\frac{2}{3}$ also have a cat as a pet. If there are 45 students in her class, how many have both a dog and a cat as pets?

30. Patrick walks $\frac{9}{10}$ mile to the gym. How far has he walked when he has covered $\frac{2}{3}$ of the distance to the gym?

31. **Construct Arguments** Which is greater, $\frac{4}{7} \times \frac{1}{4}$ or $\frac{4}{7} \times \frac{1}{6}$? Explain.

Assessment Practice

32. Choose all the multiplication sentences that have $\frac{5}{6}$ as the missing part.

- ☐ $\square \times \frac{2}{3} = \frac{5}{9}$
- ☐ $\frac{2}{3} \times \square = \frac{7}{9}$
- ☐ $\frac{11}{12} \times \frac{10}{11} = \square$
- ☐ $\square \times \frac{1}{5} = \frac{1}{6}$
- ☐ $\frac{3}{4} \times \square = \frac{5}{8}$

33. Choose all the expressions that have $\frac{8}{15}$ as a product.

- ☐ $\frac{2}{3} \times \frac{4}{5}$
- ☐ $\frac{8}{9} \times \frac{3}{5}$
- ☐ $\frac{3}{15} \times \frac{5}{15}$
- ☐ $\frac{7}{10} \times \frac{1}{5}$
- ☐ $\frac{11}{15} \times \frac{8}{11}$

Name

Practice

Video

Tools
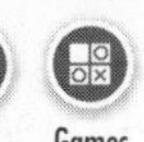
Games

Additional Practice 8-6
Area of a Rectangle

Another Look!

Cole wants to cover the back of a picture frame with colorful paper. What is the area of the back of Cole's picture frame?

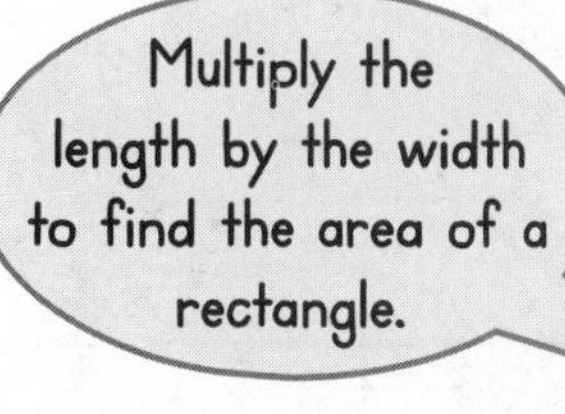

Multiply to find the area of the back of the picture frame.

$A = \frac{3}{4} \times \frac{1}{2} = \frac{3}{8}$

The area of the back of Cole's picture frame is $\frac{3}{8}$ square foot.

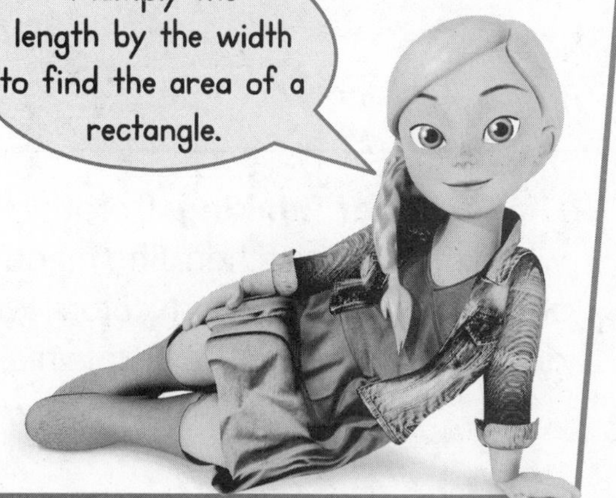

Multiply the length by the width to find the area of a rectangle.

In **1–5**, find each area.

1. $\frac{1}{4}$ yd, $\frac{1}{4}$ yd, 1 yd, 1 yd

$\frac{1}{4} \times \frac{1}{4} = \square$ sq yd

2.

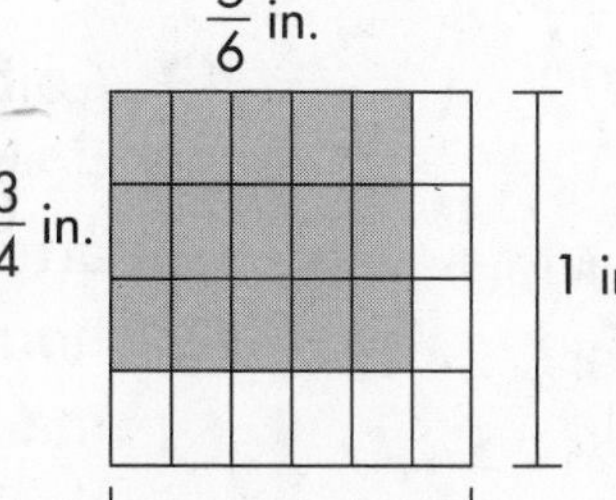

$\square \times \square = \square = \square$ sq in.

3.

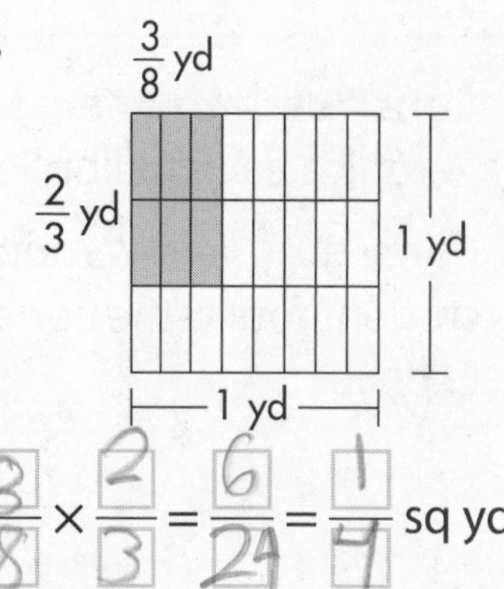

$\square \times \square = \square = \square$ sq yd

4.

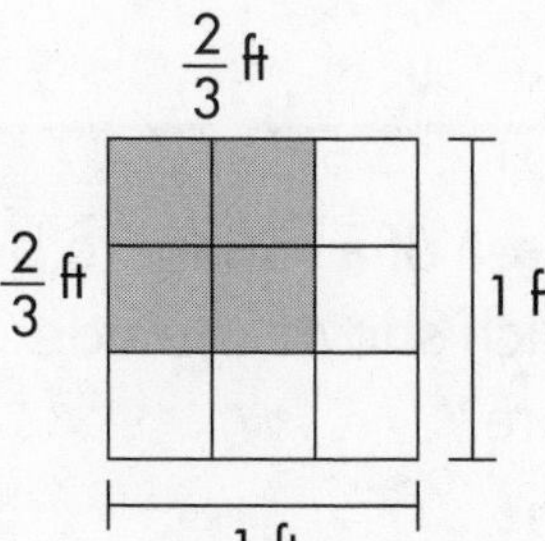
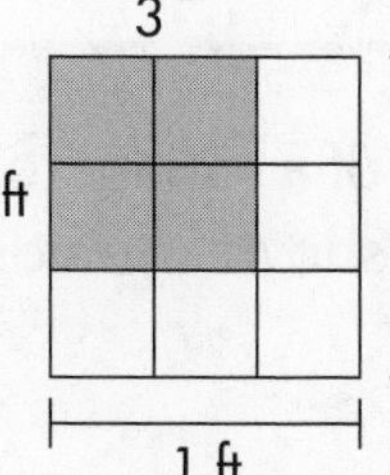

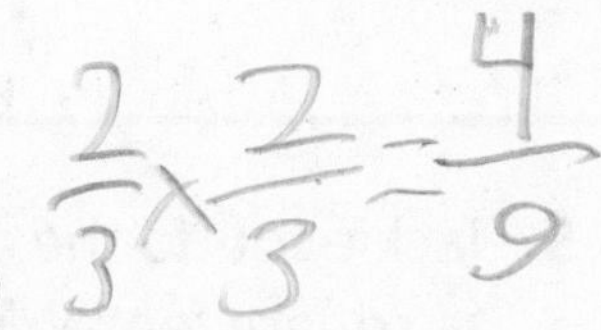

5.

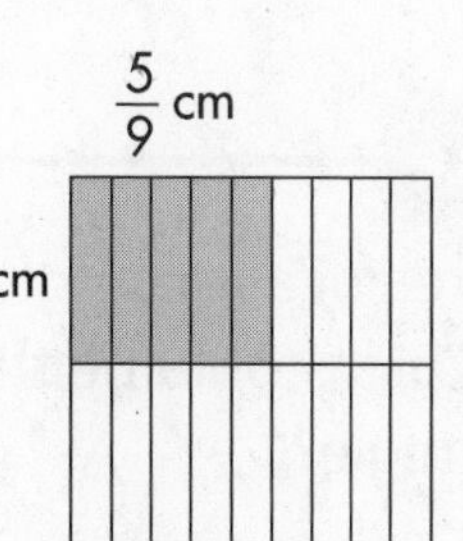

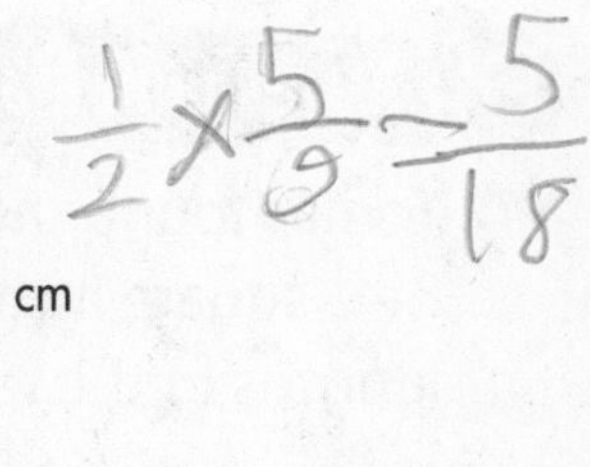

6. Find the area of a square with side length $\frac{3}{4}$ yard.

7. Find the area of a rectangle with side lengths $\frac{5}{4}$ feet and $\frac{5}{3}$ feet.

8. Find the area of a square with side length $\frac{7}{12}$ inch.

9. A crate is $\frac{3}{4}$ yard long and $\frac{2}{3}$ yard wide. The crate is also 2 feet tall. What is the area of the top of the crate?

10. Mike is making macaroni salad. For each bowl of macaroni salad, he needs $\frac{1}{3}$ cup of macaroni. How many cups of macaroni will he use if he makes 27 bowls of macaroni salad?

11. Higher Order Thinking Dorothy is installing purple and white tile in her kitchen. She made a diagram of the layout showing the area of both colors. Write two expressions that describe the area of the purple tile.

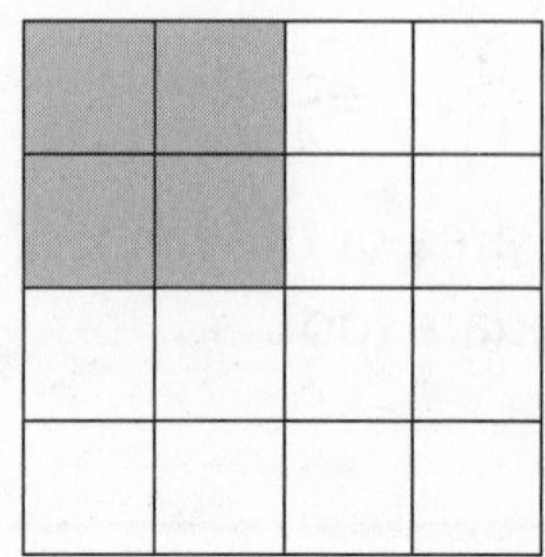

12. Construct Arguments Corey and Veronica each multiplied $\frac{1}{2} \times \frac{5}{2}$. Corey got $\frac{6}{4}$ and Veronica got $\frac{5}{4}$. Which student found the correct answer? Explain.

13. Colby attends barber school. So far, he has completed 612 hours. If Colby attended school the same number of hours each day for a total of 68 days, how many hours did he attend school each day?

Assessment Practice

14. Tomás found the area of a rectangle to be $\frac{1}{6}$ square inch. Which could be the side lengths of the rectangle?

Ⓐ $\frac{1}{4}$ inch and $\frac{2}{3}$ inch
Ⓑ $\frac{1}{3}$ inch and $\frac{1}{3}$ inch
Ⓒ $\frac{1}{6}$ inch and $\frac{1}{6}$ inch
Ⓓ $\frac{1}{2}$ inch and $\frac{1}{12}$ inch

15. Jackie found the area of a square to be $\frac{25}{16}$ square feet. Which shows the side length of the square?

Ⓐ $\frac{5}{4}$ feet
Ⓑ $\frac{5}{8}$ foot
Ⓒ $\frac{5}{16}$ foot
Ⓓ $\frac{25}{4}$ feet

Name ______________________

Additional Practice 8-7
Multiply Mixed Numbers

Another Look!

Millwood City is constructing a new highway through town. The construction crew can complete $5\frac{3}{5}$ miles of road each month. How many miles will they complete in $6\frac{1}{2}$ months?

Step 1	Step 2	Step 3	Step 4
Round the mixed numbers to whole numbers to estimate the product. $5\frac{3}{5} \times 6\frac{1}{2}$ → $6 \times 7 = 42$ So, they can complete about 42 miles.	Rename the mixed numbers. $5\frac{3}{5} \times 6\frac{1}{2} = \frac{28}{5} \times \frac{13}{2}$	Multiply the numerators and the denominators. $\frac{28}{5} \times \frac{13}{2} = \frac{364}{10} = 36\frac{2}{5}$ The construction crew will complete $36\frac{2}{5}$ miles of highway in $6\frac{1}{2}$ months.	Check for reasonableness. Compare your product to your estimate. $36\frac{2}{5}$ is close to 42, so the answer is reasonable.

In **1–4**, estimate the product. Then complete the multiplication.

1. $1\frac{1}{4} \times 2\frac{1}{4} = \frac{\square}{4} \times \frac{9}{\square} = \frac{5 \times \square}{\square \times 4} = \frac{45}{\square} = \square\frac{\square}{16}$

2. $3\frac{1}{2} \times 2\frac{2}{3} = \frac{7}{\square} \times \frac{\square}{3} = \frac{\square \times 8}{2 \times \square} = \frac{\square}{6} = \square\frac{1}{\square}$

3. $5\frac{1}{3} \times 2\frac{3}{4} = \frac{\square}{3} \times \frac{11}{\square} = \square$

4. $4\frac{1}{5} \times 2\frac{1}{4} = \frac{\square}{5} \times \frac{\square}{4} = \square$

In **5–12**, estimate the product. Then find each product.

5. $4 \times 6\frac{1}{4}$

6. $3\frac{2}{3} \times 2\frac{3}{4}$

7. $\frac{7}{8} \times 4\frac{1}{6}$

8. $1\frac{1}{2} \times 2\frac{3}{4}$

9. $8\frac{1}{10} \times \frac{2}{3}$

10. $4\frac{1}{12} \times 7$

11. $3\frac{4}{5} \times 7\frac{1}{2}$

12. $6\frac{2}{3} \times 4\frac{4}{5}$

13. How can you use estimation to find $9\frac{1}{2}+9\frac{1}{2}+9\frac{1}{2}+9\frac{1}{2}+9\frac{1}{2}$?

14. A model of a house is built on a base that measures $7\frac{3}{4}$ in. wide and $9\frac{1}{5}$ in. long. What is the area of the model house's base?

15. Algebra Write a mixed number for t so that $2\frac{3}{4}\times t$ is more than $2\frac{3}{4}$.

16. A-Z **Vocabulary** Give an example of a benchmark fraction and an example of a mixed number.

17. Make Sense and Persevere Leon and Marisol biked the Brookside Trail to the end and back. Then they biked the Forest Glen Trail to the end and back before stopping to eat. How far did they bike before they stopped to eat?

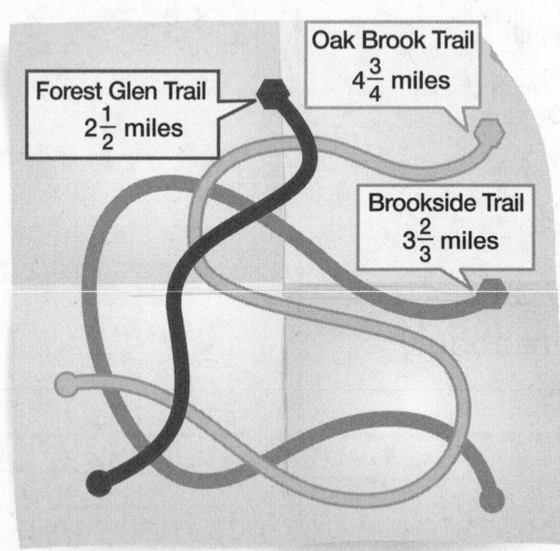

18. The One World Trade Center in New York City is about $3\frac{1}{5}$ times as tall as the Washington Monument in Washington, D.C. The Washington Monument is 555 feet tall. About how tall is the One World Trade Center?

19. Higher Order Thinking Lucie can walk about $3\frac{4}{5}$ miles each hour. About how far can she walk in 2 hours 45 minutes?

Assessment Practice

20. Choose all that are true.

- ☐ $\frac{1}{4}\times 1\frac{7}{8}=\frac{15}{32}$
- ☐ $2\frac{1}{2}\times 2\frac{1}{2}=5\frac{1}{2}$
- ☐ $3\frac{1}{5}\times 2\frac{1}{4}=6\frac{2}{5}$
- ☐ $4\frac{1}{2}\times 1\frac{1}{3}=6$
- ☐ $5\frac{1}{4}\times \frac{1}{2}=2\frac{5}{8}$

21. Choose all that are true.

- ☐ $4\frac{1}{12}\times \frac{3}{4}=\frac{49}{16}$
- ☐ $8\frac{5}{6}\times 2=17\frac{2}{3}$
- ☐ $5\frac{1}{2}\times 5\frac{1}{2}=30\frac{1}{4}$
- ☐ $9\frac{1}{5}\times \frac{3}{5}=9\frac{4}{5}$
- ☐ $6\frac{3}{4}\times 3\frac{1}{4}=19$

Name

Practice Video Tools Games

Additional Practice 8-8
Multiplication as Scaling

Another Look!

Theodore and Pam are rolling out modeling clay for an activity in art class. Theodore rolled out his clay until it was 5 inches long. Pam rolled hers $\frac{2}{3}$ times as far. Did Pam roll her clay out less than, more than, or the same as Theodore?

Step 1

Use a number line to find out how far Pam rolled out her clay. The arrows show $5 \times \frac{2}{3}$.

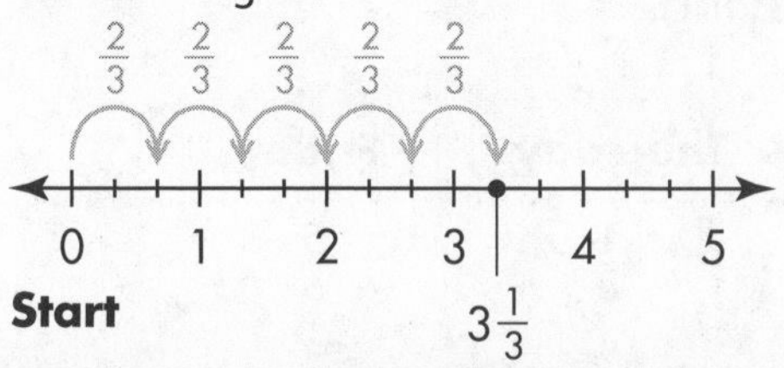

Step 2

Use a number line to compare the lengths of clay.

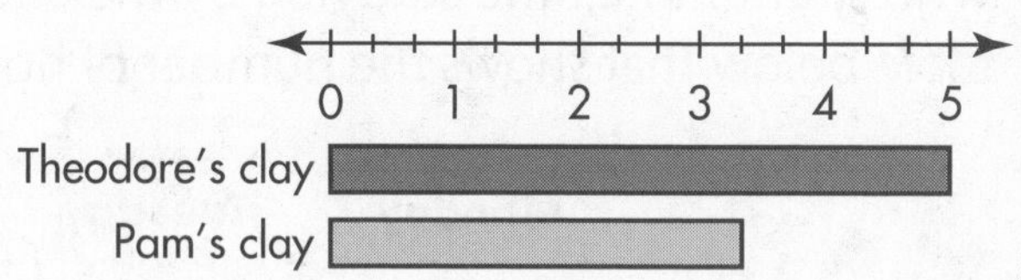

Pam rolled her clay out less than Theodore.

In **1** and **2**, decide which symbol belongs in the box: <, >, or =. Use the number line to help find the answer.

1. $5 \times \frac{3}{4}$ ☐ 5

2. $1\frac{1}{2} \times 3$ ☐ 3

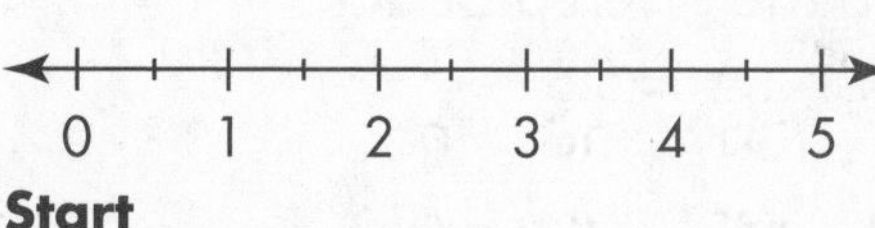

In **3–8**, without multiplying, decide which symbol belongs in the box: <, >, or =.

3. $5\frac{1}{3} \times 2\frac{3}{4}$ ☐ $5\frac{1}{3}$

4. $10\frac{3}{4} \times \frac{2}{2}$ ☐ $10\frac{3}{4}$

5. $\frac{1}{12} \times 1\frac{6}{7}$ ☐ $1\frac{6}{7}$

6. $5\frac{1}{5} \times 5\frac{1}{10}$ ☐ $5\frac{1}{10}$

7. $\frac{1}{4} \times 4\frac{1}{2}$ ☐ $4\frac{1}{2}$

8. $3\frac{9}{10} \times 1\frac{2}{3}$ ☐ $1\frac{2}{3}$

In **9** and **10**, without multiplying, order the following products from least to greatest.

9. $\frac{5}{6} \times 1\frac{8}{9}$ $\quad \frac{5}{6} \times \frac{1}{4}$ $\quad \frac{5}{6} \times 10\frac{1}{12}$ $\quad \frac{5}{6} \times \frac{6}{6}$

10. $\frac{1}{12} \times \frac{1}{4}$ $\quad 3\frac{1}{4} \times \frac{1}{4}$ $\quad 4\frac{1}{3} \times \frac{1}{4}$ $\quad \frac{1}{10} \times \frac{1}{4}$

11. Higher Order Thinking Without multiplying, decide which symbol belongs in the box: <, >, or =. Explain how you decided.

$2\frac{1}{3} \times \frac{1}{8} \square 2\frac{1}{2}$

12. Erin is making fruit salad. For each bowl of fruit salad, she needs $\frac{2}{3}$ cup of strawberries. How many cups of strawberries will she use if she makes 18 bowls of fruit salad?

13. Who spent more time studying by the end of the week? Use the table below that shows the number of hours spent studying.

DATA

	Monday	Tuesday	Wednesday	Thursday	Friday
Mark	$2\frac{1}{6}$	$1\frac{5}{6}$	$3\frac{3}{4}$	$2\frac{1}{8}$	$\frac{5}{6}$
Diane	$2\frac{1}{2}$	$\frac{5}{6}$	$3\frac{2}{3}$	$3\frac{2}{3}$	$\frac{3}{4}$

14. Make up two decimals with an answer close to the given product.

__.__ × __.__ = 5.5

15. Use Structure Put the following products in order from greatest to least, without multiplying.

$3\frac{1}{8} \times \frac{1}{8}$ $\quad \frac{2}{3} \times 3\frac{1}{8}$ $\quad 3\frac{1}{8} \times 3\frac{1}{8}$ $\quad 3\frac{1}{8} \times \frac{4}{4}$

Assessment Practice

16. Write each expression in the correct answer space to show products less than $\frac{2}{3}$ and those greater than $\frac{2}{3}$.

Less than $\frac{2}{3}$	Greater than $\frac{2}{3}$

$\frac{2}{3} \times 1\frac{1}{2}$ $\quad \frac{2}{3} \times \frac{2}{3}$ $\quad \frac{2}{3} \times \frac{1}{2}$ $\quad 2\frac{2}{3} \times \frac{2}{3}$

17. Write each expression in the correct answer space to show products less than $10\frac{1}{2}$ and those greater than $10\frac{1}{2}$.

Less than $10\frac{1}{2}$	Greater than $10\frac{1}{2}$

$1\frac{1}{12} \times 10\frac{1}{2}$ $\quad \frac{1}{12} \times 10\frac{1}{2}$ $\quad 10\frac{1}{3} \times 10\frac{1}{2}$

$1\frac{1}{9} \times 10\frac{1}{2}$

Name ______________________

Practice

Video

Tools

Games

Additional Practice 8-9

Make Sense and Persevere

Another Look!

Last weekend Troy spent $\frac{3}{4}$ hour doing math problems. He took 3 times as long to finish his science project. Then he spent $1\frac{1}{4}$ hours writing an essay. How much time did Troy spend on these assignments?

Make sense of the problem and then plan how to solve it.

Tell how you can make sense of the problem.

I know that Troy spent $\frac{3}{4}$ hour doing math problems and 3 times as long on his science project.

He spent $1\frac{1}{4}$ hours writing an essay.

Tell how you can persevere in solving the problem.

I need to determine how much time Troy spent on the assignments.

First, you need to find the amount of time Troy spent on his science project.

$3 \times \frac{3}{4} = \frac{3}{1} \times \frac{3}{4} = \frac{9}{4} = 2\frac{1}{4}$ hours

Then add to calculate the total time.

$\frac{3}{4} + 2\frac{1}{4} + 1\frac{1}{4} = 4\frac{1}{4}$ hours

Troy spent $4\frac{1}{4}$ hours on the assignments.

Make Sense and Persevere

Debra's rectangular vegetable garden measures $9\frac{1}{3}$ yards by 12 yards. A bottle of garden fertilizer costs $14.79. If Debra needs to mix $\frac{1}{8}$ cup of fertilizer with water for each square yard of her garden, how many cups of fertilizer does she need?

1. How can you make sense of the problem?

2. Is there any information that is not needed to solve the problem?

Remember to check that your work makes sense.

3. How can you persevere in solving this problem? What is the answer?

Children's Costumes

Mrs. Lin is sewing costumes for her grandchildren. She is making three lion costumes, one zebra costume, and two bear costumes. Fabric costs $7.49 per yard. How much fabric does Mrs. Lin need?

DATA

Children's Costumes	
Costume	**Fabric (yards)**
Bear	$2\frac{1}{4}$
Lion	$1\frac{2}{3}$
Zebra	$2\frac{5}{8}$

4. **Make Sense and Persevere** What do you know? What are you asked to find? Is there any information you do not need?

5. **Make Sense and Persevere** What do you need to find before you can answer the final question?

6. **Model with Math** Write equations to represent the information you described in Exercise 5.

7. **Make Sense and Persevere** Solve the problem.

8. **Construct Arguments** Explain why your answer makes sense.

Remember that good problem solvers keep asking themselves if their work makes sense.

Name ______________________

Practice Video Tools Games

Additional Practice 9-1
Fractions and Division

Another Look!

If 3 pizzas are shared equally among 8 people, what fraction of a pizza will each person get?

Step 1

Partition each pizza into 8 equal pieces. Each piece is $\frac{1}{8}$ of the whole.

Since there are more people than pizzas, each person will get less than a whole pizza.

Step 2

Each person gets 1 piece of each pizza. This is the same as $\frac{3}{8}$ of one pizza.

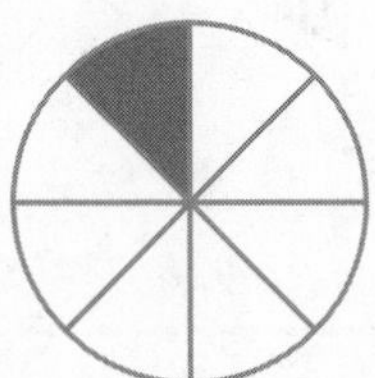

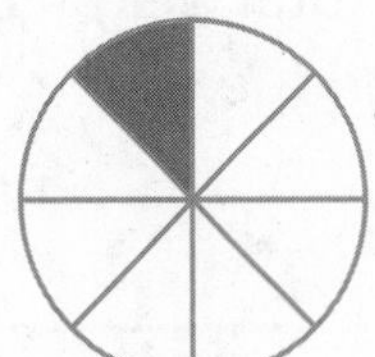

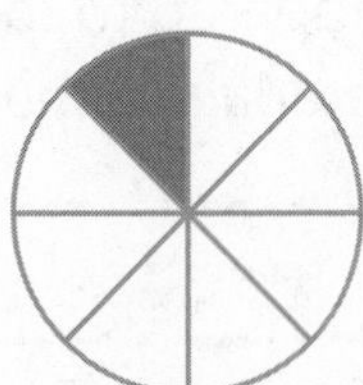

So, $3 \div 8 = \frac{3}{8}$. Each person gets $\frac{3}{8}$ of a pizza.

In **1–5**, write a division expression for each fraction.

1. $\frac{1}{2}$ **2.** $\frac{5}{6}$ **3.** $\frac{9}{15}$ **4.** $\frac{10}{25}$ **5.** $\frac{16}{31}$

In **6–10**, write each division expression as a fraction.

6. $5 \div 9$ **7.** $1 \div 12$ **8.** $4 \div 21$ **9.** $8 \div 30$ **10.** $15 \div 45$

In **11–14**, tell what fraction each person gets when they share equally.

11. 6 friends share 3 apples.

12. 8 people share 1 pizza.

13. 10 students share 1 hour to give their science reports.

14. 5 women each run an equal part of a 3-mile relay.

Use the table for **15** and **16**. The table shows the weights of different materials used to build a bridge.

15. Model with Math Write a division expression that represents the weight of the steel structure divided by the total weight of the bridge's materials.

DATA

Bridge	Materials
Concrete	1,000 tons
Steel structure	400 tons
Glass and granite	200 tons

16. Write a fraction that represents the weight of glass and granite in the bridge compared to the total weight of the materials in the bridge.

17. Higher Order Thinking A group of students shared 3 rolls of clay equally. If each student got $\frac{1}{2}$ of a roll of clay, how many students were in the group? Explain.

18. A-Z **Vocabulary** Write a division equation. Identify the dividend, divisor, and quotient.

19. One lap around the school track is $\frac{1}{4}$ of a mile. If Patrick runs 7 laps around the track and then runs $1\frac{1}{2}$ miles to get home, how far will he run in all?

20. There were 16 teams at a gymnastics meet. Each team had 12 members. How many gymnasts participated in the meet?

Assessment Practice

21. Which equation would be made true with the number 4?

Ⓐ $4 \div 5 = \square$

Ⓑ $\square \div 4 = \frac{3}{4}$

Ⓒ $1 \div \square = 4$

Ⓓ $\square \div 5 = \frac{4}{5}$

22. Which equation would be made true with the number 10?

Ⓐ $\square \div 10 = \frac{1}{10}$

Ⓑ $3 \div \square = \frac{3}{10}$

Ⓒ $4 \div 40 = \square$

Ⓓ $\square \div 21 = \frac{21}{10}$

Name ______________________

Practice

Video

Tools

Games

Additional Practice 9-2

Fractions and Mixed Numbers as Quotients

Another Look!

Max has 5 clementines (a type of small orange). He shares them equally with his friend Tyler. How many clementines will each friend get?

Find the quotient of $5 \div 2$ as a mixed number.

Divide each clementine into 2 equal parts. Each piece is $\frac{1}{2}$ of the whole.

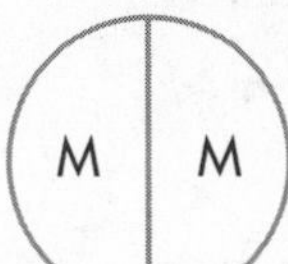

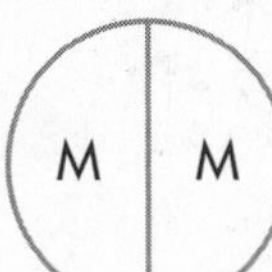

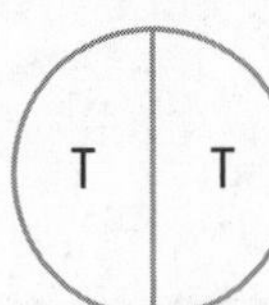

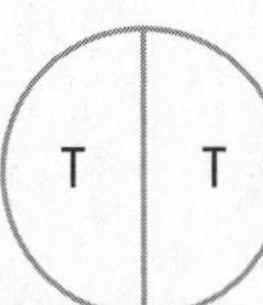

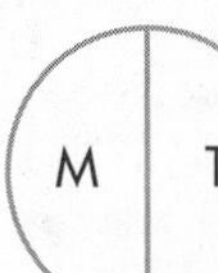

Each friend gets 2 clementines plus $\frac{1}{2}$ of a clementine or $2 + \frac{1}{2} = 2\frac{1}{2}$ clementines in all.

So, $5 \div 2 = \frac{5}{2} = 2\frac{1}{2}$.

Since there are more clementines than people, each person will get more than 1 clementine.

1. Find $5 \div 8$ and $8 \div 5$. Write each quotient as either a fraction or mixed number.

In **2–9**, find each quotient. Write each answer as either a fraction or mixed number.

2. $7 \div 5$

3. $2 \div 3$

4. $15 \div 4$

5. $51 \div 25$

6. $6 \div 11$

7. $17 \div 12$

8. $16 \div 6$

9. $92 \div 30$

In **10–13**, tell how much each person gets when they share equally.

10. 3 friends share 5 pounds of trail mix.

11. 6 people share 12 muffins.

12. 2 sisters share 3 hours of babysitting.

13. 4 students share 10 yards of fabric.

14. Carol jogged $1\frac{3}{4}$ miles on 5 days last week. She jogged $2\frac{1}{4}$ miles on 4 days this week. Was her total distance greater last week or this week? How much greater? Explain.

15. Construct Arguments How can you tell before dividing that the first digit of the quotient $2,874 \div 3$ is in the hundreds place?

16. Which car traveled the farthest on 1 gallon of gas? Show your work.

	Distance	Gasoline
Car A	302 mi	10 gal
Car B	174 mi	5 gal
Car C	292 mi	8 gal

17. Vocabulary Complete the sentence using one of the terms below.

common denominator
benchmark fraction **mixed number**

A ______________ for the fractions $\frac{1}{3}$ and $\frac{1}{4}$ is 12.

18. enVision® STEM The smallest bone in the human body is the stapes bone. It is located in the ear and is about 2.8 millimeters in length. Write this number in expanded form.

19. At Dee's Pizza Kitchen, 7 pizzas were shared equally among 3 families. How much pizza did each family get? Write an equation to represent the problem.

20. Higher Order Thinking Everett says that $1\frac{1}{4}$ equals $4 \div 5$. Is he correct? Explain.

Assessment Practice

21. Amira has 27 feet of ribbon to make 5 braided bracelets. How much ribbon goes to each bracelet?

Ⓐ $\frac{5}{27}$ feet

Ⓑ $5\frac{1}{5}$ feet

Ⓒ $5\frac{2}{5}$ feet

Ⓓ $5\frac{3}{5}$ feet

22. Leonard divides 70 by 8. Between what two whole numbers is his answer?

Ⓐ 11 and 12

Ⓑ 10 and 11

Ⓒ 9 and 10

Ⓓ 8 and 9

Name ______________________

Practice Video Tools Games

Additional Practice 9-3

Use Multiplication to Divide

Another Look!

How many sixths are in 4?

Find $4 \div \frac{1}{6}$. Use a model to help.

There are 6 sixths in each whole, so 4 wholes contain $4 \times 6 = 24$ sixths.

$4 \div \frac{1}{6} = 24$

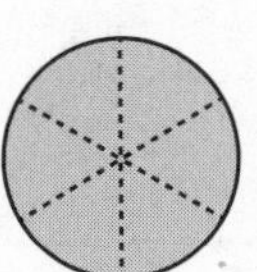
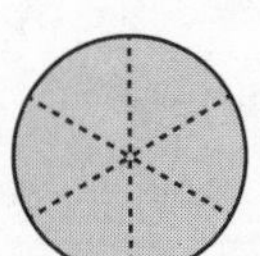
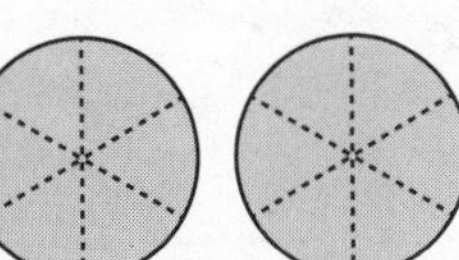
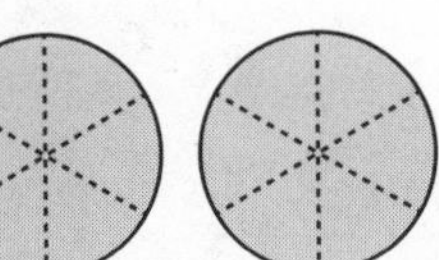

Check your answer.

$24 \times \frac{1}{6} = \frac{24}{6} = 4$

The answer checks.

You can use multiplication to check division.

In **1–4**, use the model to find each quotient. Use multiplication to check your answer.

1. $2 \div \frac{1}{9}$

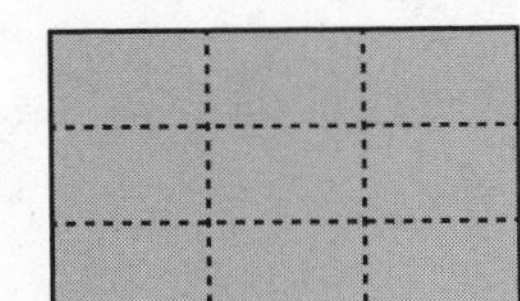
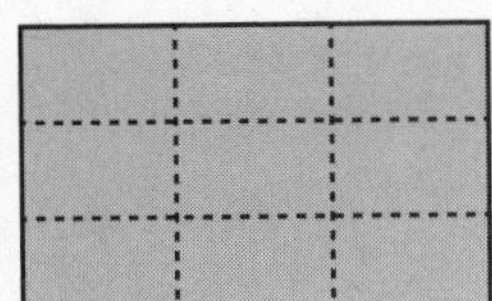

2. $4 \div \frac{1}{4}$

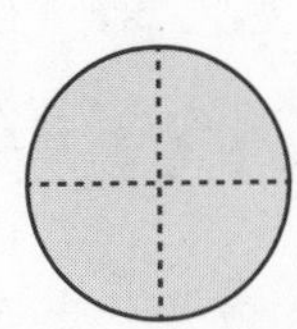
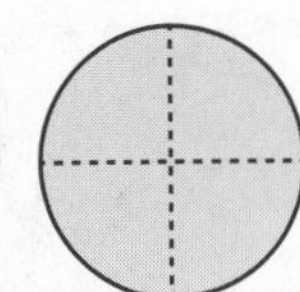
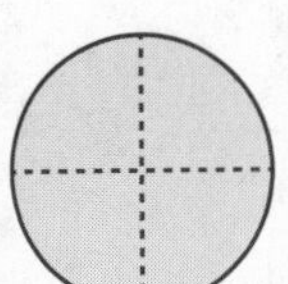
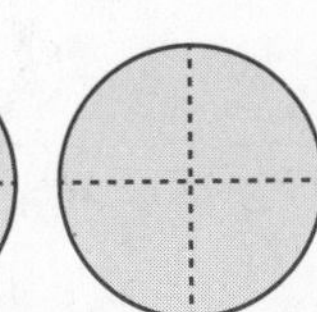

3. $7 \div \frac{1}{3}$

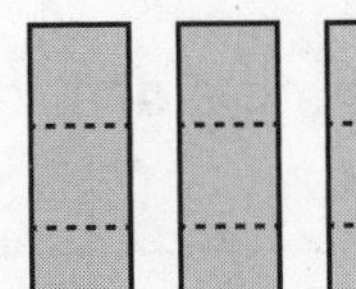
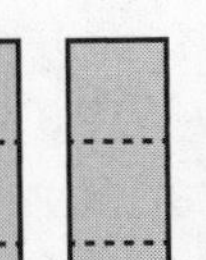
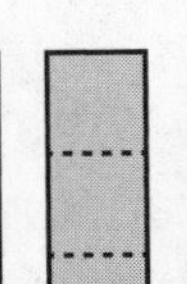
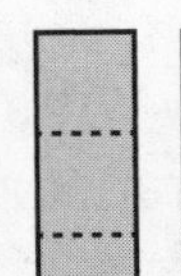

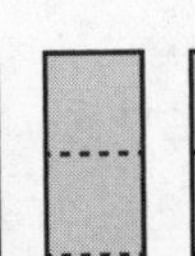
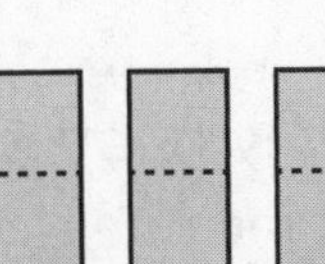
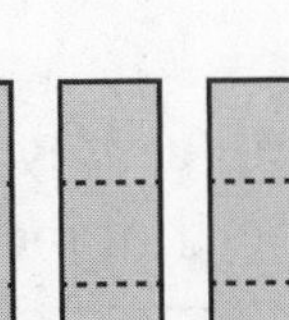

4. $3 \div \frac{1}{2}$

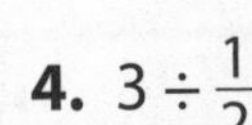
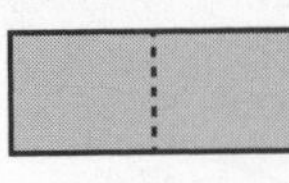
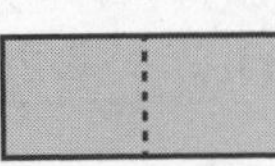
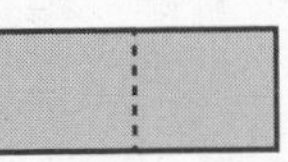

In **5–7**, draw a model to find each quotient. Use multiplication to check your answer.

5. $4 \div \frac{1}{6}$

6. $2 \div \frac{1}{8}$

7. $3 \div \frac{1}{12}$

8. **Use Structure** Use the numbers in the multiplication equation $45 \times \frac{1}{9} = 5$ to write a division equation involving division by a fraction.

9. A square has a side length of 6.2 centimeters. What is the perimeter of the square?

10. Denise makes beaded bracelets for a craft fair. She uses $\frac{1}{4}$ yard of yarn for each bracelet. How many bracelets can she make from 10 yards of yarn?

11. Arthur paid $0.84 for 0.25 pound of potato salad. How much does one pound cost?

12. **Higher Order Thinking** A company donated 5 acres of land to the city. How many more small garden plots would fit on the land than medium garden plots? Explain.

DATA

Community Garden Plots	Size (fraction of an acre)
Small	$\frac{1}{6}$
Medium	$\frac{1}{4}$
Large	$\frac{1}{3}$

Assessment Practice

13. Audrey drew a model to determine how many eighths are in 5.

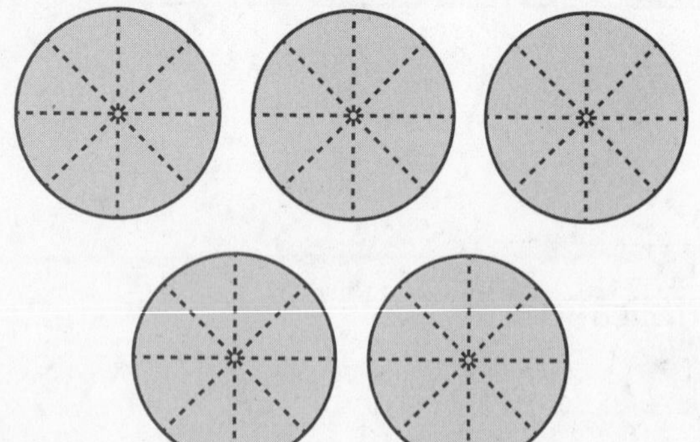

Part A

Describe Audrey's work by writing a division equation that includes a fraction.

Part B

Check your answer by using the numbers in your division equation to write a multiplication equation.

Name ______________________

Practice

Video

Tools

Games

Additional Practice 9-4

Divide Whole Numbers by Unit Fractions

Another Look!

Ned has a 2-foot-long piece of rope. He cuts the rope into $\frac{1}{3}$-foot pieces. How many pieces of rope does Ned have now?

Think: How many $\frac{1}{3}$s are in 2? Use a model or a number line to help.

Count how many $\frac{1}{3}$s there are in 2. There are three $\frac{1}{3}$s in 1, so there are six $\frac{1}{3}$s in 2.

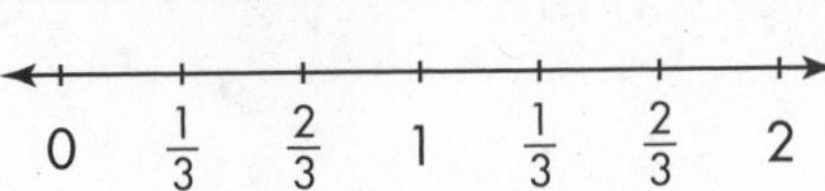

$2 \div \frac{1}{3} = 6$

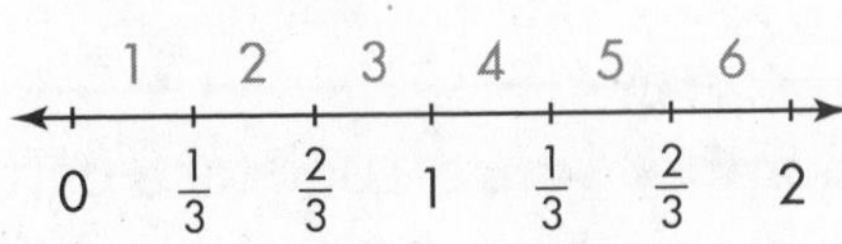

You can use multiplication to check your answer.

$6 \times \frac{1}{3} = 2$

Ned has 6 pieces of rope.

In **1** and **2**, use the picture to find each quotient.

1. How many $\frac{1}{5}$s are in 1? ____

$1 \div \frac{1}{5} =$ ____

2. How many $\frac{1}{5}$s are in 4? ____

$4 \div \frac{1}{5} =$ ____

In **3–10**, find each quotient. You may draw a picture or use a number line to help.

3. $12 \div \frac{1}{2} =$

4. $9 \div \frac{1}{4} =$

5. $3 \div \frac{1}{7} =$

6. $10 \div \frac{1}{10} =$

7. $20 \div \frac{1}{3} =$

8. $7 \div \frac{1}{5} =$

9. $6 \div \frac{1}{6} =$

10. $15 \div \frac{1}{2} =$

11. Use the number line. How many $\frac{1}{4}$-yard long pieces of pipe can be cut from two 1-yard long pieces of pipe?

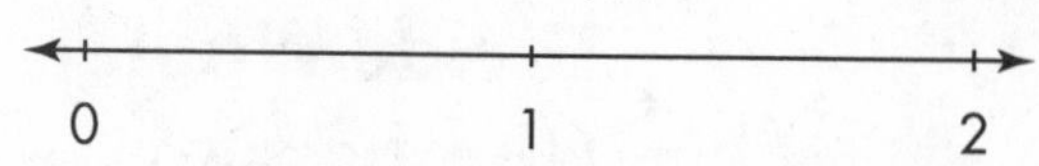

12. A-Z **Vocabulary** Define a unit fraction and then give an example.

13. Built in 2005, the world's largest leather work boot is 16 feet tall. A typical men's work boot is $\frac{1}{2}$ foot tall. How many times as tall as a typical work boot is the largest boot?

14. Higher Order Thinking When you divide a whole number by a unit fraction, explain how you can find the quotient.

15. Number Sense Look for a pattern in the table. Find the missing addends and sums.

Addends	$\frac{1}{8}+\frac{1}{4}$	$\frac{1}{4}+\frac{1}{4}$	$\frac{3}{8}+\frac{1}{4}$	
Sum	$\frac{3}{8}$	$\frac{1}{2}$		

16. Make Sense and Persevere David made a line plot of how many miles he biked each day for two weeks. How many miles did he bike in all?

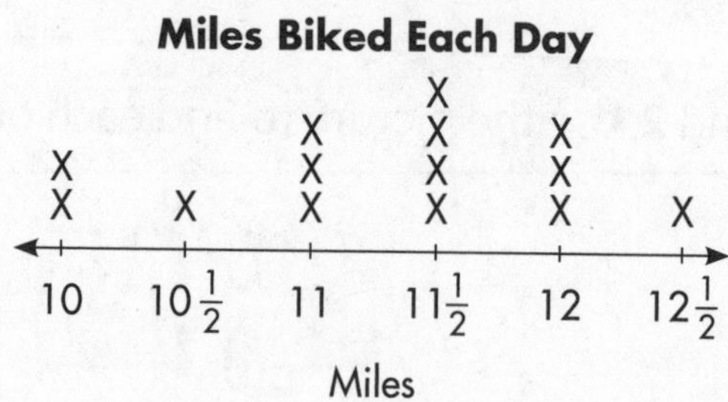

Assessment Practice

17. Omar has 8 cups of cornmeal. How many batches of corn muffins can he make?

Ⓐ 4 batches

Ⓑ 6 batches

Ⓒ 16 batches

Ⓓ 32 batches

DATA

Cornmeal Recipes

Item	Amount Needed
Cornbread	$\frac{3}{4}$ cup per loaf
Corn Muffins	$\frac{1}{2}$ cup per batch
Hush Puppies	$\frac{5}{8}$ cup per batch

Name ________________

Additional Practice 9-5

Divide Unit Fractions by Non-Zero Whole Numbers

Another Look!

Sal has $\frac{1}{3}$ of a sheet of poster board. Four friends are sharing the $\frac{1}{3}$ sheet equally. What fraction of the original sheet does each friend get?

How can you divide $\frac{1}{3}$ into 4 equal parts?

Step 1

Use a drawing.

Divide 1 whole sheet into 3 equal parts.

Shade to show Sal's $\frac{1}{3}$.

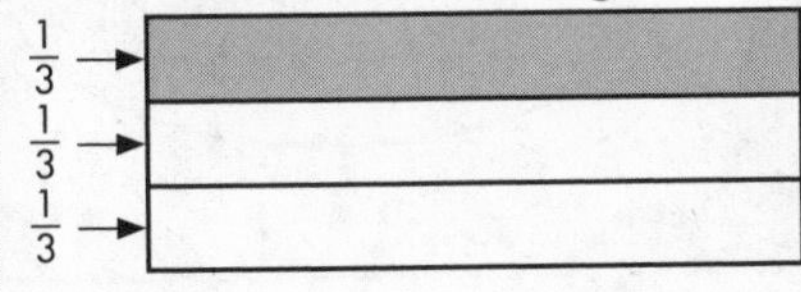

Step 2

Next, divide each third into 4 equal parts.

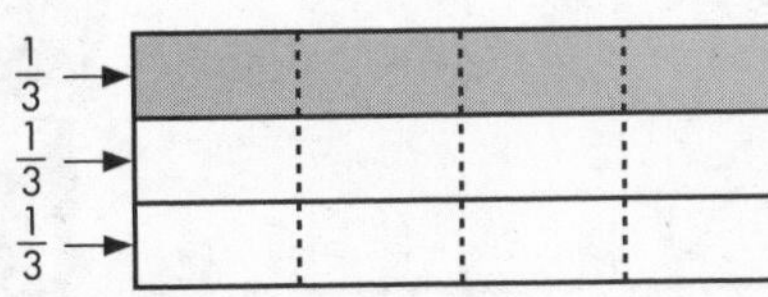

Step 3

Count the total number of parts. The total is the denominator.

$\frac{1}{12}$ ← each friend's part; 12 ← total number of parts

So, each friend gets $\frac{1}{12}$ of the original sheet.

Leveled Practice In **1–11**, find each quotient. Draw a picture or use a number line to help.

1. $\frac{1}{2} \div 4$

2. $\frac{1}{3} \div 2$

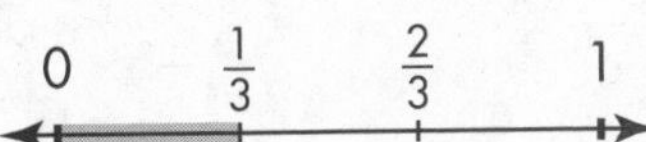

3. $\frac{1}{3} \div 5$

4. $\frac{1}{5} \div 3$

5. $\frac{1}{2} \div 5$

6. $\frac{1}{8} \div 2$

7. $\frac{1}{5} \div 4$

8. $\frac{1}{5} \div 2$

9. $\frac{1}{6} \div 4$

10. $\frac{1}{4} \div 3$

11. $\frac{1}{8} \div 2$

12. Marge and Kimo equally shared one fourth of a pie that was left over. What fraction of the original pie did each friend get? Use the picture to help you find the solution.

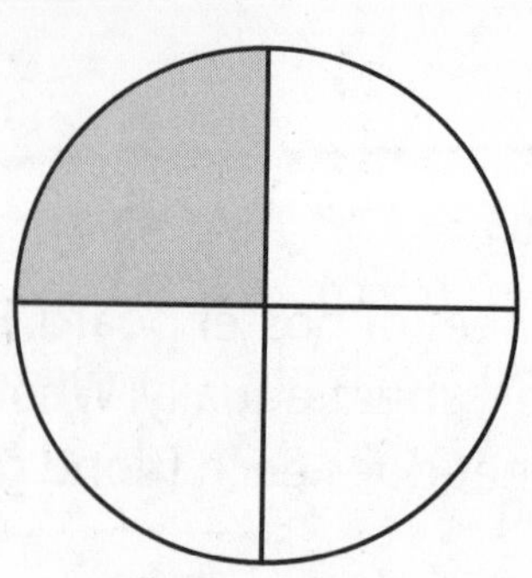

13. Higher Order Thinking Eve and Gerard each have $\frac{1}{2}$ of a poster to paint. Eve divided her half into 6 equal sections. She painted one section blue. Gerard divided his half into 5 equal sections. He painted one section blue. Whose blue section is larger? Explain.

14. Number Sense What are two decimals whose product is close to 10?

Use compatible numbers to help you find a product.

15. Use Structure Without multiplying, order the following products from least to greatest.

$2 \times \frac{3}{5}$ $\quad \frac{1}{4} \times \frac{3}{5}$ $\quad 1\frac{2}{5} \times \frac{3}{5}$ $\quad \frac{6}{6} \times \frac{3}{5}$

16. Tom plans to replace a rectangular piece of drywall. Find the area of the piece of drywall that Tom needs to replace.

16 feet

$\frac{3}{4}$ foot

Assessment Practice

17. Mrs. Sims cut a melon into fifths. She gave 1 piece to each of her four children. She used equal amounts of the leftover melon to make three fruit cups. What fraction of the original melon did she use to make each fruit cup?

Ⓐ $\frac{1}{4}$

Ⓑ $\frac{1}{12}$

Ⓒ $\frac{1}{15}$

Ⓓ $\frac{1}{20}$

18. Steven has $\frac{1}{3}$ of a package of biscuit mix left. He will use equal parts of the leftover mix to make three batches of biscuits. What fraction of the original package will he use for each batch?

Ⓐ $\frac{1}{9}$

Ⓑ $\frac{1}{6}$

Ⓒ $\frac{1}{2}$

Ⓓ $\frac{2}{3}$

Name ______________________

Additional Practice 9-6

Divide Whole Numbers and Unit Fractions

Another Look!

Find $8 \div \frac{1}{4}$.

You can use an area model to solve the problem.

First, draw a rectangle and divide it into 8 equal parts to represent 8 wholes.

Then use another color to divide each of the 8 parts into fourths and count the total number of fraction parts.

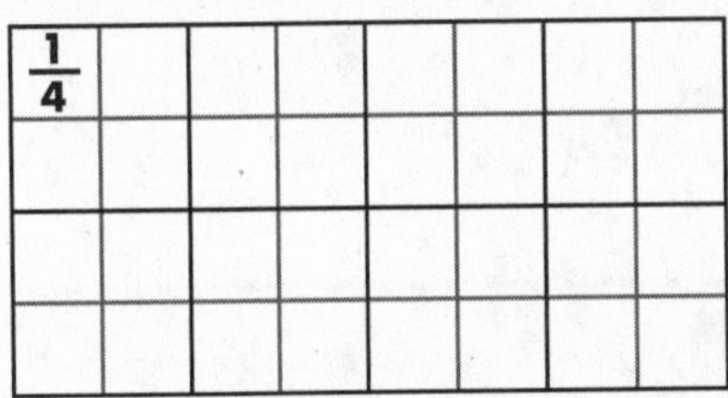

There are 32 small squares, so you know that $8 \div \frac{1}{4} = 32$.

Find $\frac{1}{4} \div 8$.

You can also divide unit fractions by whole numbers.

Think: the quotient times the divisor must equal the dividend.

What times 8 equals $\frac{1}{4}$?

$\frac{1}{32} \times 8 = \frac{1}{4}$

So, $\frac{1}{4} \div 8 = \frac{1}{32}$.

In **1–12**, find each quotient. Use a number line or model to help.

1. $6 \div \frac{1}{2}$

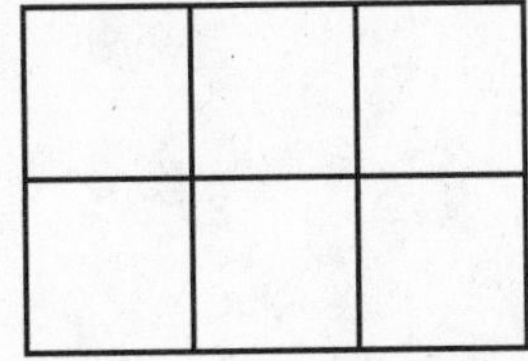

2. $4 \div \frac{1}{4}$

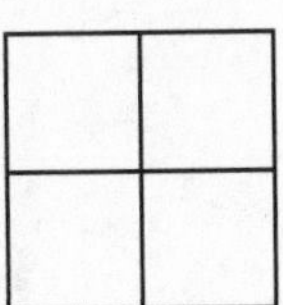

3. $5 \div \frac{1}{3}$

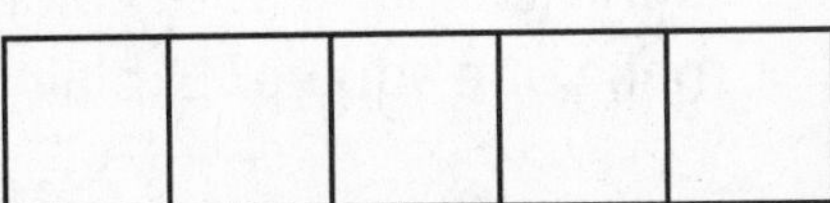

4. $\frac{1}{2} \div 6$

5. $\frac{1}{5} \div 2$

6. $\frac{1}{8} \div 3$

7. $\frac{1}{7} \div 8$

8. $5 \div \frac{1}{5}$

9. $\frac{1}{3} \div 9$

10. $\frac{1}{4} \div 8$

11. $6 \div \frac{1}{7}$

12. $\frac{1}{6} \div 5$

13. Cynthia has a piece of wood that is 6 feet long. She cuts it into $\frac{1}{2}$-foot pieces. How many pieces does she have? Use the number line to help you solve the problem.

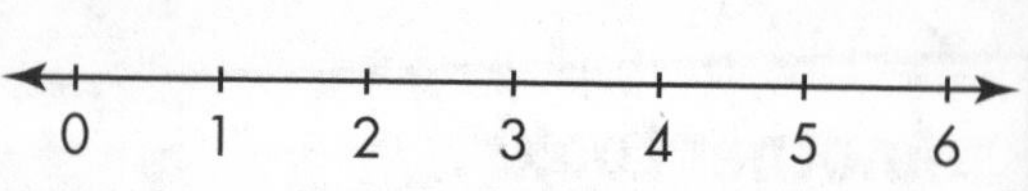

14. Gregg has a coin collection album with 275 pages. Each coin is displayed on $\frac{1}{6}$ of a page. How many coins will fit in the album?

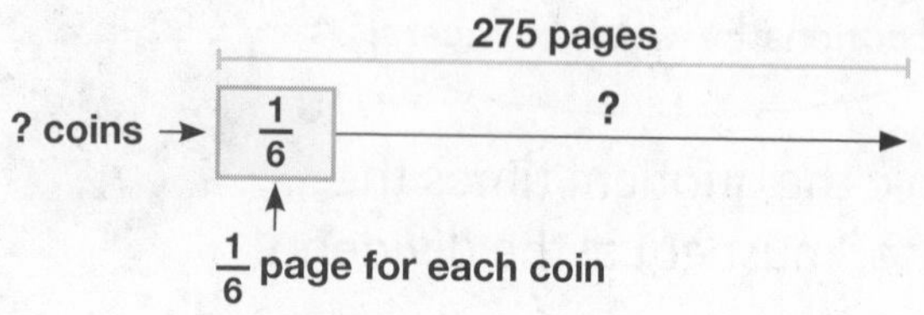

15. **enVision® STEM** Suppose a wind turbine requires $\frac{1}{6}$ square mile of land. How many turbines can be built on 8 square miles of land?

16. **Reasoning** Meredith modeled a division problem on the number line. What division problem did she model? Find the quotient.

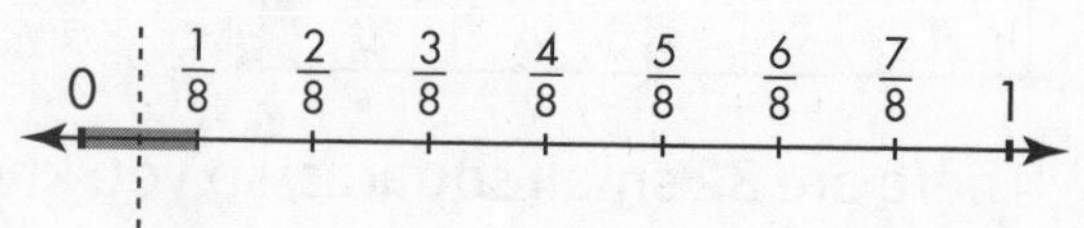

17. **Higher Order Thinking** Millie has 5 yards of blue fabric and 7 yards of pink fabric. How many quilt squares can she make with the fabric she has if both colors are needed to make one square? Explain your reasoning.

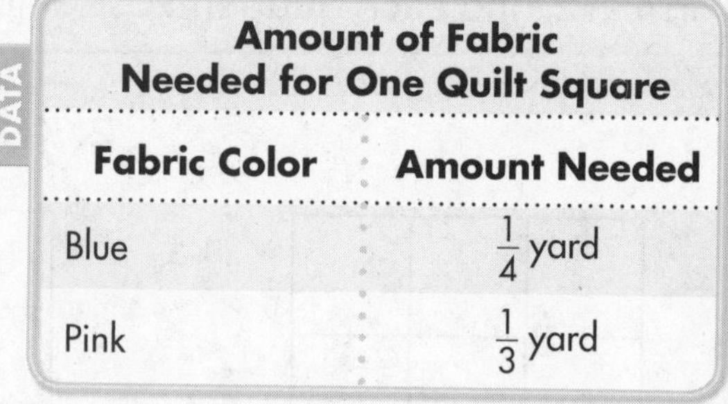

DATA

Amount of Fabric Needed for One Quilt Square

Fabric Color	Amount Needed
Blue	$\frac{1}{4}$ yard
Pink	$\frac{1}{3}$ yard

Assessment Practice

18. Cindy says that $\frac{1}{4} \div 12 = 3$. Is she correct? If not, justify your reasoning and give the correct quotient.

Name ______________________________

Practice Video Tools Games

Additional Practice 9-7

Solve Problems Using Division

Another Look!

Nell participated in a 3-day charity walk. She raised \$0.50 for each $\frac{1}{3}$ mile that she walked. The first day, Nell walked 12 miles. The second day, she walked 8 miles. The third day, she walked 16 miles. How much money did Nell raise?

What do you know?

Nell walked 12 miles, 8 miles, and 16 miles.

She raised \$0.50 for each $\frac{1}{3}$ mile she walked.

What do you need to find?

How much money Nell raised

How can you use what you know to solve the problem?

Write an equation to answer each question.

a What is the total number of miles Nell walked?

Nell walked $12 + 8 + 16 = 36$, or 36 miles.

b How many $\frac{1}{3}$ miles did Nell walk?

Nell walked $36 \div \frac{1}{3} = 108$, or 108 one-third miles.

c How much money did Nell raise?

Nell raised $108 \times \$0.50 = \$54$.

Write the equations needed to solve each problem. Then solve.

How many steps do you need to solve each problem?

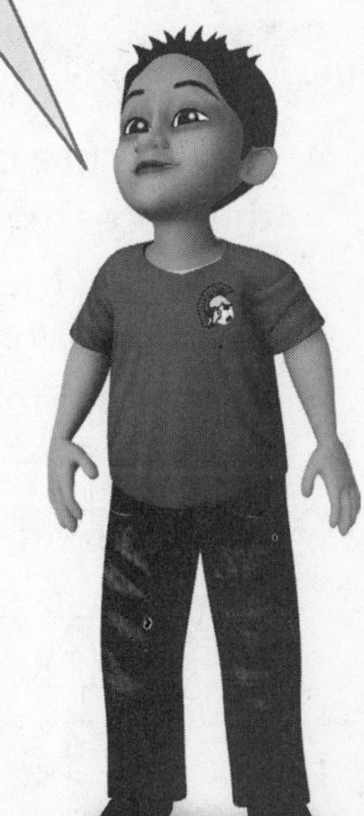

1. Anna plants peas in $\frac{3}{8}$ of her garden and herbs in $\frac{1}{8}$ of it. She divides the rest of the garden into 6 sections. What fraction of the original garden is each section?

Equations: ______________________________

Answer: ______________________________

2. Ryan has 4 cups of grape juice, and Kelsey has 7 cups of lemonade. They want to combine what they have to make punch. How many $\frac{1}{2}$-cup servings of punch can they make?

Equations: ______________________________

Answer: ______________________________

3. **Be Precise** Benjamin is making bow ties. How many $\frac{1}{2}$-yard-long bow ties can he make if he has 18 feet of fabric?

4. Cole's rectangular garden has an area of 54 square feet. What could be the dimensions of the garden?

5. One batch of fruit punch contains $\frac{1}{4}$ quart grape juice and $\frac{1}{2}$ quart apple juice. Colby makes 9 batches of fruit punch. How much grape juice did he use for 9 batches?

6. **Higher Order Thinking** Ms. James has a 6-square-foot bulletin board and a 12-square-foot bulletin board. She wants to cover both boards with index cards without gaps or overlaps. Each index card has an area of $\frac{1}{4}$ square foot. How many index cards does she need?

7. **Number Sense** Craig has 36 ounces of flour left in one bag and 64 ounces of flour in another bag. Use the Baking Flour Equivalents table to find how many cups of flour Craig has in all.

DATA

Baking Flour Equivalents

Number of Ounces	Number of Cups
16	3.6
10	2.3
8	1.8

8. Doris uses 8 square pieces of fabric to make one scarf. Each side of a square piece of fabric is $\frac{1}{4}$ foot in length. Doris can buy large pieces of fabric that are $\frac{1}{4}$ foot long and 2 feet wide. How many large pieces of fabric should she buy to make 7 scarves? Show your work.

Assessment Practice

9. Debbie cut a cord into sixths. She used five of the pieces to make necklaces. She used equal lengths of the remaining cord for each of four bracelets. What fraction of the original cord did Debbie use for each bracelet?

Ⓐ $\frac{1}{6}$

Ⓑ $\frac{1}{12}$

Ⓒ $\frac{1}{16}$

Ⓓ $\frac{1}{24}$

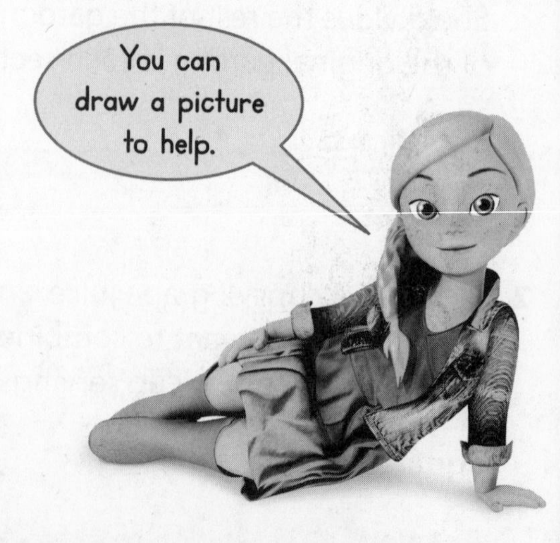
You can draw a picture to help.

Name ______________________

Practice Video Tools Games

Additional Practice 9-8
Repeated Reasoning

Another Look!

Study each set of problems. Then make a generalization about each set.

Set A

$\frac{1}{4} \div 6 = \frac{1}{24}$ $\quad \frac{1}{4} \times \frac{1}{6} = \frac{1}{24}$

$\frac{1}{3} \div 5 = \frac{1}{15}$ $\quad \frac{1}{3} \times \frac{1}{5} = \frac{1}{15}$

Set B

$6 \div \frac{1}{4} = 24$ $\quad 6 \times 4 = 24$

$5 \div \frac{1}{3} = 15$ $\quad 5 \times 3 = 15$

Generalizing can help you find general methods for solving division problems involving unit fractions and whole numbers.

Set A

$\frac{1}{4} \div 6 = \frac{1}{4} \times \frac{1}{6}$

$\frac{1}{3} \div 5 = \frac{1}{3} \times \frac{1}{5}$

Generalization:

Dividing a unit fraction by a whole number other than zero is the same as multiplying the unit fraction by a unit fraction with the whole number as the denominator.

Set B

$6 \div \frac{1}{4} = 6 \times 4$

$5 \div \frac{1}{3} = 5 \times 3$

Generalization:

Dividing a whole number by a unit fraction is the same as multiplying a whole number by the denominator of the unit fraction.

Mrs. Miller brought 7 apples to a picnic. She cut each apple in half. How many pieces did she wind up with?

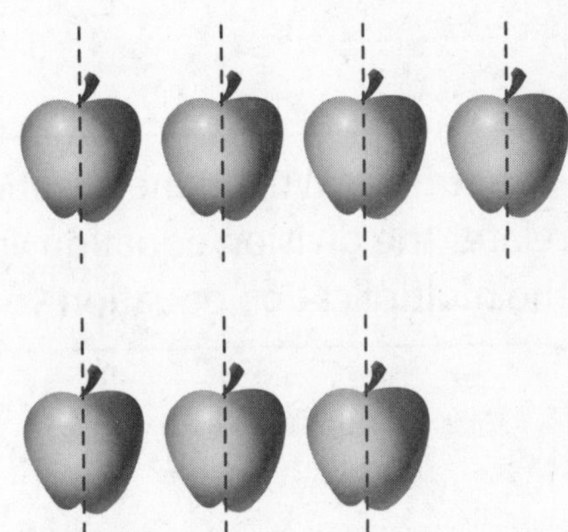

1. Write and solve a division equation to find the total number of apple pieces. Explain your reasoning.

2. Suppose Mrs. Miller decided to cut each apple into fourths rather than into halves. Find how many apple pieces she would have then. Can you repeat the method you used in Exercise 1 to solve this problem? Explain.

3. When you divide a whole number by a unit fraction, how does the quotient compare to the whole number? Explain.

Performance Task

Craft Project

Mariah has the spool of ribbon shown at the right and $\frac{1}{2}$ yard of fabric for a craft project. She wants to cut the ribbon into 6 equal pieces. How long is each piece of ribbon?

$\frac{1}{3}$ yard

?	?	?	?	?	?

$\frac{1}{3}$ yard

4. Model with Math Find the length of each ribbon piece in yards. Write a division equation to model the problem.

5. Reasoning Explain how you can use multiplication to check your answer to Exercise 4.

6. Be Precise Find the length of each ribbon piece in inches. Show your work.

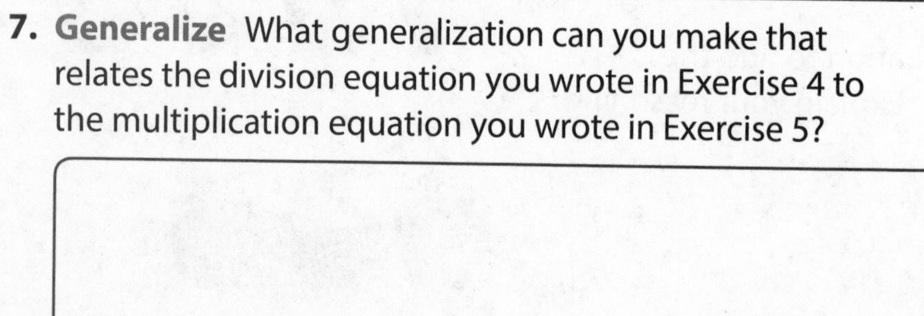

7. Generalize What generalization can you make that relates the division equation you wrote in Exercise 4 to the multiplication equation you wrote in Exercise 5?

Repeated reasoning can help you find shortcuts.

8. Generalize Mariah has $\frac{1}{3}$ yard of a gold ribbon. She wants to cut this ribbon into 2 equal pieces. How long is each piece of gold ribbon in yards? Can you repeat the method you used in Exercises 4 and 5 to solve this problem? Explain.

Name ______________________________

Additional Practice 10-1
Analyze Line Plots

Another Look!

For an experiment, Bea recorded how much each of 14 seedlings grew in one month. She made a line plot to show the data. Which value occurred most often?

DATA

Plant Growth (in cm)						
5.1	5.5	4.9	4.8	5.0	5.1	5.1
5.0	4.9	5.1	5.0	5.1	5.0	5.2

Step 1

Read the labels on the line plot. Values are listed in order on a number line.

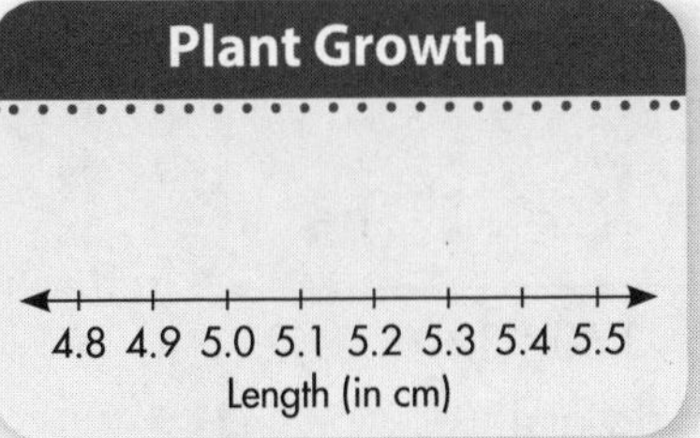

Step 2

Each dot stands for one time the value occurred. Dots are stacked when a value occurs more than once.

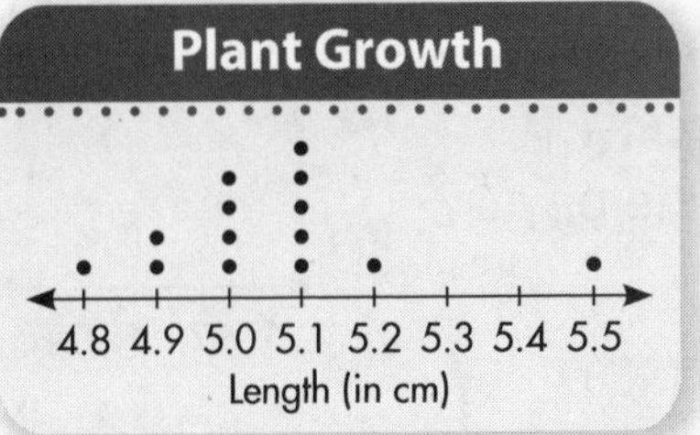

Step 3

Use the dot plot to solve.

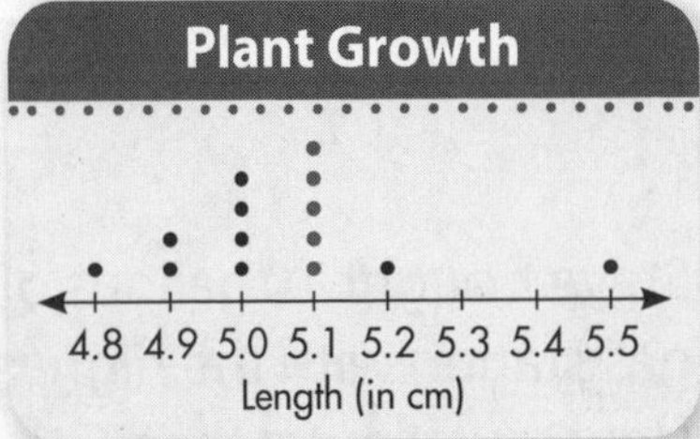

The value of 5.1 has the most dots, so 5.1 cm growth occurred most often.

In **1–4**, use the line plots to solve.

Turn 4th, 4

1. Ani and her friends recorded their bowling shoe sizes. Which two bowling shoe sizes occurred most often?

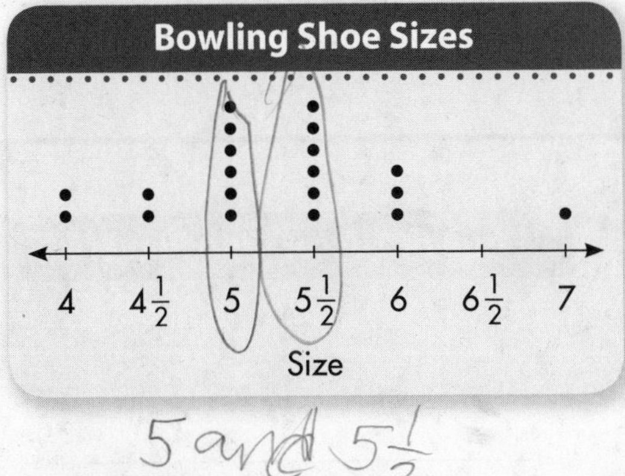

5 and $5\frac{1}{2}$

2. A pearl diver recorded the sizes of the pearls in a batch. Which three pearl sizes occurred least often?

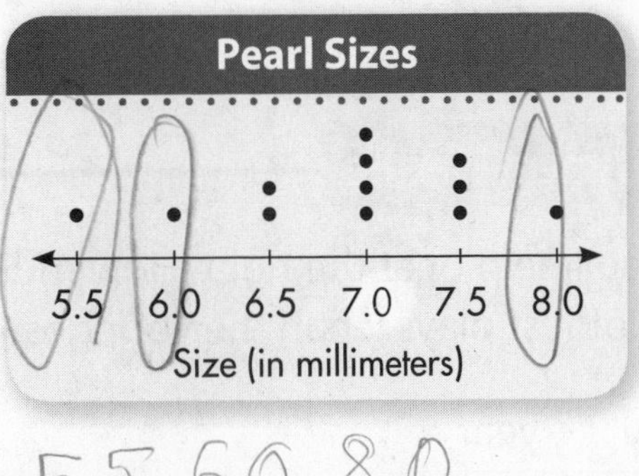

5.5, 6.0, 8.0

3. In Exercise 1, how many of Ani's bowling friends have size $6\frac{1}{2}$ shoes? Explain how you know.

none because there are no Dots

4. In Exercise 2, how many pearls were in the batch? Explain how you know.

12 because there are 12 Dots in total in the

In **5–8**, use the data set and line plot.

5. On Thursday, Cole collected data on the gas prices at different gas stations. How many gas stations are in Cole's data set?

6. Which gas price occurred most often?

7. Cole bought 10 gallons of gas at the gas station with the lowest price. He paid with two $20 bills. Write and solve an equation to find his change.

8. Steve bought 10 gallons of gas at the gas station with the highest price. How much more than Cole did he pay for gas?

DATA

Prices of One Gallon of Gas on Thursday (in dollars)

3.61	3.60	3.59	3.58	3.59
3.59	3.60	3.61	3.62	3.61
3.58	3.57	3.59	3.60	3.59

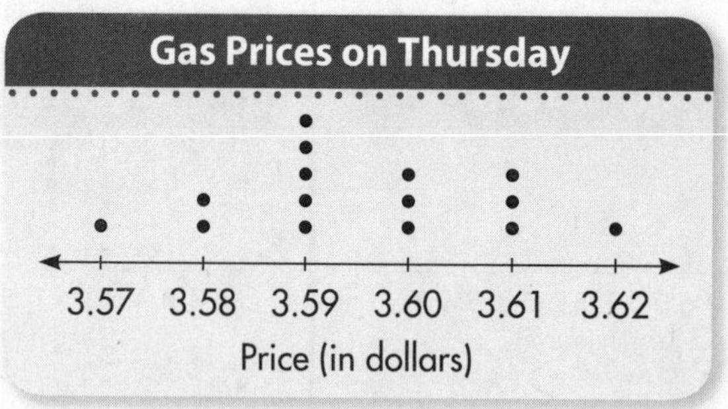

9. Be Precise Mrs. Dugan plans to serve 100 barbecue sandwiches at the company picnic. How many packages of barbecue buns will she need if buns come in packages of 8? Packages of 12?

10. Algebra Janet had $9.25 this morning. She spent $4.50 for lunch, and then spent $3.50 on school supplies. Write and solve an equation to find m, the amount of money Janet had left at the end of the day.

Assessment Practice

11. Use the line plot at the right. How much older is the oldest player than the youngest player?

Ⓐ $\frac{1}{2}$ year

Ⓑ $1\frac{1}{2}$ years

Ⓒ 2 years

Ⓓ 11 years

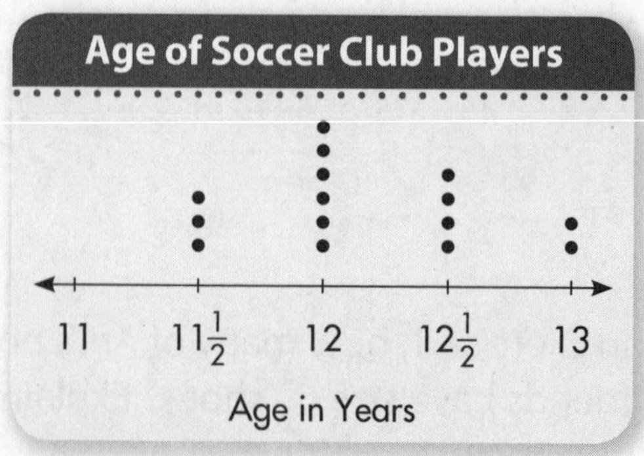

Name ______________________

 Practice  Video  Tools  Games

Additional Practice 10-2
Make Line Plots

Another Look!

Mick recorded the lengths of 10 Steller sea lions. Which length occurs most often?

Steller Sea Lion Lengths (in feet)

$9\frac{1}{4}$	$9\frac{1}{8}$	$8\frac{3}{4}$	$9\frac{1}{4}$	$9\frac{1}{4}$
$9\frac{3}{8}$	$9\frac{1}{4}$	$9\frac{1}{8}$	$9\frac{1}{4}$	$9\frac{1}{8}$

Step 1

Make a frequency table to organize the data.

Value	Tally	Frequency
$8\frac{3}{4}$	I	1
$9\frac{1}{8}$	III	3
$9\frac{1}{4}$	~~IIII~~	5
$9\frac{3}{8}$	I	1

Step 2

Make a line plot. Draw a dot for each value. Stack dots for values that occur more than once.

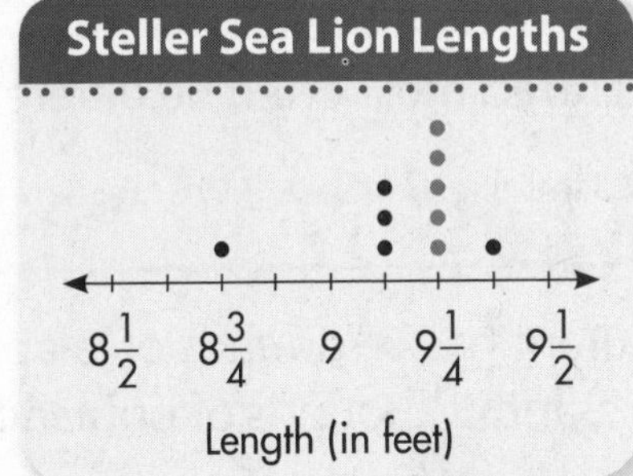

The length $9\frac{1}{4}$ feet occurs most often.

1. Jacob and his father measured the lengths of scrap wood in their yard. Make a line plot of their data.

Scrap Wood Lengths (in inches)

$4\frac{1}{2}$	$4\frac{7}{8}$	5	$4\frac{1}{4}$	$4\frac{1}{2}$	$4\frac{3}{8}$
$4\frac{1}{8}$	$4\frac{1}{2}$	$4\frac{1}{4}$	$4\frac{3}{4}$	$4\frac{1}{2}$	$4\frac{1}{2}$
$4\frac{5}{8}$	$4\frac{3}{4}$	$4\frac{1}{4}$	$4\frac{1}{8}$	$4\frac{1}{2}$	$4\frac{7}{8}$

2. What is the difference between the longest and shortest pieces of scrap wood?

In **3** and **4**, use the table showing data from recipes used in a chili cooking contest.

3. **Make Sense and Persevere** Draw a line plot of the data.

Cups of Beans in One Batch				
5	$5\frac{1}{2}$	$4\frac{1}{2}$	$4\frac{1}{2}$	$4\frac{1}{2}$
$4\frac{1}{2}$	$4\frac{1}{2}$	$4\frac{1}{2}$	$4\frac{3}{4}$	$4\frac{1}{2}$

4. **Higher Order Thinking** Suppose the contestants were asked to make two batches of their recipe instead of one batch. Would the value for the amount of beans that occurred most often be different? Explain.

5. A restaurant has $6\frac{1}{2}$ pounds of jalapeño peppers, $4\frac{3}{4}$ pounds of red bell peppers, and $5\frac{1}{4}$ pounds of poblano peppers. How many pounds of peppers does the restaurant have in all?

6. Jessica and her friend measured the lengths of the fish they caught one day. Make a line plot of their data.

Fish Lengths (in cm)			
10.25	10.50	11.75	12.00
10.75	11.00	11.25	11.50
11.25	11.25	11.50	11.00

Assessment Practice

7. The list below shows the weight in ounces of various rock samples. Use the data to complete the line plot on the right.

$8\frac{1}{4}, 7\frac{1}{2}, 5\frac{1}{4}, 6\frac{3}{4}, 7, 7, 8\frac{1}{4}, 5\frac{1}{4},$
$5\frac{1}{4}, 7\frac{1}{2}, 7, 7, 6\frac{3}{4}, 7$

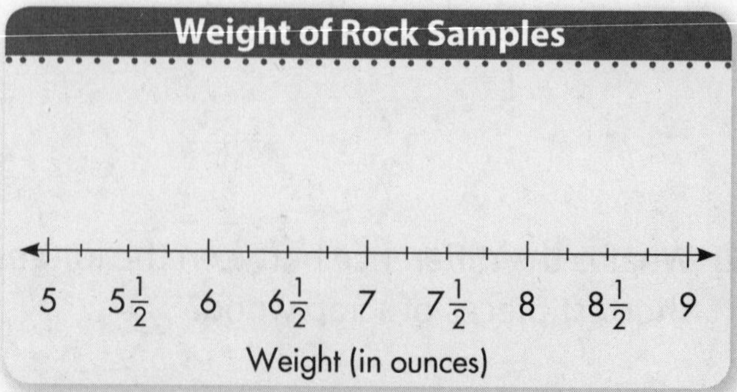

Name ______________________________

Additional Practice 10-3
Solve Word Problems Using Measurement Data

Another Look!

Mr. Culver made a line plot to show the number of hours students worked on a class project. What was the total number of hours that the students worked?

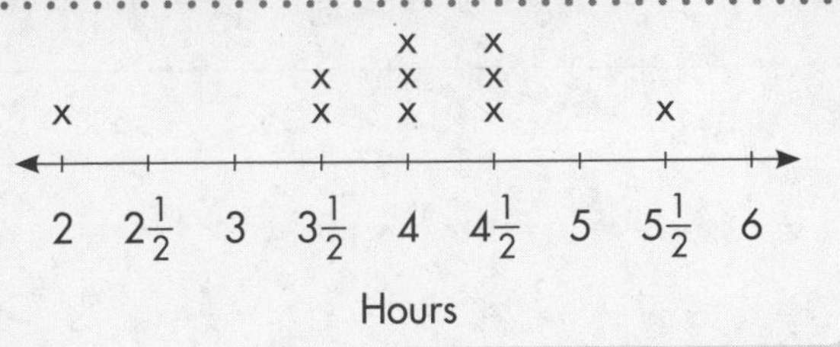

Use the line plot to make a frequency table.

Multiply each number of hours by its frequency. The product is the total amount for that value.

Add the products.

$$2 + 7 + 12 + 13\frac{1}{2} + 5\frac{1}{2} = 40$$

The students spent a total of 40 hours on the project.

Hours	Frequency	Multiplication
2	1	$1 \times 2 = 2$
$3\frac{1}{2}$	2	$2 \times 3\frac{1}{2} = 7$
4	3	$3 \times 4 = 12$
$4\frac{1}{2}$	3	$3 \times 4\frac{1}{2} = 13\frac{1}{2}$
$5\frac{1}{2}$	1	$1 \times 5\frac{1}{2} = 5\frac{1}{2}$

In **1** and **2**, use each line plot to answer the question.

1. Wai recorded the length of each wire needed for a science project. What is the total length of wire needed?

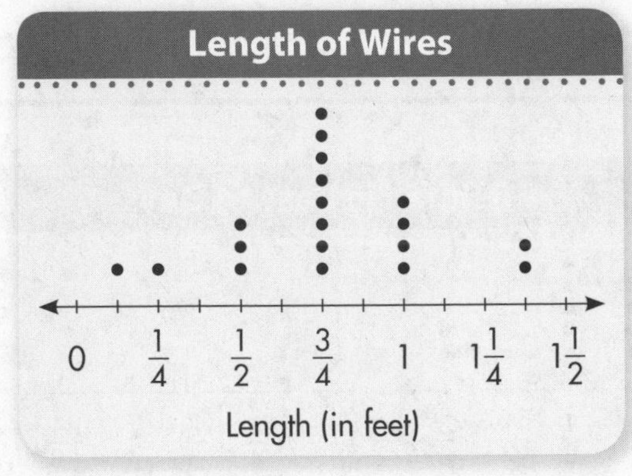

2. Trey measured the mass of some pebbles. What is the combined mass of the pebbles that are $4\frac{1}{2}$ grams or more?

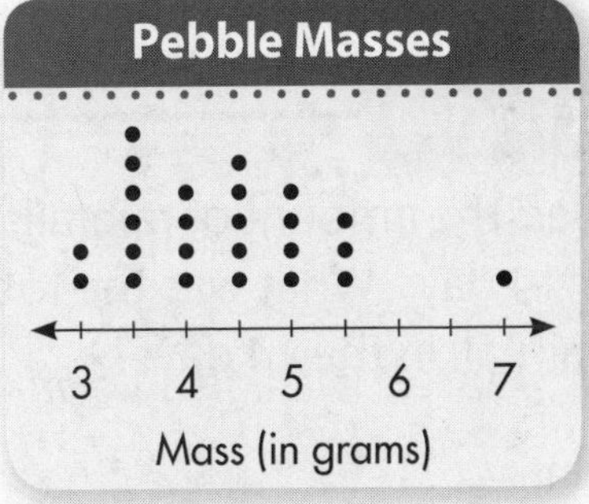

In **3** and **4**, Dominick's class flew toy gliders. He recorded the flight distances in a line plot.

3. What is the difference between the longest and shortest distances the gliders flew?

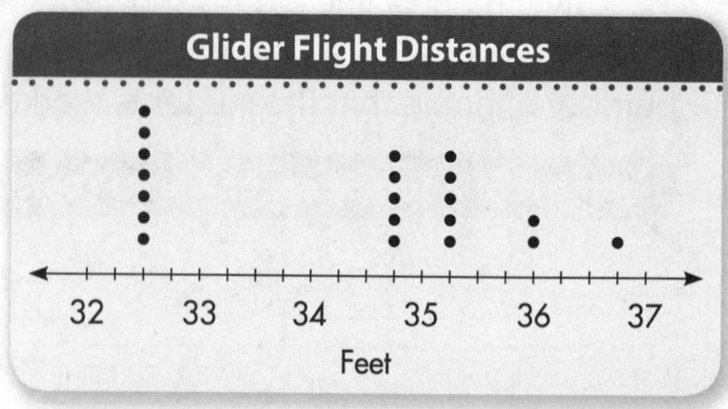

4. Did more gliders fly farther or shorter than 35 feet? Explain.

5. **enVision® STEM** On June 1, 2013, the number of hours of daylight in Anchorage, Alaska was $18\frac{1}{4}$ hours. What was the number of hours without daylight?

6. **Number Sense** How could you estimate the quotient $162 \div 19$?

7. **Reasoning** Nolan listed the weights of oranges in a box in the frequency table. Which is greater, the total weight of the 6.25-ounce oranges or the total weight of the 7.25-ounce oranges? How much more? Explain.

DATA

Weight (in ounces)	Frequency	Multiplication
6.25	13	?
6.5	16	$16 \times 6.5 = 104$
6.75	20	$20 \times 6.75 = 135$
7.0	14	$14 \times 7.0 = 98$
7.25	9	?

Assessment Practice

8. Anita recorded the amount of rainfall each day for 14 days. What was the total amount of rainfall in the 14 days?

Ⓐ $6\frac{7}{8}$ in.

Ⓑ $4\frac{1}{2}$ in.

Ⓒ $3\frac{3}{8}$ in.

Ⓓ $\frac{1}{8}$ in.

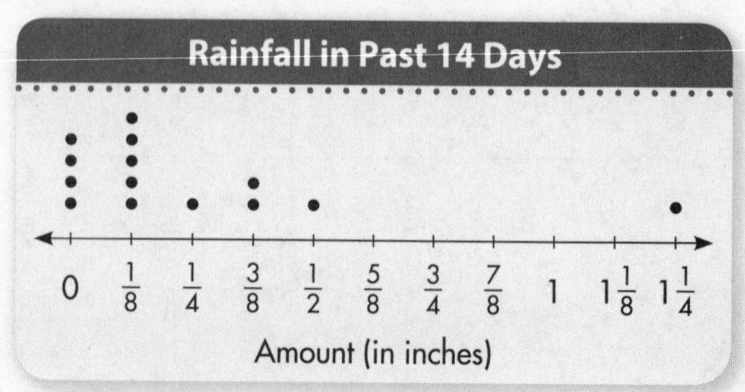

Name ______________________________

Practice Video Tools Games

Additional Practice 10-4
Critique Reasoning

Another Look!

A cooking class needs 20 quarts of raspberries. The instructor, Mr. Romano, made a line plot to show how many quarts of raspberries each student picked at a raspberry farm. Then he said, "We need another $\frac{3}{4}$ quart." He showed the class:

$$(2 \times 3) + 3\tfrac{1}{4} + \left(2 \times 3\tfrac{3}{4}\right) + 4\tfrac{1}{4} =$$
$$6 + 3\tfrac{1}{4} + 5\tfrac{3}{4} + 4\tfrac{1}{4} = 19\tfrac{1}{4}.$$

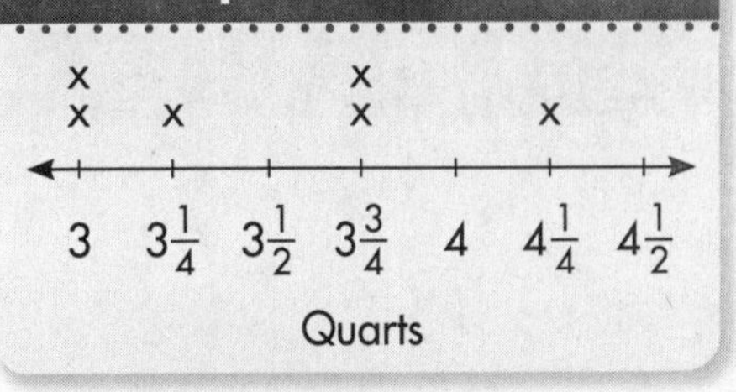

Tell how you can critique Mr. Romano's reasoning.

- I can decide if his strategy makes sense.
- I can look for flaws in his calculations.
- I can clarify or correct his reasoning.

When you critique reasoning, you explain why someone's thinking is correct or incorrect.

Critique Mr. Romano's reasoning.

Mr. Romano's strategy makes sense, but he made a careless mistake in his calculations. $\left(2 \times 3\frac{3}{4}\right) = 7\frac{1}{2}$, not $5\frac{3}{4}$. So, the class picked $6 + 3\frac{1}{4} + 7\frac{1}{2} + 4\frac{1}{4} = 21$ quarts. They have enough raspberries.

Critique Reasoning

Gillian said that if all the students and Mr. Romano had each picked just $2\frac{1}{2}$ quarts of raspberries, they would have had enough. She estimated $7 \times 3 = 21$.

1. Tell how you can critique Gillian's reasoning.

2. Critique Gillian's reasoning.

3. Identify the flaw in Gillian's thinking.

Performance Task

Video Game

Lydia is playing *Galaxy 8RX*. After three misses, the game is over. Last week, Lydia kept track of how long her games lasted. She made a line plot of her data. Lydia said, "My best time is $2\frac{3}{4}$ minutes longer than my worst time because $4\frac{1}{4} - 1\frac{1}{2} = 2\frac{3}{4}$."

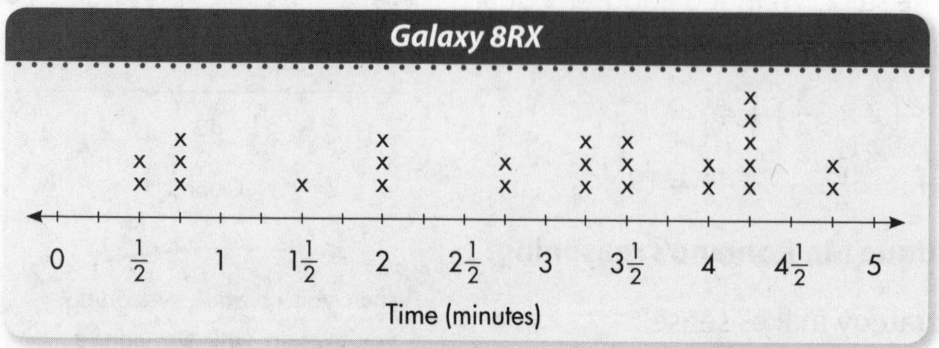

4. Model With Math Is subtraction the correct operation to compare Lydia's best and worst times? Explain.

5. Be Precise Are Lydia's calculations accurate? Show how you know.

6. Make Sense and Persevere In the line plot, what do the numbers Lydia subtracted represent?

7. Critique Reasoning Does Lydia's conclusion make sense? How did you decide? If not, what can you do to improve her reasoning?

When you critique reasoning, you need to carefully consider all parts of a person's reasoning.

Name ______________________________

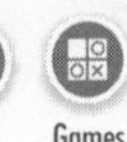

Practice Video Tools Games

Additional Practice 11-1
Model Volume

Another Look!

Volume is the measure of space inside a solid figure.

Volume is measured in cubic units.

Find the volume of this solid by counting the number of unit cubes.

There are 8 cubes in the bottom layer and there are 4 layers. The total number of unit cubes is 32.

So, the volume is 32 cubic units.

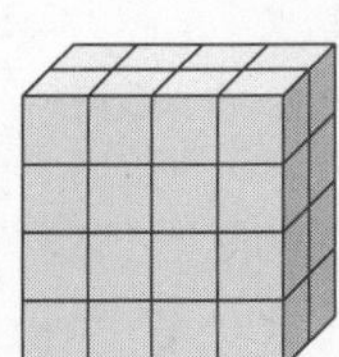

In **1–9**, find the volume of each solid. Use unit cubes to help.

1.

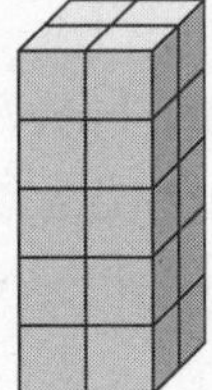

2.

3.

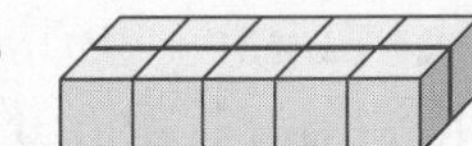

4.

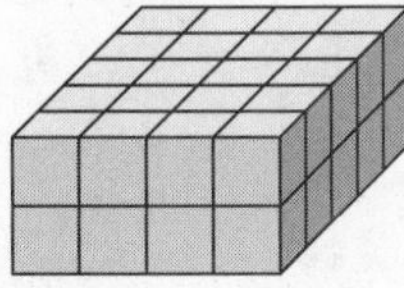

5.

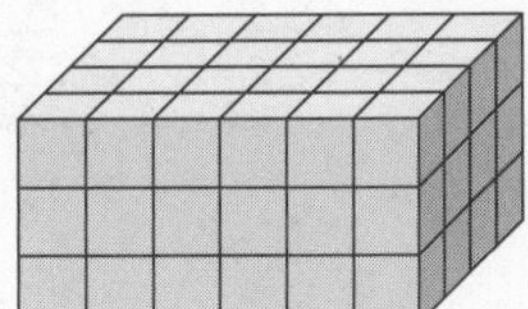

6.

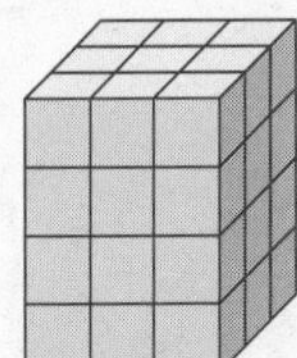

7.

8.

9.

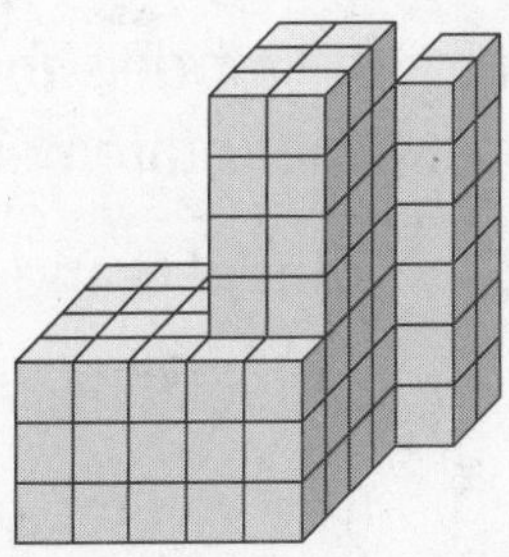

In **10–12**, use the table.

10. Higher Order Thinking Complete the table. Show some different ways that a rectangular prism can have a volume of 12 cubic units.

11. Look for Relationships Look across each row of the table. What pattern do you see?

12. Use the table to help. How many unit cubes are needed to make a model of a rectangular prism that is 4 units long, 3 units wide, and 2 units tall?

Number of Cubes Long	Number of Cubes Wide	Number of Cubes Tall
1	1	12
2	2	3
2	3	
2		1
3	1	
3	2	
3		1
4	1	
6		1

13. Number Sense A building is 509 feet tall. Each floor is about 14 feet tall. About how many floors does the building have?

Do you need an estimate or an exact answer?

14. Velma and Bruce combined their model buildings to make one building. How can they change each building part to make the parts equal in volume? Explain your reasoning.

Assessment Practice

15. Both of the models shown are made up of 1-inch cubes. Which statement about these models is true?

Ⓐ Model Q and Model R have the same volume.

Ⓑ Model R has a greater volume than Model Q.

Ⓒ The volume of Model Q is 7 cubic inches greater than the volume of Model R.

Ⓓ The volume of Model Q and Model R combined is 54 cubic inches.

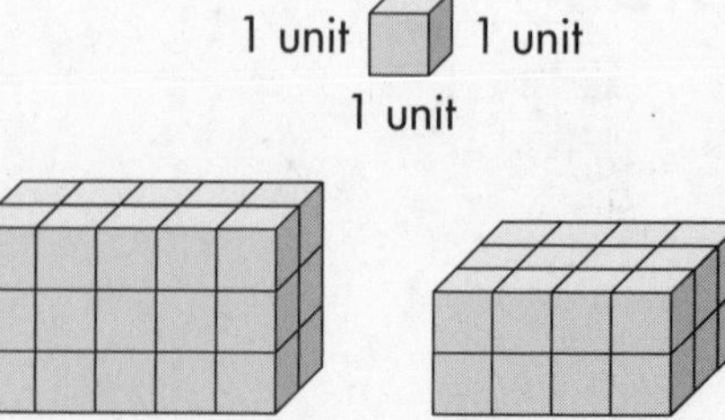

Name

Practice Video Tools Games

Additional Practice 11-2

Develop a Volume Formula

Another Look!

What is the volume of the rectangular prism?

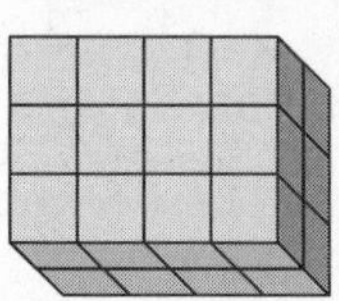

Use the formula $V = b \times h$ and cubes to help.

$V = b \times h$

$b =$ the area of the base

$h =$ height

What is the area of the base?

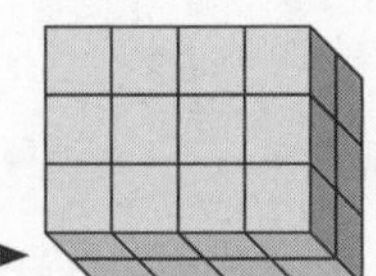

$A = \ell \times w$

$A = 4 \times 2$

$A = 8$ units^2

What is the height, h?

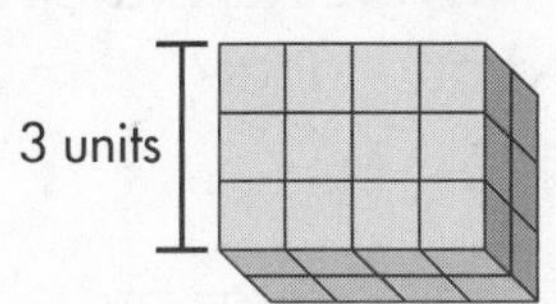

The prism is 3 units tall.

Use the values to complete the formula.

$V = b \times h$

$V = 8 \times 3$

$V = 24$ units^3

In **1–6**, find the volume of each rectangular prism.

1.

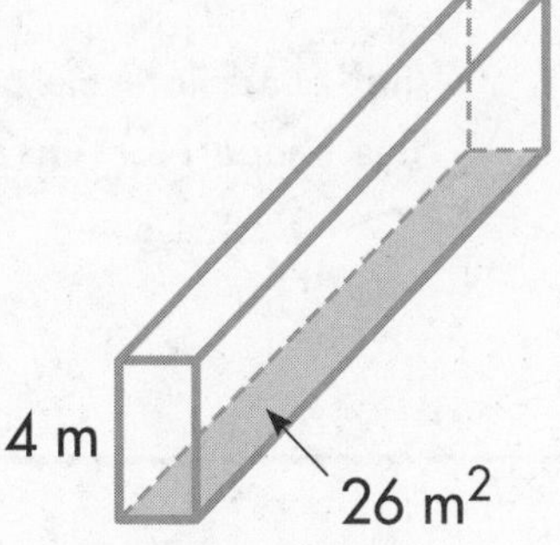

2.

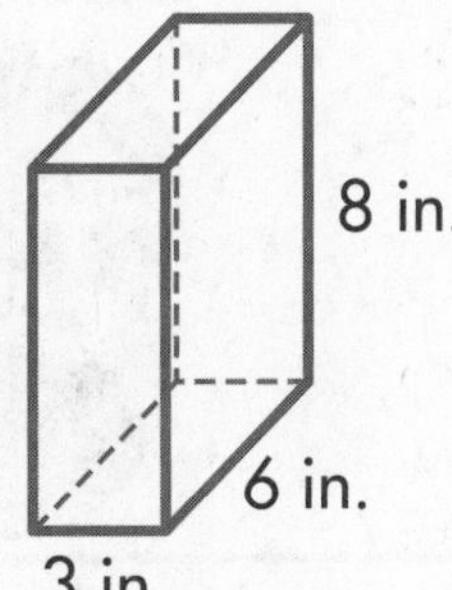

3.

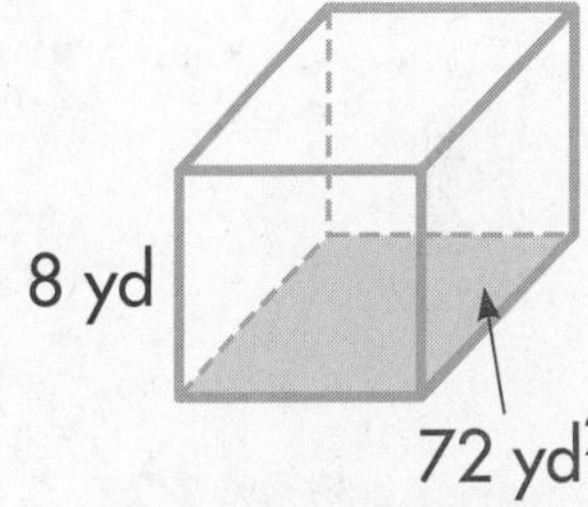

4.

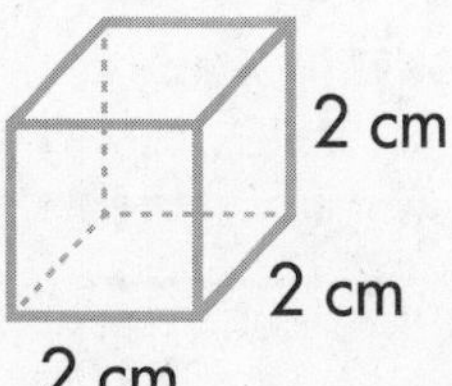

5.

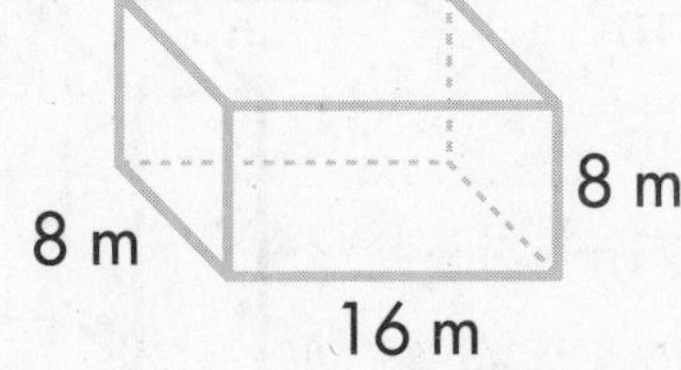

6.

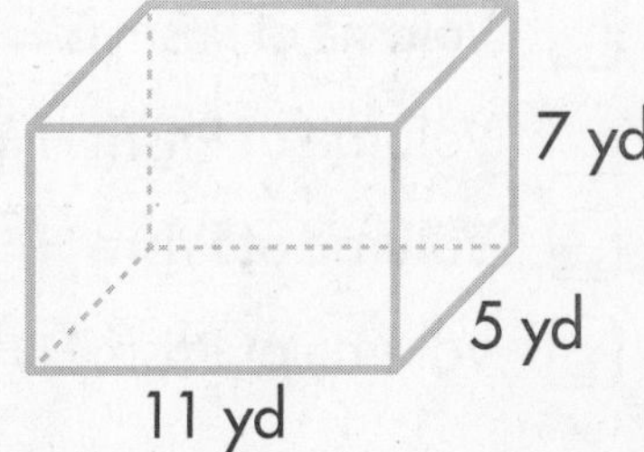

7. Model with Math Write an expression for the volume of the bar magnet.

0.5 in. N S 0.25 in.
2.25 in.

---

8. The front door of a house is 80 inches tall. What is the volume of the door?

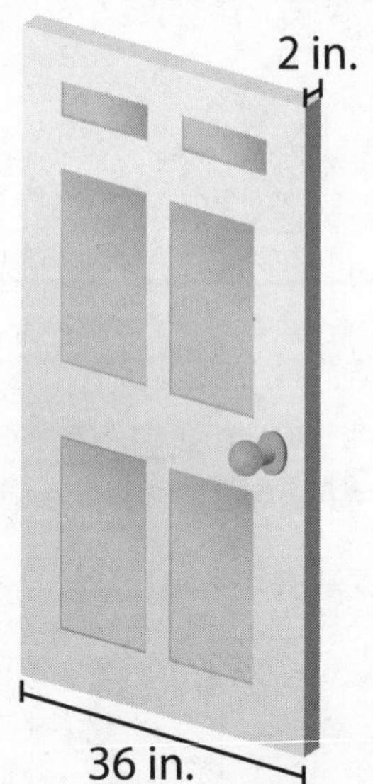

9. A bedroom door in the house has the same dimensions as the front door, but the area of the base is 60 inches rather than 72 inches. How much greater is the volume of the front door than the bedroom door?

10. The living room in the house has an area of 224 square feet and a width of 14 feet. What is the length of the room?

---

11. Higher Order Thinking A cube has a volume of 1,000 cubic feet. What is the length of an edge of the cube? Show how you found your answer.

12. A quadrilateral has all sides the same length and no right angles. What is the name of the quadrilateral?

What quadrilaterals can this shape NOT be?

Assessment Practice

13. Choose all the statements that are true.

- ☐ Volume of Prism G $= 40 + 12$ m^3
- ☐ Volume of Prism G $= 40 \times 12$ m^3
- ☐ Volume of Prism H $= 70 \times 7$ m^3
- ☐ Volume of Prism H $= 14 \times 12$ m^3
- ☐ Volume of Prism H $= (14 \times 5) \times 7$ m^3

Rectangular Prism G

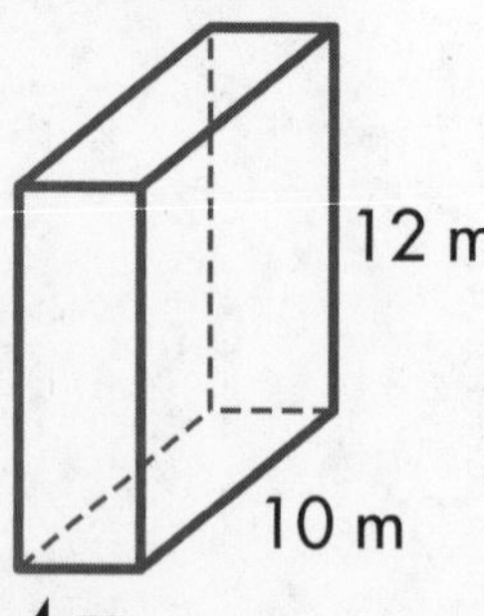

Rectangular Prism H

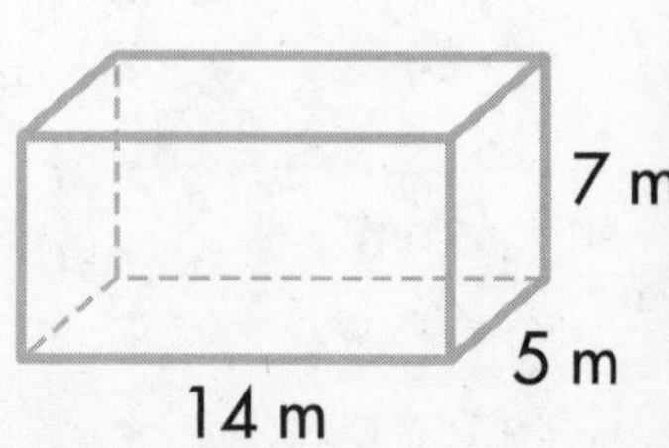

Name

Practice Video Tools Games

Additional Practice 11-3

Combine Volumes of Prisms

Another Look!

What is the volume of the solid figure?

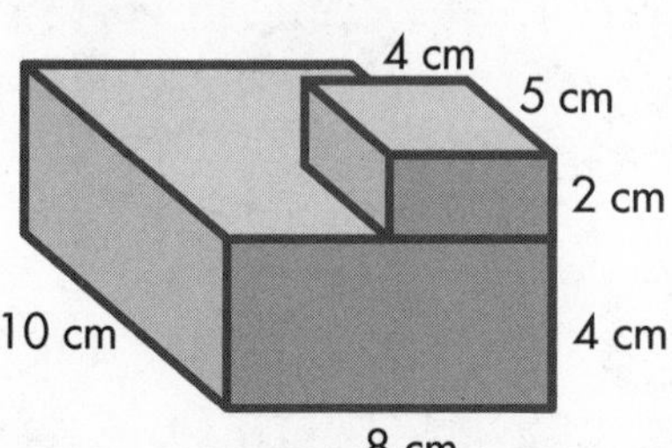

Make sure you find the ℓ, w, and h of each rectangular prism.

Separate the solid figure into rectangular prisms.

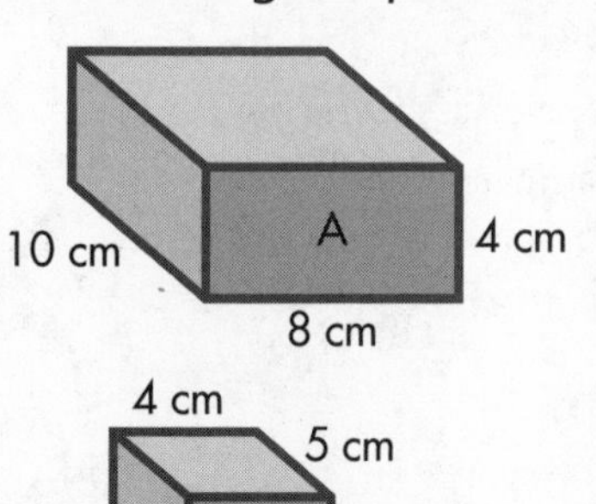

Find the volume of each rectangular prism.

Prism A:	Prism B:
$V = \ell \times w \times h$	$V = \ell \times w \times h$
$V = 8 \times 10 \times 4$	$V = 4 \times 5 \times 2$
$V = 80 \times 4$	$V = 20 \times 2$
$V = 320$	$V = 40$

Add the volumes.

$320 + 40 = 360$

So, the volume of the solid figure is 360 cm^3.

In **1–6**, find the volume of each solid figure.

1.

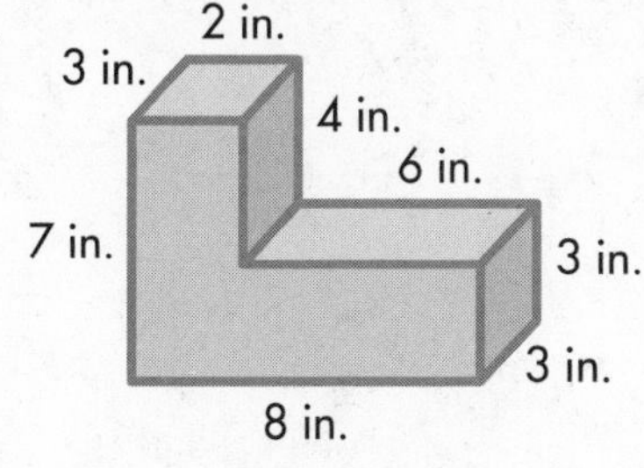

2.

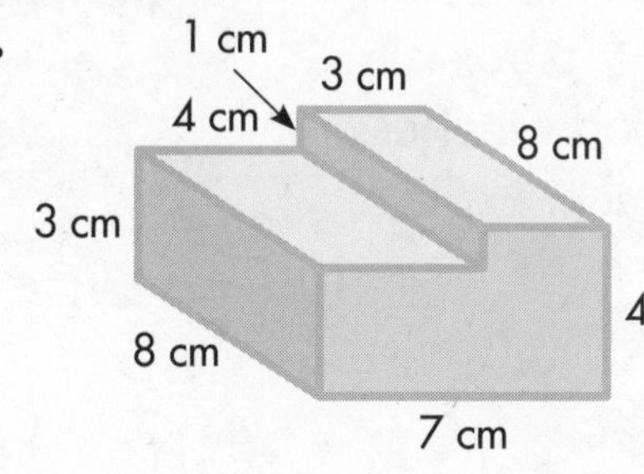

3.

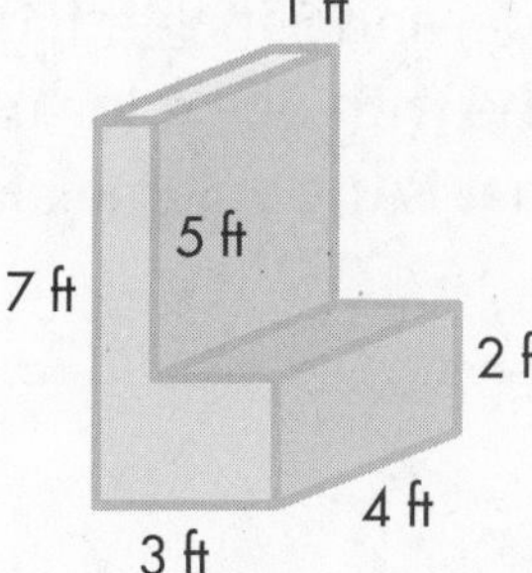

4.

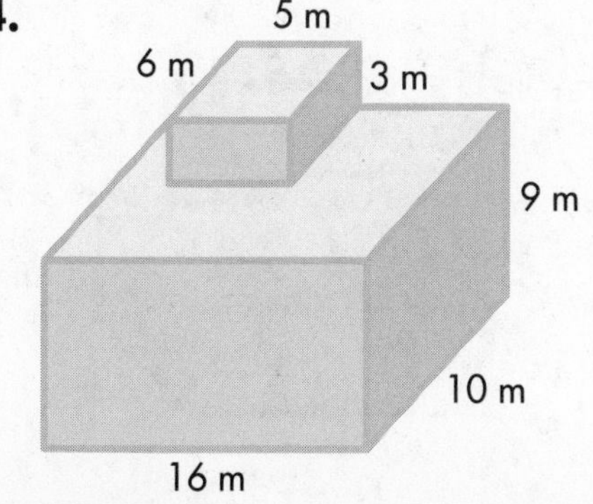

5.

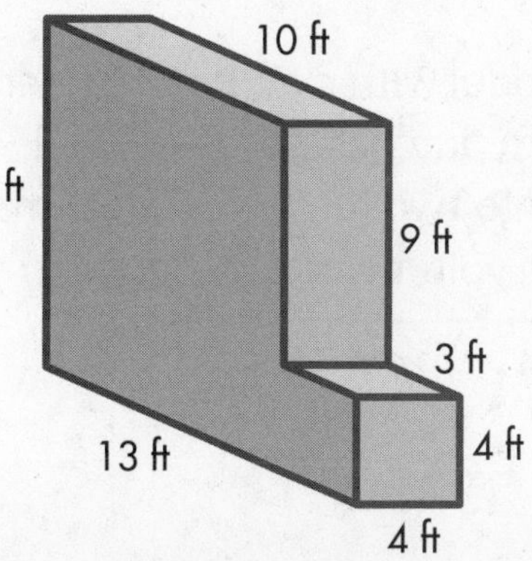

6.

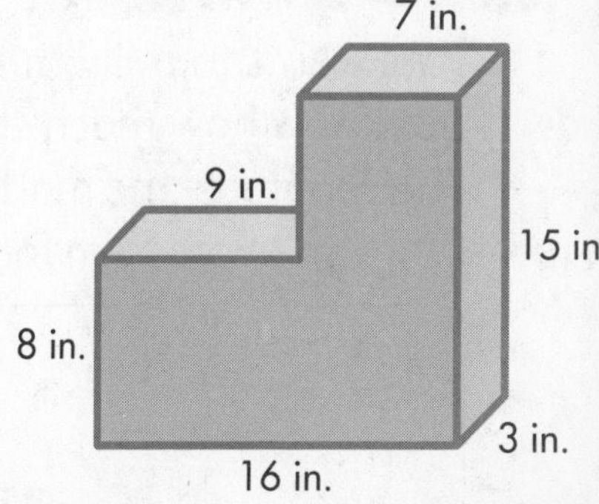

In **7** and **8**, use the drawing of the solid figure.

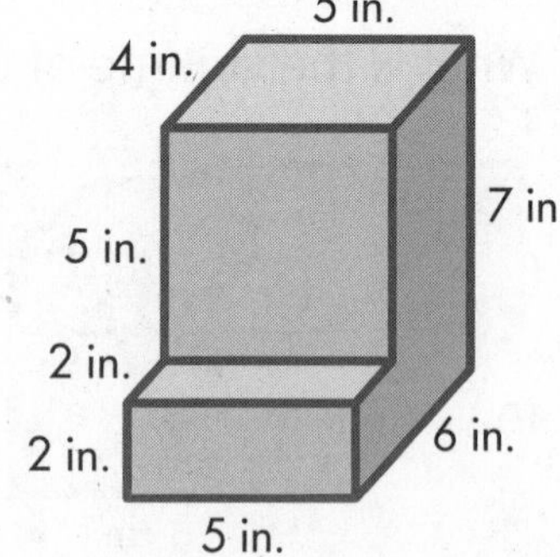

7. Find two different ways to separate the solid figure into two rectangular prisms. Draw a line on each figure below to show each way.

One Way

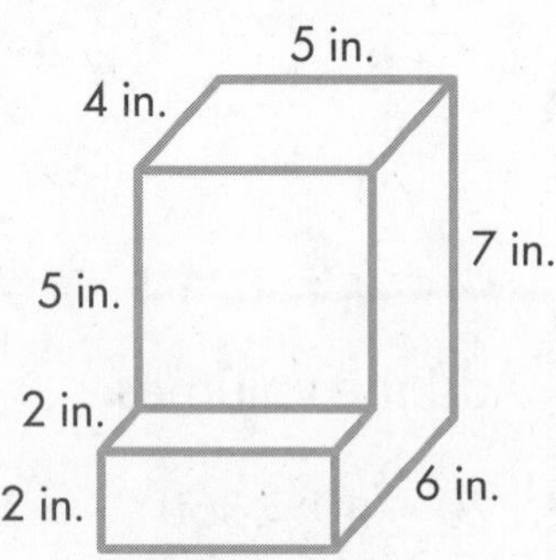

Another Way

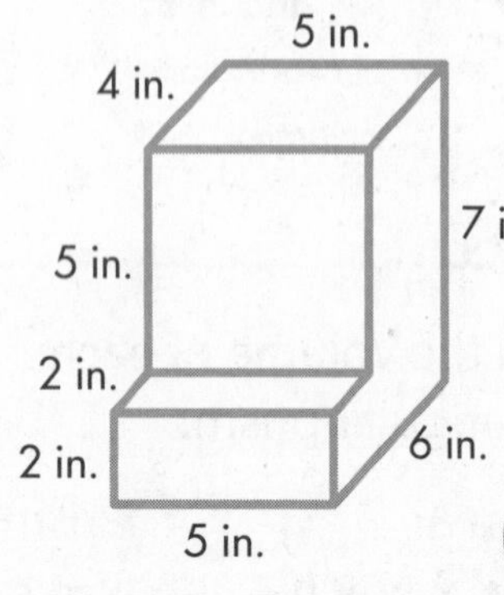

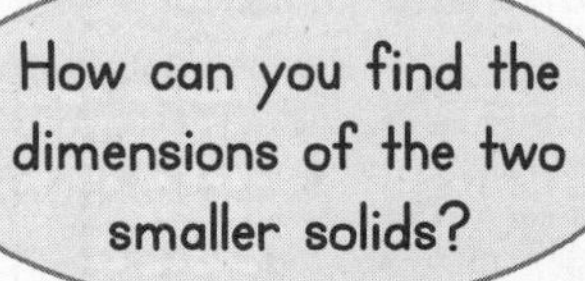

How can you find the dimensions of the two smaller solids?

8. Model with Math Choose one way that you found. Write and solve an equation for the volume of each rectangular prism. Then find the volume of the solid figure.

9. Higher Order Thinking Ashley is stacking two boxes on a shelf. The bottom box measures 6 inches long, 5 inches wide, and 5 inches high. The top box is a cube with one edge measuring 4 inches. What is the volume of this stack? Explain.

10. Algebra Write an expression you can use to find the volume of the cube. Then find the volume if $y = 9$ feet.

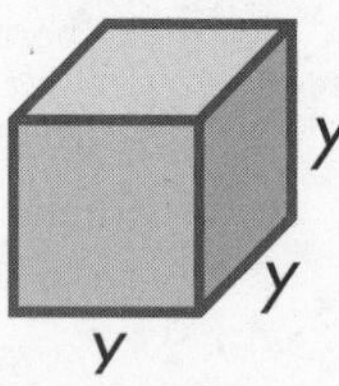

Assessment Practice

11. Paul wants to build this model with clay, but he does not know how much clay to purchase. A horizontal line separates the model into two rectangular prisms. Write an expression for the volume of the model.

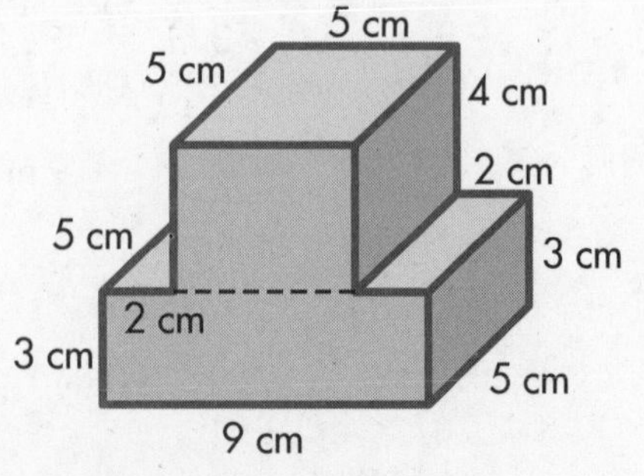

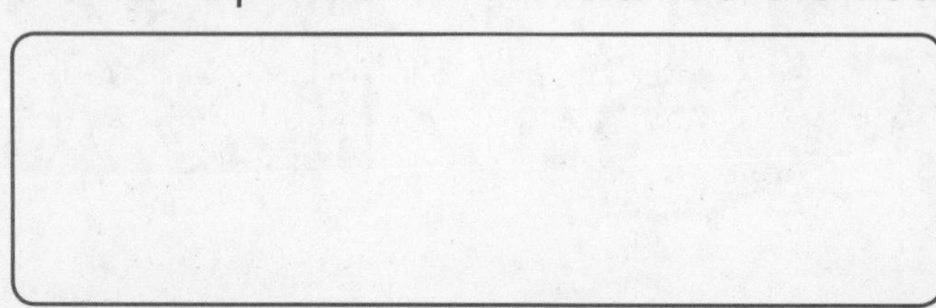

Name ____________________

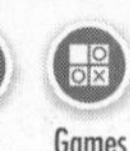

Practice Video Tools Games

Additional Practice 11-4
Solve Word Problems Using Volume

Another Look!

The shape of a swimming pool is a rectangular prism. The pool is 9 meters long and 4 meters wide. It holds 108 cubic meters of water. How deep is the pool if the entire pool is the same depth?

Use the volume formula.

$V = \ell \times w \times h$
$108 = 4 \times 9 \times h$
$108 = 36 \times h$

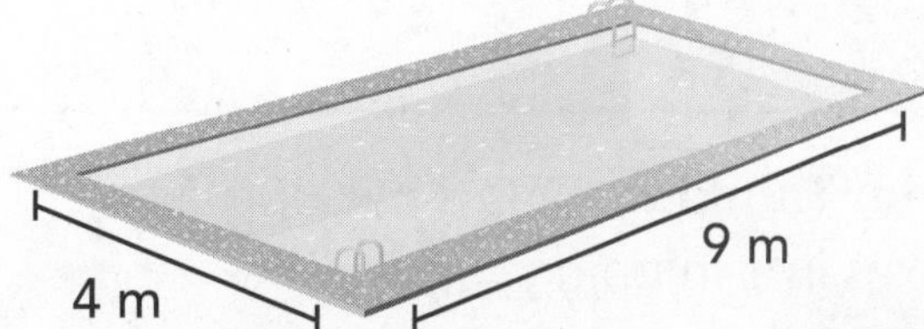

Divide to find the answer.

$108 \div 36 = 3$

The swimming pool is 3 meters deep.

Think about the operation that can help you find a missing factor.

1. A garage is shaped like a rectangular prism. What is the volume of the garage? Show your work.

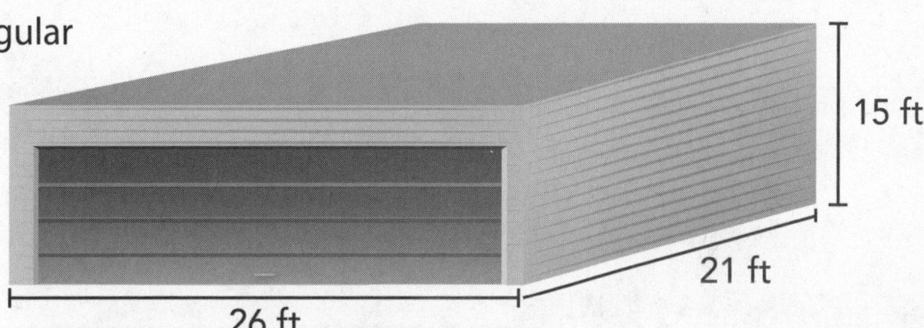

2. Nabeel's sand box is 7 feet wide, 5 feet long and 2 feet deep. What is the volume of the sand box?

3. A box of oat cereal measures 24 centimeters long by 5 centimeters wide by 25 centimeters high. A box of rice cereal measures 26 centimeters long by 4 centimeters wide by 28 centimeters high. Which box has the greater volume? How much greater?

4. Marin has a jewelry box with a volume of 440 cubic inches. The box is 5 inches high and 11 inches long. What is the width of the box?

5. Walter is building a storage shed shaped like a rectangular prism. It will be 7 feet high and 8 feet long. How wide should it be if Walter wants 280 cubic feet of storage space? Explain how you found your answer.

6. **Generalize** Use multiplication to describe the relationship between the dividend, the divisor, and the quotient. Then use that relationship to show that $\frac{1}{8} \div 6 = \frac{1}{48}$.

7. **Higher Order Thinking** Otis is packing two gift boxes in a shipping carton. The rest of the space in the carton will be filled with packing pellets. What is the volume of the space that needs to be filled with packing pellets? Explain how you found your answer.

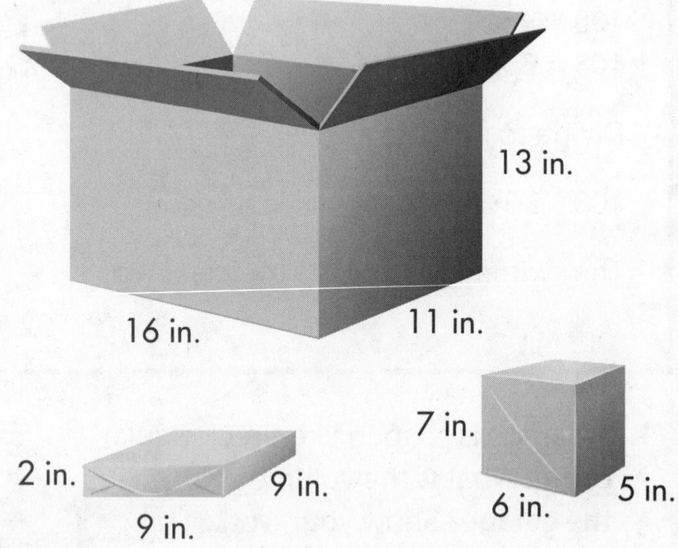

Assessment Practice

8. Marie built a sand castle that is made of two rectangular prisms. She used one bag of sand. If there are 2,000 cubic inches of sand in a bag of sand, how much sand was left after Marie built her sand castle?

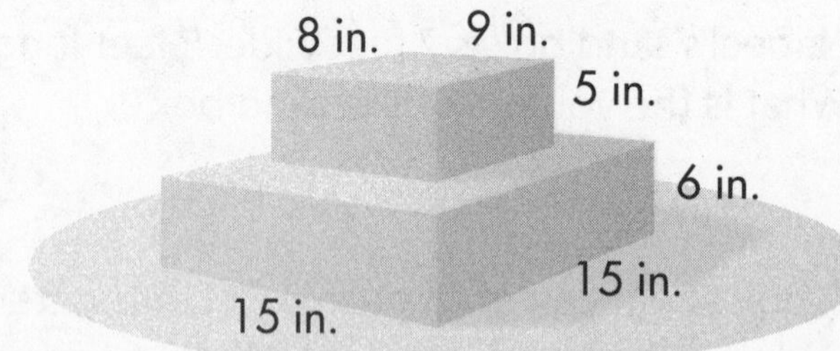

Ⓐ 248 in^3

Ⓑ 290 in^3

Ⓒ 578 in^3

Ⓓ none

Name ______________________________

Additional Practice 11-5
Use Appropriate Tools

Another Look!

Francine is designing a small birdhouse shaped like a rectangular prism. It needs to have a volume of 120 cubic inches. She wants the height to be 10 inches. What could the length and width of the floor be?

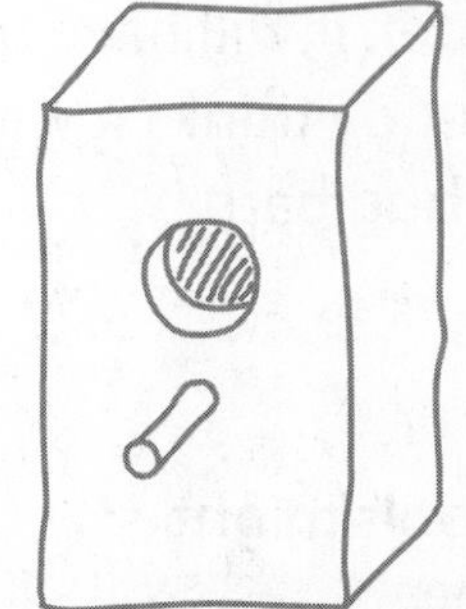

One Way

Build a model with cubes. Since the volume is 120 cubic inches, use 120 cubes.

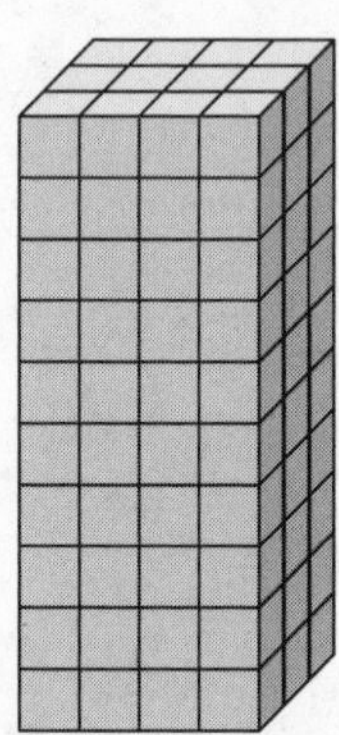

So, one possibility is that the length is 4 inches and the width is 3 inches.

Another Way

Use grid paper to design the floor.

The height is 10 inches, so the area of the floor is $120 \div 10 = 12$. Use grid paper to draw some possible floors with an area of 12 square inches.

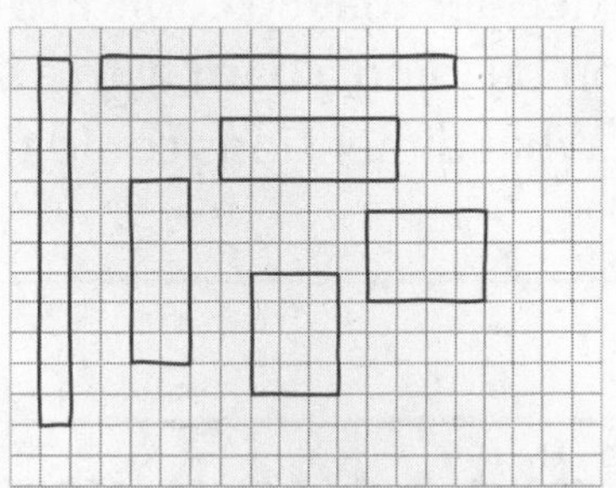

One possibility is that the length is 4 inches and the width is 3 inches.

Use Appropriate Tools

An architect is designing different vacation cottages that are shaped like rectangular prisms that are side-by-side.

Sometimes there is more than one tool that can help you solve problems.

1. The height of one cottage will be 3 meters, and the volume will be 108 cubic meters. What tool can help you find different dimensions for the floor? Give two different possible pairs of dimensions for the floor. Explain.

2. Can you think of a different tool to use to solve this problem? Explain.

Performance Task

Making a Bug Barn
Wendy is going to use screening and wood to make a bug barn for her little sister. It will have the shape of a rectangular prism. Wendy thinks it will take about 2 hours to make the bug barn.

3. **Use Appropriate Tools** What tools might Wendy use?

4. **Reasoning** Wendy wants the volume to be 80 cubic inches. What dimensions could the bug barn have?

5. **Reasoning** Wendy decides that 80 cubic inches is too small. So she plans on building a barn with a volume of 108 cubic inches. What dimensions could this bug barn have?

6. **Make Sense and Persevere** Wendy searches the Internet and finds a bug barn that is 7 inches long, 4 inches wide, and 3 inches tall. If she wants to build a bug barn with volume greater than this, would either of the above barns work? Explain.

7. **Critique Reasoning** Wendy thinks that if she doubles all of the dimensions of a bug barn, its volume will also double. Do you agree? Use one of the above bug barns to show your work.

Name ______________________

Additional Practice 12-1
Convert Customary Units of Length

Another Look!

Remember:
1 foot equals 12 inches.
1 yard equals 3 feet, or 36 inches.
1 mile equals 1,760 yards, or 5,280 feet.

How to change from one customary unit of length to another:

Converting from a smaller unit to a larger unit:

6 feet = ______ yards

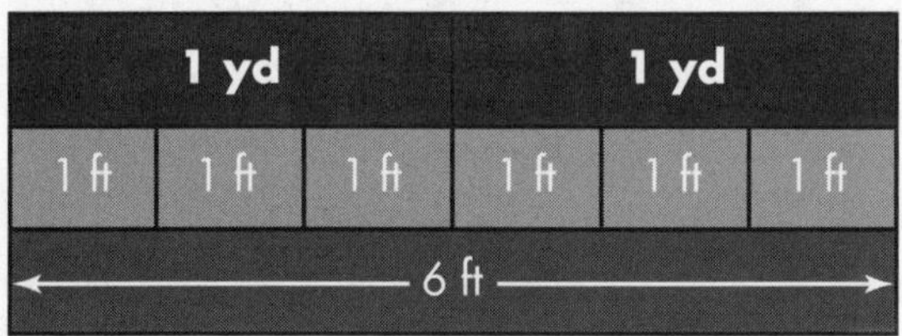

You know 3 ft = 1 yd. **Divide** 6 ÷ 3.

So, 6 ft = 2 yd.

Converting from a larger unit to a smaller unit:

2 feet = ______ inches

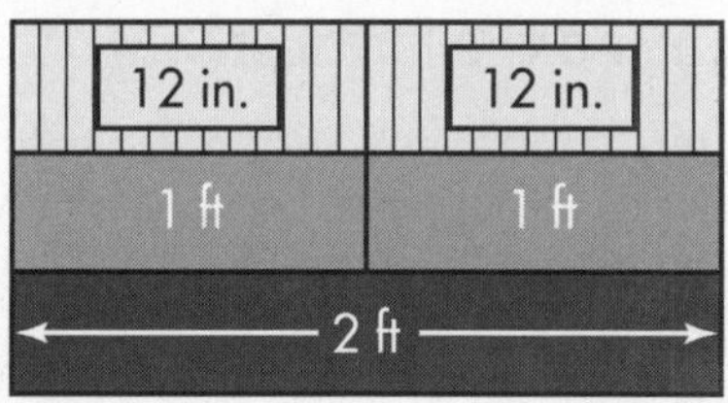

You know 1 ft = 12 in. **Multiply** 2 × 12.

So, 2 ft = 24 in.

In **1–9**, convert each unit of length.

1. 12 ft = ______ yd

2. 2 mi = ______ yd

3. 46 in. = ______ ft ______ in.

4. 7 ft = ______ in.

5. 3 mi = ______ ft

6. 108 in. = ______ ft

7. 72 in. = ______ yd

8. 2 ft 3 in. = ______ in.

9. 45 in. = ______ yd ______ in.

In **10–15**, compare lengths. Write >, <, or = for each ◯.

10. 64 in. ◯ 5 ft

11. 2 mi ◯ 3,333 yd

12. 36 yd 2 ft ◯ 114 ft 2 in.

13. 9 yd ◯ 324 in.

14. 4 ft 7 in. ◯ 56 in.

15. 25 ft ◯ 8 yd 11 in.

16. Find the perimeter of the rectangle in yards.

33 in.

75 in.

17. Lucy wants to make different types of cheesecake. Each cheesecake uses $\frac{2}{3}$ pound of cream cheese. She has 2 pounds of cream cheese. How many cheesecakes can she make?

For **18** and **19**, use the table.

18. Four friends each took a different path walking from the lunchroom to the gymnasium. The table shows the distance that each of them walked. Who walked the farthest?

DATA

Distance Walked	
Rowan	150 yd
Janelle	429 ft 8 in.
Domingo	130 yd 2 ft
Lydia	460 ft

19. Write the distance Domingo walked in feet and in inches.

20. Be Precise Jordan is 4 feet 8 inches tall. Her mother is 5 feet 10 inches tall. How much taller is Jordan's mother than Jordan? Give your answer in feet and inches.

21. Higher Order Thinking How can you find the number of inches in 1 mile? Show your work.

Assessment Practice

22. Select all of the measurements greater than 100 inches.

- ☐ 8 feet 6 inches
- ☐ 8 feet
- ☐ 3 yards
- ☐ 2 yards 19 inches

23. Select all of the measurements less than 4 yards.

- ☐ 143 inches
- ☐ 47 feet
- ☐ 12 feet
- ☐ 11 feet

Name ______________________

Practice Video Tools Games

Additional Practice 12-2

Convert Customary Units of Capacity

Another Look!

Remember:
1 gallon equals 4 quarts,
1 quart equals 2 pints,
1 pints equals 2 cups, and
1 cup equals 8 fluid ounces.

How to change from one customary unit of capacity to another:

Converting from a smaller unit to a larger unit:

4 pints = ______ quarts

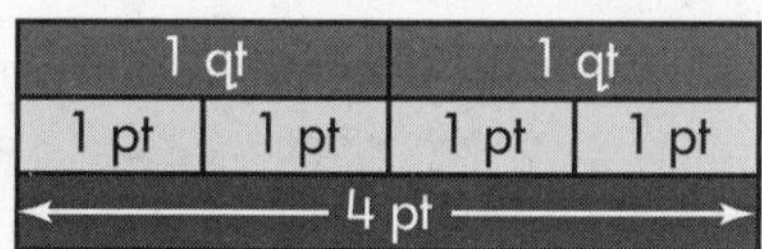

Operation: Divide.

You know 2 pt = 1 qt.

Find $4 \div 2$; 4 pt = 2 qt.

Converting from a larger unit to a smaller unit:

2 gallons = ______ quarts

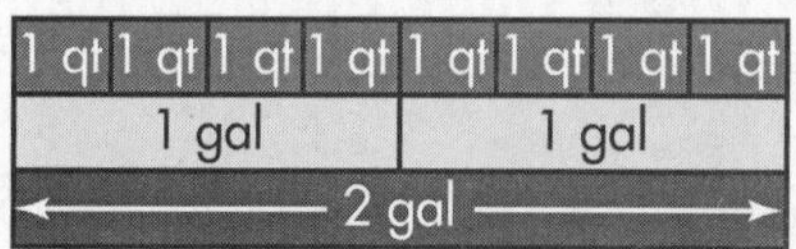

Operation: Multiply.

You know 1 gal = 4 qt.

Find 2×4; 2 gal = 8 qt.

1. Convert 2 quarts to fluid ounces. Write in the missing amounts.

2 quarts = ____ pints ____ pints = 8 cups ____ cups = ____ fluid ounces

In **2–13**, convert each unit of capacity.

2. 14 fl oz = ______ c

3. 8 gal = ______ qt

4. $3\frac{1}{4}$ pt = ______ fl oz

5. $\frac{1}{4}$ c = ______ pt

6. $6\frac{1}{4}$ qt = ______ pt

7. 28 c = ______ qt

8. 2 qt = ______ pt

9. 5 c = ______ pt ______ c

10. 3 gal = ______ pt

11. 96 fl oz = ______ c

12. 4 qt = ______ c

13. $8\frac{1}{4}$ pt = ______ c

14. Number Sense Estimate the number of pints in 445 fluid ounces. Explain your work.

15. If you needed only 1 cup of milk, what is your best choice at the grocery store—a quart container, a pint container, or a $\frac{1}{2}$-gallon container?

In **16** and **17**, use the recipe.

16. Sadie is making punch. How many more quarts of lemon-lime juice will she use than orange juice?

17. Higher Order Thinking How many gallons of punch will Sadie make?

Ingredients for Punch
8 quarts lemon-lime juice
4 pints vanilla ice cream
8 cups orange juice

18. Callie bought 2 gallons of juice for $2.58 per gallon. She sold the juice in 1-cup servings for $0.75 each. Each serving is $\frac{1}{16}$ gallon. How much more did she get for selling the juice than she paid to buy it? Tell how you found the answer.

19. Reasoning How would you convert a measurement given in fluid ounces into pints?

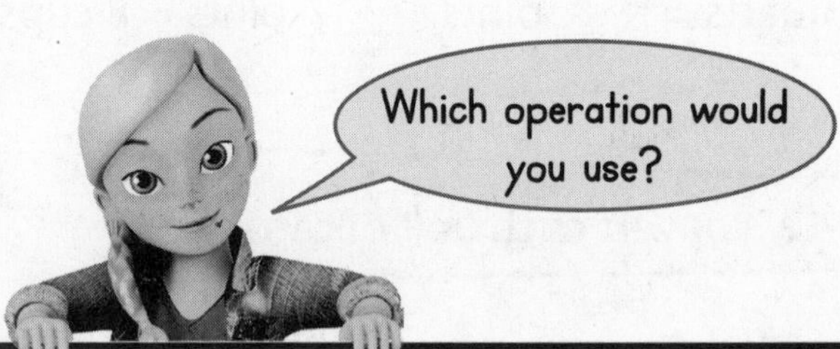

Assessment Practice

20. Choose all measurements that are equal to 4 quarts.

- ☐ 2 gallons
- ☐ 2 pints
- ☐ 8 pints
- ☐ 16 cups
- ☐ 48 fl oz

21. Choose all statements that are true.

- ☐ 7 pints > 2 quarts
- ☐ 4 pints 1 cup > 10 cups
- ☐ 1 quart > 40 fl oz
- ☐ 1 gallon < 8 pints 1 cup
- ☐ 8 quarts = 32 gallons

Name ______________________

Practice Video Tools Games

Additional Practice 12-3
Convert Customary Units of Weight

Another Look!

Remember:
1 ton equals 2,000 pounds and
1 pound equals 16 ounces.

How to change from one unit of weight to another:

Converting from a smaller unit to a larger unit:

32 ounces = ______ pounds

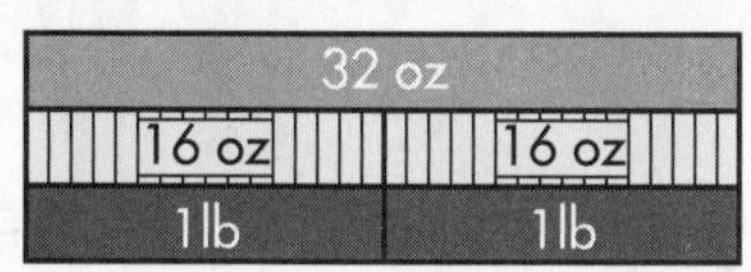

You know 16 oz = 1 lb, so divide.

Find 32 ÷ 16; 32 oz = 2 lb.

Converting from a larger unit to a smaller unit:

3 pounds = ______ ounces

3 lb		
1 lb	1 lb	1 lb
16 oz	16 oz	16 oz

You know 1 lb = 16 oz, so multiply.

Find 3 × 16; 3 lb = 48 oz.

In **1–6**, convert each unit of weight.

1. 4 T = ______ lb **2.** 5 lb = ______ oz **3.** 5,500 lb = ______ T

4. $2\frac{1}{2}$ lb = ______ oz **5.** 90 lb = ______ oz **6.** 224 oz = ______ lb

In **7–12**, compare. Write >, <, or = for each ◯.

7. 16 lb ◯ 16 oz **8.** 1,500 lb ◯ 2 T **9.** 3 T ◯ 5,999 lb

10. 1,600 oz ◯ 10 lb **11.** 19 lb ◯ 300 oz **12.** 8 oz ◯ $\frac{1}{2}$ lb

In **13** and **14**, complete each table to show equivalent measures.

13.

pounds	2,000	3,000	
tons			3

14.

ounces	16	48	
pounds			10

In **15** and **16**, use the recipe.

15. Aaron bought these ingredients to make the trail mix recipe. How many pounds of trail mix will he make?

16. **Model with Math** Aaron wants to divide the trail mix equally into 6 bags to give to his friends. How much trail mix will be in each bag? Draw a bar diagram and write an equation to help you find the answer.

DATA

Trail Mix Recipe
10 ounces dried bananas
20 ounces raisins
18 ounces nuts

17. **Number Sense** A candy maker buys a bar of chocolate weighing 162 ounces. About how many pounds does the bar weigh?

18. **Higher Order Thinking** Karla bought 2 pounds of broccoli, $1\frac{3}{4}$ pounds of green beans, and 10 ounces of kale. How much do Karla's vegetables weigh in all? Write your answer two different ways.

19. Students visited a zoo where they learned that a large white rhinoceros could weigh as much as 6,000 pounds. How many tons is this?

20. **Algebra** Complete the table. Write the expression that can be used to find the missing value in the second row.

n	12	15	21	28
$n +$ ___	18	21	27	

Assessment Practice

21. **Part A**

Paula's kitten weighs $3\frac{1}{2}$ pounds. Write this weight using pounds and ounces.

____ pounds ____ ounces

Part B

Explain how you found your answer.

Name ______________________

 Practice  Video  Tools  Games

Additional Practice 12-4

Convert Metric Units of Length

Another Look!

Remember:
1 km = 10^3 m = 1,000 m
1 m = 10^2 cm = 100 cm
1 m = 10^3 mm = 1,000 mm
1 cm = 10 mm

How to change from one metric unit of length to another:

Converting a length from a smaller to a larger metric unit:

200 centimeters = ______ meters

1 m	1 m
100 cm	100 cm
← 200 cm →	

You know 10^2 cm = 1 m, so divide.

Find 200 ÷ 100; 200 cm = 2 m.

Converting a length from a larger to a smaller metric unit:

2 kilometers = ______ meters

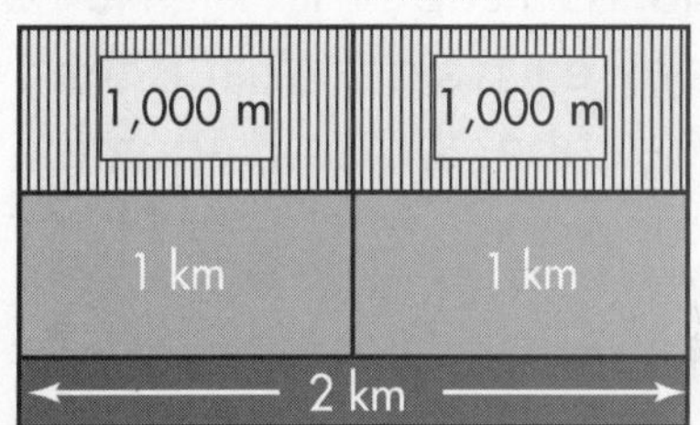

You know 1 km = 10^3 m, so multiply.

Find 2 × 1,000; 2 km = 2,000 m.

In **1–6**, convert each unit of length.

How can you double check that your answers are correct?

1. 25 m = ______ cm

2. 345 cm = ______ m

3. 4.5 m = ______ cm

4. 10 m = ______ mm

5. 987 mm = ______ cm

6. 5 km = ______ m

In **7–9**, compare lengths. Write >, <, or = for each ○.

7. 3 km ○ 5,000 m

8. 800 cm ○ 8 m

9. 38.5 mm ○ 10 cm

In **10** and **11**, complete each table to show equivalent measures.

10.

mm	5	85	
cm			90

11.

km	0.4		25
m		7,000	

12. Higher Order Thinking Park rangers at the North Rim of the Grand Canyon recorded the amounts of rainfall over 12 months. What was the total amount of rainfall in centimeters?

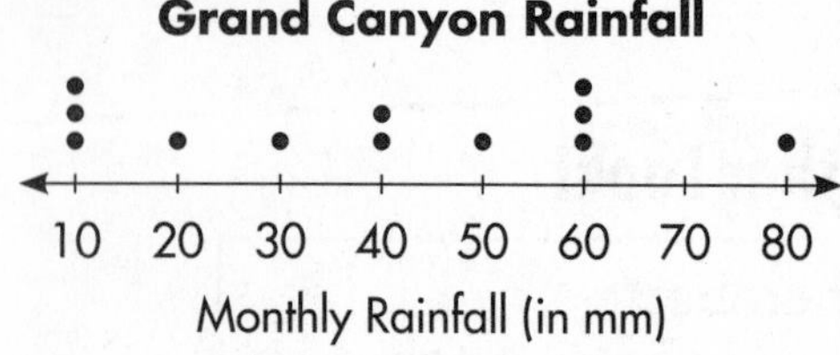

13. What is the difference between the greatest and least amounts of monthly rainfall? Write an equation to model your work.

---

14. Arturo builds a cube that measures 5 inches on each side. What is the volume of Arturo's cube? Write an equation to show your work.

15. Use Structure List three measurements with different units that are equal to 5 meters.

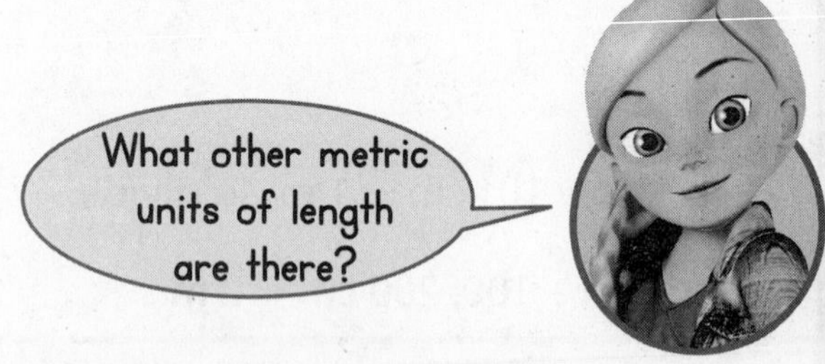

What other metric units of length are there?

---

16. If you walked all three trails in one day, how far would you walk? Write the answer in meters and in kilometers.

DATA

Trail	Length
Spring Hollow	2 km
Brookside	2,400 m
Oak Ridge	1 km 600 m

17. Explain how you can move the decimal point to convert 3,200 meters to kilometers.

Assessment Practice

18. Cory finds a leaf that is 5 cm long. Which measurement is equivalent to 5 cm?

Ⓐ 0.05 mm

Ⓑ 0.5 mm

Ⓒ 50 mm

Ⓓ 500 mm

19. Which of these number sentences is **NOT** true?

Ⓐ 4,000,000 mm = 4 km

Ⓑ 300 mm > 3 cm

Ⓒ 5 m > 5,000 mm

Ⓓ 2,000 m < 20 km

Name ______

Practice Video Tools Games

Additional Practice 12-5
Convert Metric Units of Capacity

Another Look!

Remember:
To change from liters to milliliters, multiply by 10^3. To change from milliliters to liters, divide by 10^3.

How to change from one metric unit of capacity to another:

Converting a capacity from a smaller to a larger metric unit:

2,000 milliliters = ______ liters

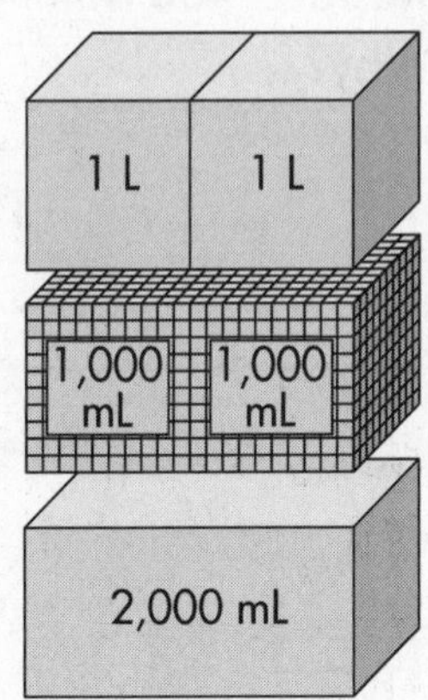

You know 10^3 mL = 1 L, so divide.

Find 2,000 ÷ 1,000; 2,000 mL = 2 L.

Converting a capacity from a larger to a smaller metric unit:

3 liters = ______ milliliters

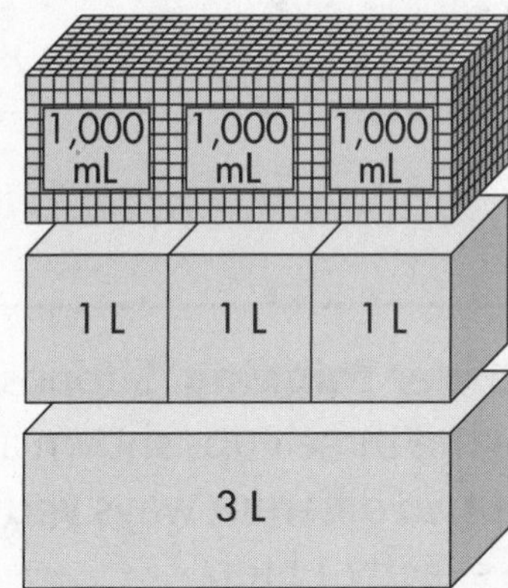

You know 1 L = 10^3 mL, so multiply.

Find 3 × 1,000; 3 L = 3,000 mL.

In **1–9**, convert each unit of capacity.

1. 5 L = ______ mL

2. 13,000 mL = ______ L

3. 1.6 L = ______ mL

4. 4,750 mL = ______ L

5. 950 mL = ______ L

6. 0.4 L = ______ mL

7. 2.7 L = ______ mL

8. 8,400 mL = ______ L

9. 0.071 L = ______ mL

In **10** and **11**, complete each table to show equivalent measures.

10.

liters	90	9	0.9
milliliters			

11.

milliliters	250	2,500	25,000
liters			

12. Construct Arguments Tell whether you would use multiplication or division to convert milliliters to liters. Explain your answer.

13. Algebra Complete the following table. Then write an equation that can be used to convert *p* pounds to *o* ounces.

Pounds	3	4	5	6	7
Ounces	48				

14. The length of a rectangular garden is 10 yards and its width is 10 feet. What is the perimeter of the garden in feet?

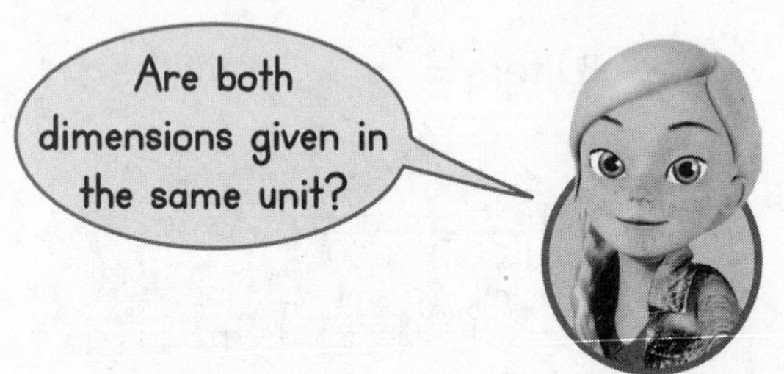

Are both dimensions given in the same unit?

15. You are preparing for a breakfast party and need enough milk for 20 people. Each person will drink about 200 milliliters of milk. Which is the better estimate of the amount of milk you should prepare: 400 milliliters or 4 liters? Why?

16. Higher Order Thinking Suppose you have the three cups shown at the right. List two different ways you can measure exactly 1 liter.

Assessment Practice

17. A community center has a swimming pool that holds 29,000,000 milliliters of water. How many liters of water can the pool hold?

Ⓐ 290,000,000 L
Ⓑ 2,900,000 L
Ⓒ 290,000 L
Ⓓ 29,000 L

18. There are 1.5 liters of punch in a pitcher. How many milliliters of punch are in the pitcher?

Ⓐ 100 mL
Ⓑ 1,500 mL
Ⓒ 1,000 mL
Ⓓ 15,000 mL

Name ______________________

Additional Practice 12-6
Convert Metric Units of Mass

Another Look!

Remember:
10^3 milligrams equals 1 gram and 10^3 grams equals 1 kilogram.

How to convert from one metric unit of mass to another:

Smaller metric unit to a larger unit:
6,000 grams = ____ kilograms

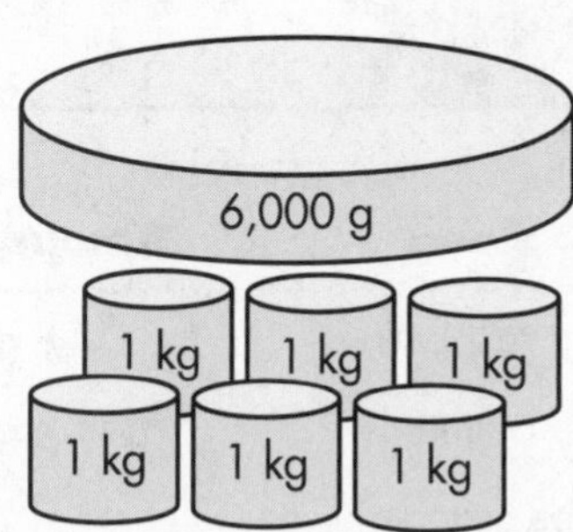

You know 10^3 g = 1 kg, so divide.

Find 6,000 ÷ 1,000; 6,000 g = 6 kg.

Larger metric unit to a smaller unit:
2 grams = ____ miligrams

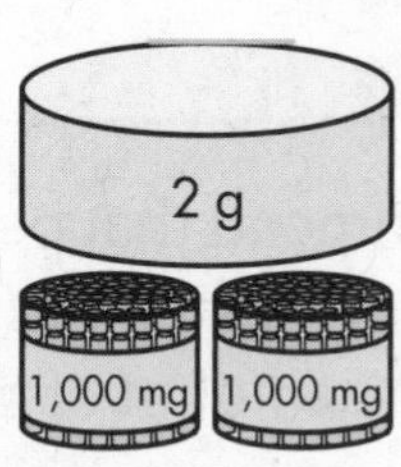

You know 1 g = 10^3 mg, so multiply.

Find 2 × 1,000; 2 g = 2,000 mg.

In **1–6**, convert each unit of mass.

1. 72 g = ________ mg
2. 8,000 g = ______ kg
3. 2,000 mg = ______ kg

4. 490 g = ______ kg
5. 0.648 g = ____ mg
6. 0.061 kg = ______ g

In **7–12**, compare. Write >, <, or = for each ◯.

7. 4,000 mg ◯ 5 g
8. 64 kg ◯ 64,000 g
9. 3 kg ◯ 40,000 mg

10. 6,000 g ◯ 6 kg
11. 93 g ◯ 92,000 mg
12. 90 kg ◯ 90,000 mg

In **13** and **14**, complete each table to show equivalent measures.

13.

grams	2		200
milligrams		20,000	

14.

grams		1,000	
kilograms	0.1		10

15. A recipe that serves two people calls for 1,600 milligrams of baking soda. You want to make enough for 10 people. How many grams of baking soda will you need? Write an equation to show your work.

16. Reasoning What steps would you take to compare 2 kilograms and 3,200 grams?

Is there more than one way to compare them?

17. Nutritionists recommend that people eat 25,000 milligrams of fiber each day. The table shows the amount of fiber Jodi has eaten today. How many more grams of fiber does she need to get the recommended daily amount of fiber?

DATA

Food	Amount of Fiber
1 cup raspberries	8 grams
1 cup oatmeal	4 grams
2 cups orange juice	1 gram

18. Classify the triangle by its sides and its angles.

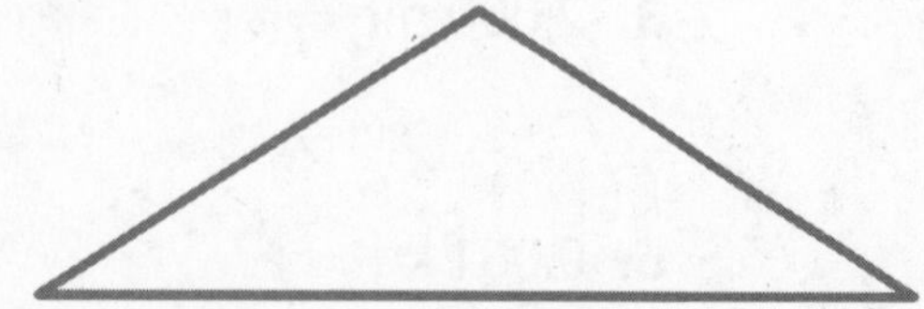

19. Higher Order Thinking How is converting grams to milligrams similar to converting pounds to ounces? How is it different?

Assessment Practice

20. Write the following masses on the lines from greatest to least.

30 g   2 kg   60,000 mg

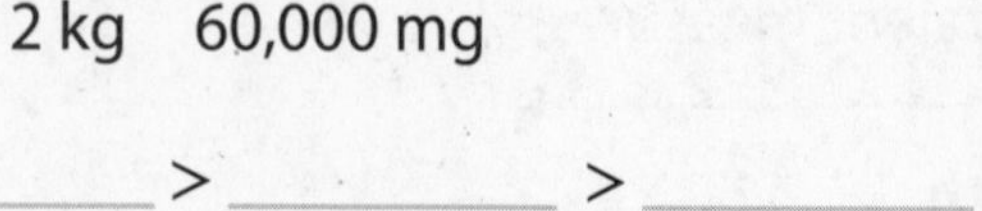

________ > ________ > ________

21. If you convert grams to kilograms, what operation would you use?

Ⓐ Addition

Ⓑ Subtraction

Ⓒ Multiplication

Ⓓ Division

Name ______________________

 Practice  Video  Tools  Games

Additional Practice 12-7

Convert Units of Time

Another Look!

Remember:
To change from hours to minutes, or from minutes to seconds, multiply by 60. To change from seconds to minutes, or from minutes to hours, divide by 60.

Change from one unit of time to another.

From a smaller unit to a larger unit:

500 seconds = ____ minutes

You know 60 seconds = 1 minute.

Divide 500 by 60.

$\frac{500}{60} = 8\frac{20}{60} = 8\frac{1}{3}$

So, 500 seconds = $8\frac{1}{3}$ minutes.

From a larger unit to a smaller unit:

4.5 hours = ____ minutes

You know 1 hour = 60 minutes.

Multiply 4.5 by 60.

$4.5 \times 60 = 270$

So, 4.5 hours = 270 minutes.

In **1–6**, convert each time.

1. 8 minutes = ______ seconds

2. 90 minutes = ______ hours

3. 5.5 hours = ______ minutes

4. 195 seconds = ______ minutes

5. 156 seconds = ____ minutes, ____ seconds

6. 4 hours, 5 minutes = ______ minutes

In **7–8**, compare. Write >, <, or = in each ◯.

7. 600 minutes ◯ 10 hours

8. 110 minutes ◯ $1\frac{1}{4}$ hours

9. A waffle iron can make a waffle in 4 minutes. How many waffles can be made in an hour?

10. Howard slept from 9:00 P.M. until 6:00 A.M. the next morning. How many minutes did he sleep?

11. Maria does weightlifting for 30 seconds and then aerobics for 60 seconds. She repeats this 10 times. If she does not take any breaks, how many minutes does she exercise?

12. **Make Sense and Persevere** Every 20 seconds, a sprinkler passes across a garden. Will it take more than an hour for the sprinkler to cross the garden 150 times? Explain.

13. **Higher Order Thinking** Gina made a playlist of children's songs. In 1 hour, how many more times could she play "Row, Row, Row Your Boat" than "Twinkle, Twinkle, Little Star"?

Favorite Children's Songs

Name	Time
Row, Row, Row Your Boat	8 seconds
Twinkle, Twinkle, Little Star	20 seconds
Hickory Dickory Dock	10 seconds

Assessment Practice

14. The last total solar eclipse in North America occurred in August 2017. The durations of the total eclipse in three U.S. cities are shown at the right. Write the names of the cities from longest duration to shortest.

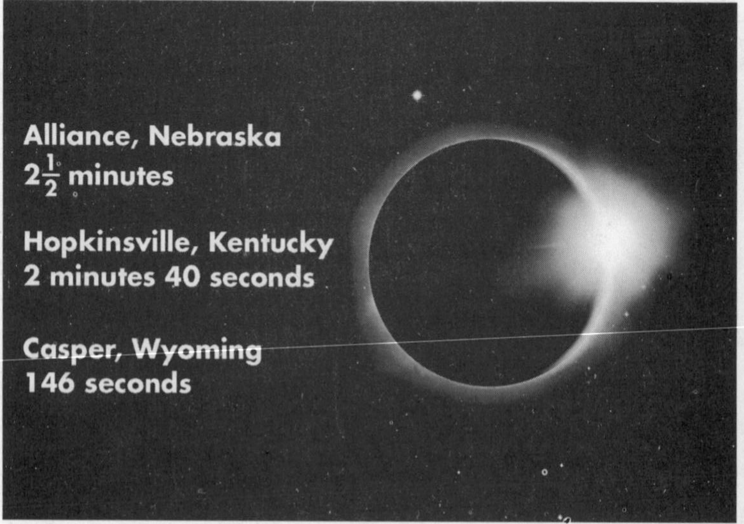

Alliance, Nebraska
$2\frac{1}{2}$ minutes
Hopkinsville, Kentucky
2 minutes 40 seconds
Casper, Wyoming
146 seconds

Name ______________________

Practice Video Tools Games

Additional Practice 12-8

Solve Word Problems Using Measurement Conversions

Another Look!

Kyle hiked 10 miles on Saturday. He hiked half as many miles on Sunday. How many total yards did Kyle hike?

What question needs to be answered first?
How many miles did Kyle hike on Sunday?

Answer this question.
$10 \div 2 = 5$ miles

What is the total number of miles hiked?
$10 + 5 = 15$ miles

Convert the answer to yards.
1 mi = 1,760 yd, so 15 miles is $15 \times 1,760 = 26,400$ yd

Kyle hiked a total of 26,400 yards.

Read the problem. Underline what you know. Circle what you are asked to find.

1. Kendra biked 10 kilometers on Monday. She biked twice as many kilometers on Tuesday. How many total meters did she bike?

   Underline what you know. Circle what you need to find.

   What question do you need to answer first?

   ____

   How many meters did Kendra bike in all? __________

Remember to check your calculations and make sure you answered the correct question.

2. Wilson made fruit punch. He used 2 quarts of orange juice and 1 pint of cranberry juice. He used one quart more ginger ale than orange juice. How many cups of fruit punch did Wilson make?

3. Claire's backyard is in the shape of a rectangle and has a length of 19.5 feet. It cost her $945 to fence in the yard. If fencing costs $15 per foot, what is the width of Claire's backyard?

4. Zayna is putting ribbon around a picture of her dog. The picture is a rectangle, 300 millimeters wide and 150 millimeters tall. How many meters of ribbon will she need?

5. Ann is putting carpet in a room that is 12 feet long and 10 feet wide. The carpet costs $3.00 per square foot. How much will the carpet for the room cost?

6. For every 3 cans of vegetables purchased, you get 1 free can. Tessie went home with 32 cans of vegetables. How many cans did she have to pay for?

7. Isabel ran around the track 6 times at the same rate of speed. It took her 24 minutes to run. John took 3 minutes to run around the track once. Which student ran faster? Explain.

8. **Construct Arguments** Badal has 120 cubic centimeters of water. He wants to pour it into a rectangular vase that is 4 centimeters high, 40 millimeters wide, and 5 centimeters long. Will all the water fit into the vase? Explain.

9. **Higher Order Thinking** Nancy is saving $2 from her allowance every week. Marco is saving $1 the first week, $2 the second week, $3 the third week, and so on. At the end of 10 weeks, who will have saved more money? How much more?

10. José is painting a backdrop for the school play. The rectangular backdrop is 60 inches by 45 inches. If his container of paint can cover 25 square feet, does he have enough to paint the backdrop?

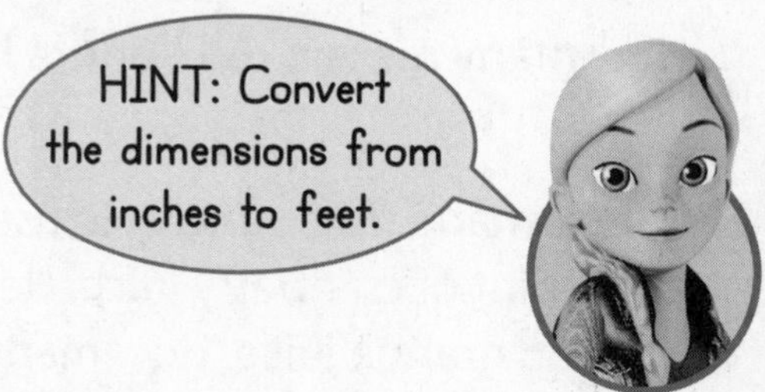

HINT: Convert the dimensions from inches to feet.

11. Darin wants to put a fence around his garden. How much fencing should he buy?

Ⓐ 26 yards

Ⓑ 40 yards

Ⓒ 46 feet

Ⓓ 120 feet

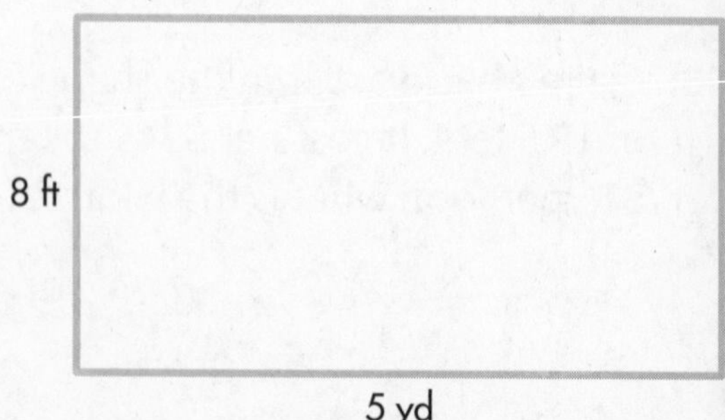

Name ____________

 Practice  Video  Tools  Games

Additional Practice 12-9
Precision

Another Look!

Meg and Tina measured the length of their classroom. They wondered how the measurements compare.

Meg	Tina
Our classroom is $9\frac{1}{3}$ yards long	Length of classroom = 28 ft

Tell how you can use precision to compare the measurements.

- I can use numbers, units, and symbols correctly.
- I can calculate accurately.
- I can give a clear answer.

Use precision to compare the measurements.

Convert $9\frac{1}{3}$ yards to feet.

$9\frac{1}{3}$ yd = ____ ft

$9\frac{1}{3} \times 3 = \frac{28}{3} \times \frac{3}{1} = \frac{84}{3} = 28$

So, $9\frac{1}{3}$ yd = 28 ft.

Since $9\frac{1}{3}$ yd = 28 ft, the measurements are equal.

Be Precise

William bought a 0.5-liter bottle of liquid plant food. He uses 40 milliliters a week.

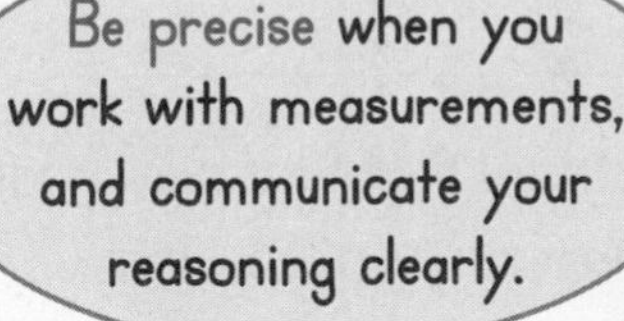

Be precise when you work with measurements, and communicate your reasoning clearly.

1. What measurements are given? Are the same units used for each measurement? Explain.

2. Explain how you can convert one of the measurements so that both use the same unit.

3. How much plant food does William need for 12 weeks? Explain.

4. Is one bottle enough for 12 weeks? Give a clear answer.

Performance Task

Buying Ribbon

Mimi needs eleven 18-inch pieces of rhinestone ribbon. She purchased 5 yards of the ribbon shown at the right.

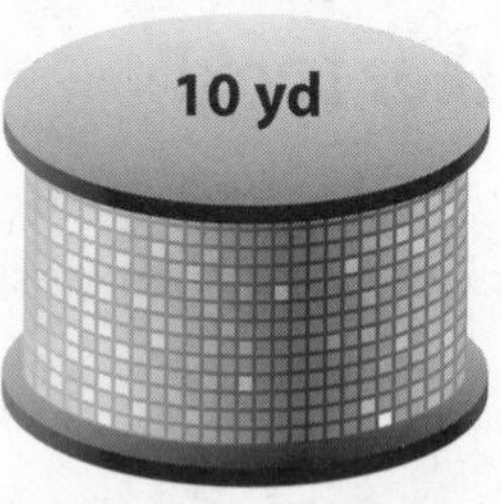

$6 per yard
or
$55 for the whole spool

5. **Be Precise** What is the total amount of ribbon Mimi needs? Explain.

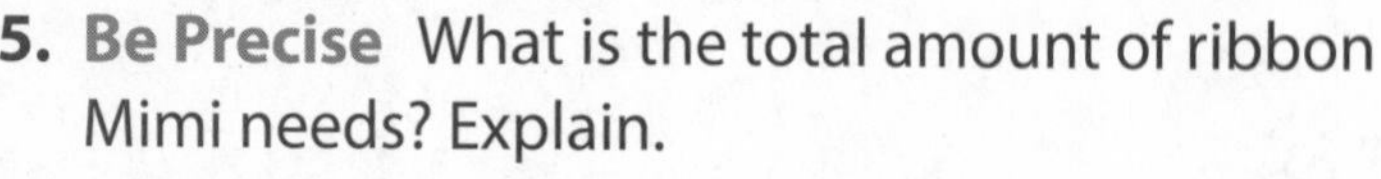

6. **Reasoning** Do you need to convert measurements to determine if Mimi purchased the right amount of ribbon? Explain.

7. **Model with Math** Show how to convert the measurements you described in Exercise 6.

8. **Be Precise** Did Mimi purchase the correct amount of ribbon? Explain.

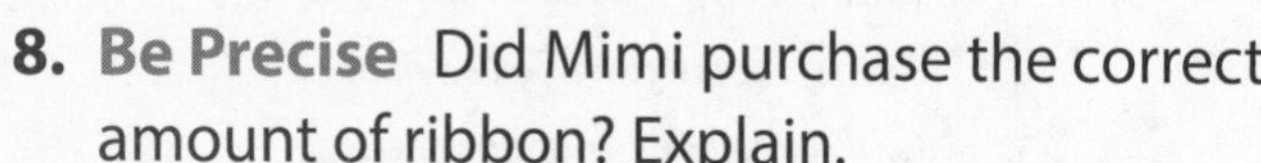

9. **Make Sense and Persevere** If Mimi purchases the additional ribbon she needs, what will be the total cost of all the ribbon? Show two different ways to find the answer.

To be precise, you need to check that you are using units of measure correctly and that your conversions are accurate.

Name ______________________

Additional Practice 13-1

Evaluate Expressions

Another Look!

When an expression contains more than one operation, **parentheses ( )** can be used to show which operation should be done first. Parentheses are one type of **grouping symbol**.

Do the operation inside the parentheses first.

Operations in grouping symbols are always done first.

Evaluate $(2 + 8) \times 3$.

$10 \times 3 = 30$

Evaluate $2 + (8 \times 3)$.

$2 + 24 = 26$

Brackets and **braces** are other types of **grouping symbols**.
Evaluate terms inside brackets after doing operations within parentheses.

Evaluate $[(4 + 9) - (30 \div 5)] \times 10$.

$[13 - 6] \times 10$

$7 \times 10 = 70$

In **1–12**, evaluate the expression.

Use the order of operations to choose which calculation to do next: Multiply and divide from left to right. Add and subtract from left to right.

1. $(16 + 4) \div 10$

______ $\div 10 =$ ______

2. $60 \div (3 \times 4)$

$60 \div$ ______ $=$ ______

3. $(16 \div 4) + (10 - 3)$

4. $64 \div (10 \times 0.8)$

5. $27 - (7.5 \times 2)$

6. $[(4 \times 6) + 6] \div 6$

7. $(5 + 2) \times (14 - 9) - 1$

8. $5 + \{[2 \times (14 - 9)] - 1\}$

9. $(52 + 48) \div (8 + 17)$

10. $[52 + (48 \div 8)] + 17$

11. $(80 + 16) \div (4 + 12)$

12. $80 + 16 \div 4 + 12$

13. Keisha bought a new pair of skis for $450. She made a payment of $120 and got a student discount of $40. Her mother paid $\frac{1}{2}$ of the remaining balance. How much does Keisha have left to pay?

14. Be Precise Ellen is $5\frac{1}{2}$ feet tall. Her sister is $\frac{3}{4}$ foot shorter than Ellen. How tall is Ellen's sister?

15. Higher Order Thinking Rewrite using parentheses to make each statement true.

a $42 + 12 \div 6 = 9$

b $33 - 14\frac{1}{2} + 3\frac{1}{2} = 15$

c $32 \div 8 \times 2 = 2$

16. Algebra What steps would you use to solve the equation $n = 7 + (32 \div 16) \times 4 - 6$? Solve the equation.

17. Make Sense and Persevere Milton makes trail mix for his hiking group. He mixes $1\frac{1}{4}$ pounds of peanuts, 14 ounces of raisins, 12 ounces of walnuts, and 10 ounces of chocolate chips. If Milton divides the trail mix equally among the 8 hikers in the group, how many ounces of trail mix does each hiker receive?

Remember:
There are 16 ounces in 1 pound.

Assessment Practice

18. Which expression has a value of 11?

Ⓐ $13 - 5 - 3$

Ⓑ $1 + (8 \times 2)$

Ⓒ $5 + 2 \times (4 - 1)$

Ⓓ $15 - 1 + (6 \div 2)$

19. Using the order of operations, which operation should you perform last to evaluate this expression?

$8 + \{[14 \div 2 \times (3 - 1)] - 1\}$

Ⓐ Addition

Ⓑ Division

Ⓒ Multiplication

Ⓓ Subtraction

Name ______________________________

Practice

Video

Tools

Games

Additional Practice 13-2

Write Numerical Expressions

Another Look!

Cole is $11\frac{1}{2}$ years old. Uncle Frank is 4 times as old as Cole. Write an expression to show how you could calculate Uncle Frank's age in 6 years.

You could use properties to write other expressions for Frank's age.

Uncle Frank's current age:

$4 \times 11\frac{1}{2}$

Uncle Frank's age in 6 years:

$\left(4 \times 11\frac{1}{2}\right) + 6$

The expression $\left(4 \times 11\frac{1}{2}\right) + 6$ shows the calculations that will determine Uncle Frank's age in 6 years.

In **1–7**, write a numerical expression for each calculation.

1. Multiply 16, 3, and 29, and then subtract 17.

2. Add 13.2 and 0.9, and then divide by 0.6.

3. Subtract $12\frac{1}{2}$ from the product of $\frac{9}{10}$ and 180.

4. Add the quotient of 120 and 60 to the quotient of 72 and 9.

5. Multiply 71 by 8, and then add 379.

6. Find 3 times the difference of 7.25 and 4.5.

7. Write an expression to show the calculations you could use to determine how much greater the area of the larger rectangle is than the area of the smaller rectangle.

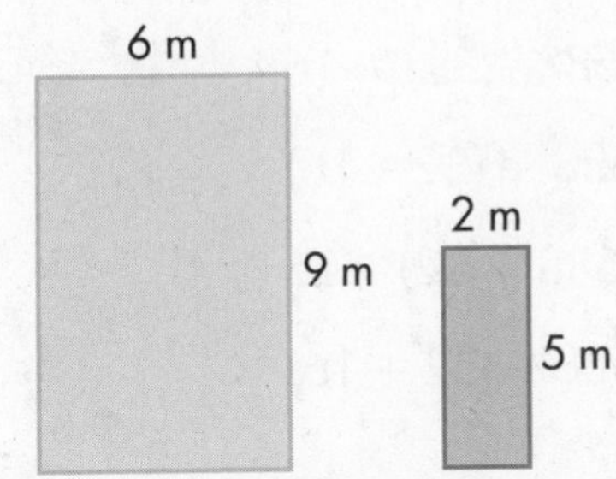

8. **Model with Math** Lola uses 44 beads to make a bracelet and 96 beads to make a necklace. Write an expression to show how you could calculate the total number of beads Lola used to make 13 bracelets and 8 necklaces.

9. Bart works 36 hours a week and makes \$612. Charles works 34 hours a week and makes \$663. Who makes more per hour? How do you know?

10. Use a property to write an equivalent expression for $12 \times (100 - 5)$. Which property did you use?

11. Doreen solved the following problem:
$\frac{1}{6} \div 5 = \frac{1}{30}$
Show how to use multiplication to check Doreen's answer.

12. **Higher Order Thinking** Stephen is combining all of the juice shown to make fruit punch. Does the expression $(64 + 28 + 76) \div 6$ show how you could calculate the number of $\frac{3}{4}$-cup servings? Explain.

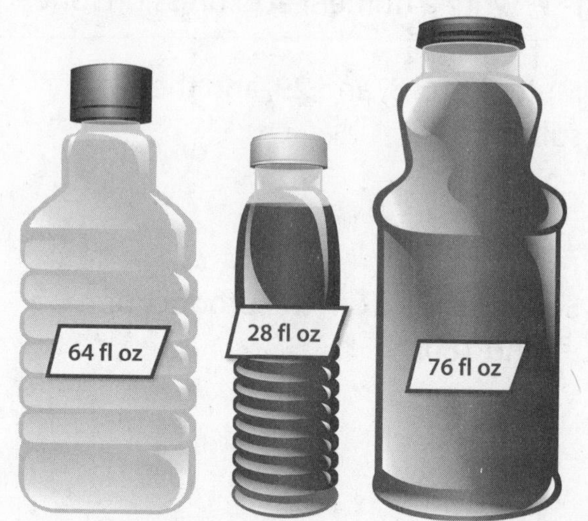

Assessment Practice

13. Which expression represents the following calculation?

Divide 688 by 32, and then add 16.

Ⓐ $(688 \div 32) + 16$

Ⓑ $688 + (32 \div 16)$

Ⓒ $(688 + 32) \div 16$

Ⓓ $688 \div (32 + 16)$

14. Which is the first step in evaluating the expression?

$(25 - 9) \div 8 \times 3$

Ⓐ Multiply 8 and 3

Ⓑ Subtract 25 and 9

Ⓒ Divide 9 by 8

Ⓓ Multiply 9 and 3

Name ______________________

 Practice  Video  Tools 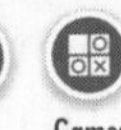 Games

Additional Practice 13-3
Interpret Numerical Expressions

Another Look!

Audrey and Donald played a video game. The expressions below show the number of points each player scored.

Audrey: 32,700 + 6,140 + 5,050

Donald: (32,700 + 6,140 + 5,050) − 8,815

How does Donald's score compare to Audrey's?

You can compare some expressions without doing any calculations.

Both expressions contain the same sum.

Audrey: 32,700 + 6,140 + 5,050

Donald: (32,700 + 6,140 + 5,050) − 8,815

The expression for Donald's score shows 8,815 subtracted from the sum.

So, Donald's score is 8,815 points less than Audrey's score.

In **1** and **2**, without doing any calculations, describe how Expression A compares to Expression B.

1. **A** (23,000 − 789) × 19
B 23,000 − 789

2. **A** $6\frac{4}{5} + \left(88 \times \frac{3}{10}\right)$
B $88 \times \frac{3}{10}$

In **3–6**, without doing any calculations, write >, <, or =.

3. (714 ÷ 32) − 20 ◯ (714 ÷ 32) − 310

4. 0.1 × (716 + 789) ◯ 716 + 789

5. $\frac{1}{2}$ × (228 + 4,316) ◯ (228 + 4,316) ÷ 2

6. (3.9 × 8) + (3.9 × 4) ◯ 3.9 × 15

7. Which expression is 16 times as large as 18,233 − 4,006?

Ⓐ (18,233 − 4,006) + 16
Ⓑ (18,233 − 4,006) × 16
Ⓒ (18,233 − 4,006) ÷ 16
Ⓓ (18,233 × 16) − 4,006

8. Use Structure Sid paid \$6.80 for wrapping paper and \$7.35 for ribbon. He wrapped identical gifts for all of his cousins. Sid wrote the expression $(6.80 + 7.35) \div 8$ to help him calculate how much it cost him to wrap each gift. How many gifts did Sid wrap? Explain.

9. Construct Arguments Yolanda bought $3 \times \left(\frac{1}{4} + \frac{7}{8} + 1\frac{1}{2}\right)$ pounds of cheese. Sam bought $2 \times \left(\frac{1}{4} + \frac{7}{8} + 1\frac{1}{2}\right)$ pounds of cheese. Without doing any calculations, determine who bought more cheese. Explain.

10. Jack bought the fishing gear pictured. The sales tax was calculated by multiplying the total cost of the fishing gear by 0.07 and rounding to the nearest cent. How much did Jack pay for the fishing gear including sales tax?

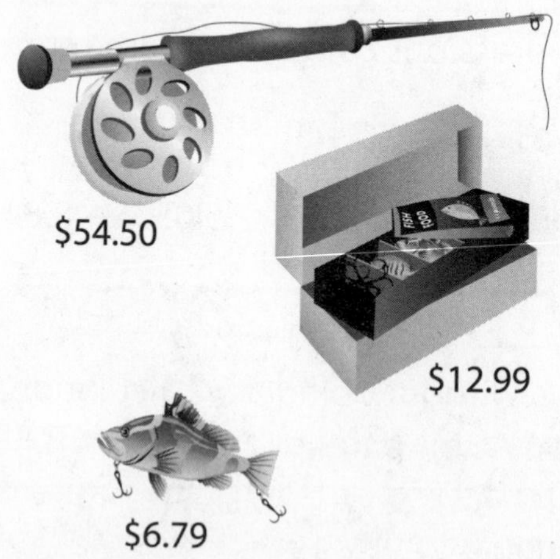

11. Cy bought a laptop computer, a printer, and a router. Cy used a \$35 coupon to make the purchase. He wrote $(1{,}415.00 + 277.50 + 44.95) - 35$ to show how he can calculate the final cost, not including sales tax. Write an expression that can be used to find the total price of the items he bought before sales tax and the coupon.

12. Higher Order Thinking Arrange expressions A, B, C, D, and E in order from least to greatest.

A $(9{,}311 + 522) \times 4.8$

B $9{,}311 + 522$

C $(9{,}311 + 522) \times \frac{1}{2}$

D $25 \times (9{,}311 + 522)$

E $(9{,}311 \times 5) + (522 \times 5)$

Assessment Practice

13. Which statement describes the expression $4 \times (17 - 9 + 28)$?

Ⓐ Four times the sum of 9 and 28 subtracted from 17

Ⓑ Four times 17 minus 9 plus 28

Ⓒ Twenty-eight added to the difference of 17 and 9, then multiplied by 4

Ⓓ Nine plus 28 subtracted from the product of 4 and 17

Name ______________________

Practice

Video

Tools

Games

Additional Practice 13-4
Reasoning

Another Look!

There are 37 cars parked in the school parking lot at 5:00. There are 9 more cars at 5:30. At 6:00, there are twice as many cars as at 5:30. How many cars are in the lot at 6:00?

Use expressions to represent the quantities and relationships in the problem. You can use diagrams to help.

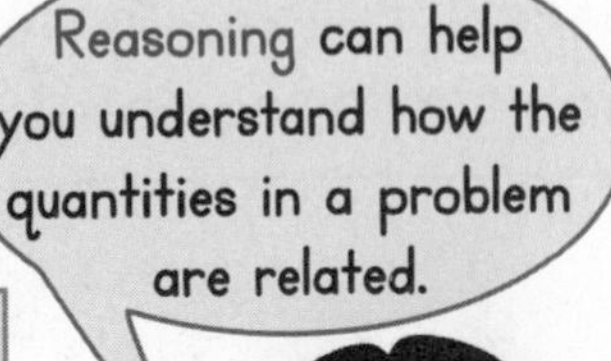

37 cars at 5:00	**9 more at 5:30**	**Twice as many at 6:00**
[37]	[37 | 9]	[37 | 9] [37 | 9]
37	$37 + 9$	$(37 + 9) \times 2$

$$(37 + 9) \times 2 = 46 \times 2 = 92$$

So, there are 92 cars at 6:00.

Reasoning

Ms. Lang lives in St. Paul, Minnesota. Last year, she made 4 round trips to Madison, Wisconsin, and 3 round trips to Bismarck, North Dakota. How many more miles did she travel in her trips to Bismarck than in her trips to Madison?

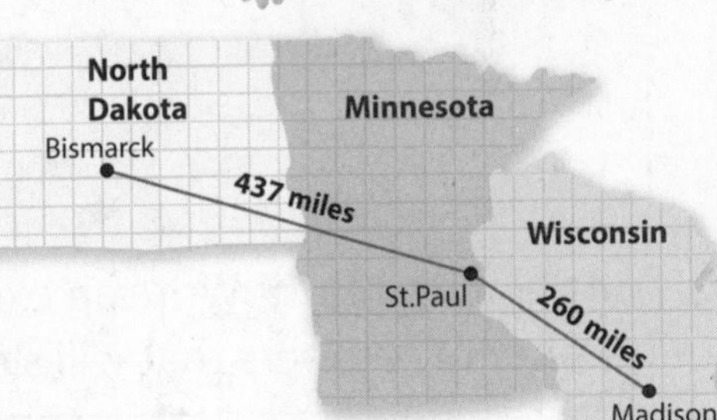

1. Write an expression to represent the difference between the total number of miles in the Bismarck trips and the total number of miles in the Madison trips. You can use a diagram to help.

2. Explain how the numbers, symbols, and operations in your expression represent the problem.

3. How many more miles did Mrs. Lang travel in her trips to Bismarck than in her trips to Madison? Explain how you solved the problem.

Performance Task

Camping Trip

Ross is planning a camping trip for 136 scouts. He has reserved 4 buses. The scouts will sleep in tents or cabins. If they fill every bed in the cabins, how many campers will sleep in tents?

State Park
14 cabins
Each cabin has 4 single beds.

4. **Make Sense and Persevere** What information in the problem do you need?

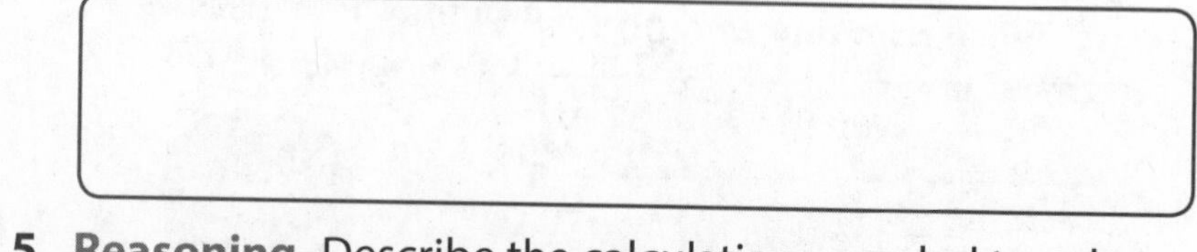

5. **Reasoning** Describe the calculations needed to solve the problem and explain the order in which you need to do them. You can use a diagram to help.

6. **Model with Math** Write an expression to represent the number of campers that will sleep in tents.

7. **Critique Reasoning** Ross says he does not need grouping symbols in the expression that represents this problem. Is he correct? Explain.

8. **Be Precise** Find the number of campers that will sleep in tents. Explain how you found the answer.

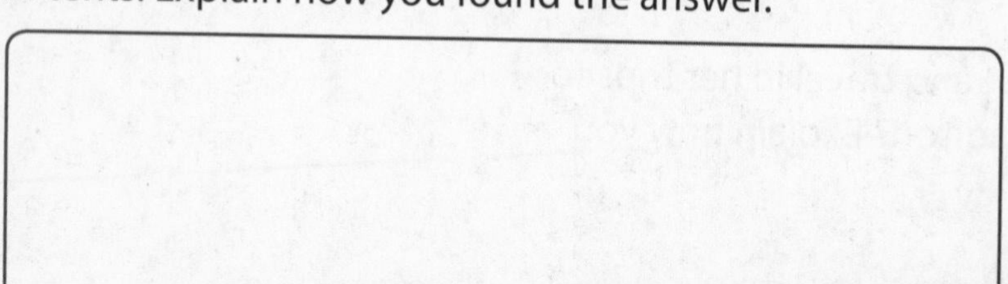

When you use reasoning, you can use properties and diagrams to help make sense of the quantities.

Name ______________________

Practice

Video

Tools

Games

Additional Practice 14-1
The Coordinate System

Another Look!

Point *P* gives the location of the playground. Find the coordinates of Point *P*.

Start at (0, 0). Move a distance of 4 units to the right along the *x*-axis.

Move a distance of 3 units up.

The coordinates of Point *P* are (4, 3).

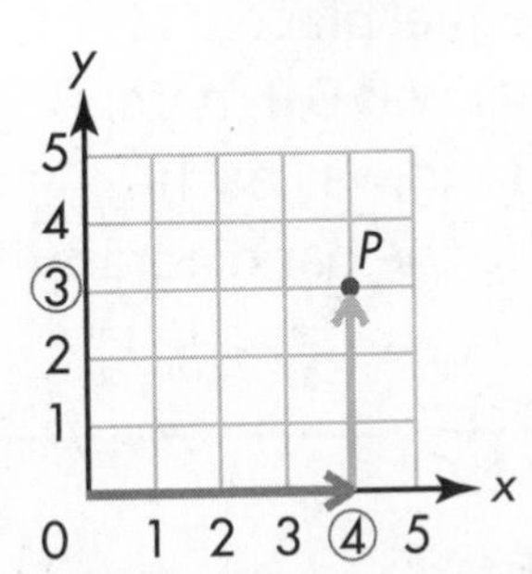

In **1–6**, write the ordered pair for each point on the grid.

1. *A*

2. *B*

3. *C*

4. *D*

5. *E*

6. *F*

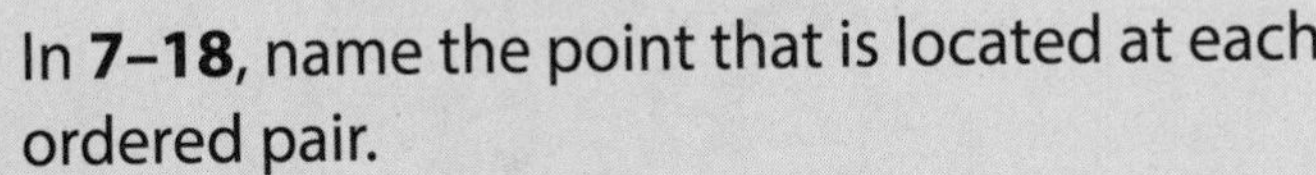

In **7–18**, name the point that is located at each ordered pair.

7. (4, 3) Point ______

8. (3, 7) Point ______

9. (0, 3) Point ______

10. (5, 2) Point ______

11. (6, 8) Point ______

12. (6, 4) Point ______

13. (4, 5) Point ______

14. (2, 8) Point ______

15. (5, 5) Point ______

16. (2, 6) Point ______

17. (2, 3) Point ______

18. (3, 2) Point ______

19. Describe to a friend how to graph a point at (2, 5).

20. Reasoning How are the locations on a coordinate grid different for the ordered pairs (7, 0) and (0, 7)?

21. Steven cut a wire into 5 equal pieces. He started with a wire that was 6.8 meters long. How many meters long was each piece that Steven cut? Use the bar diagram to help you.

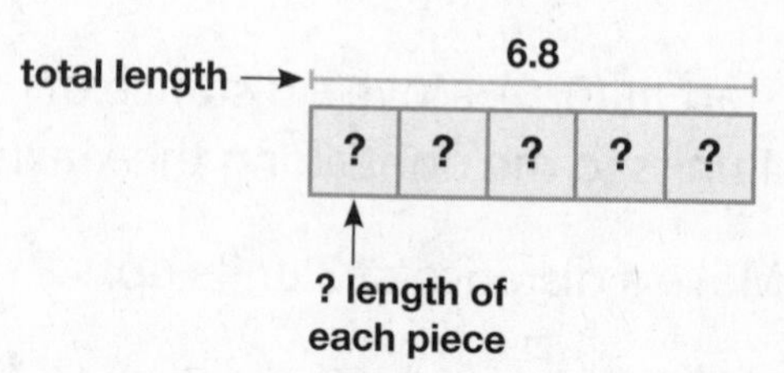

In **22** and **23**, use the chessboard.

22. Higher Order Thinking A chessboard is similar to a coordinate grid. The pieces that look like horses are knights. What letter-number combinations name the locations of the white knights?

23. Andre moves the pawn located at (e, 7) down 2 units. What letter-number combination names the pawn's new location? Explain.

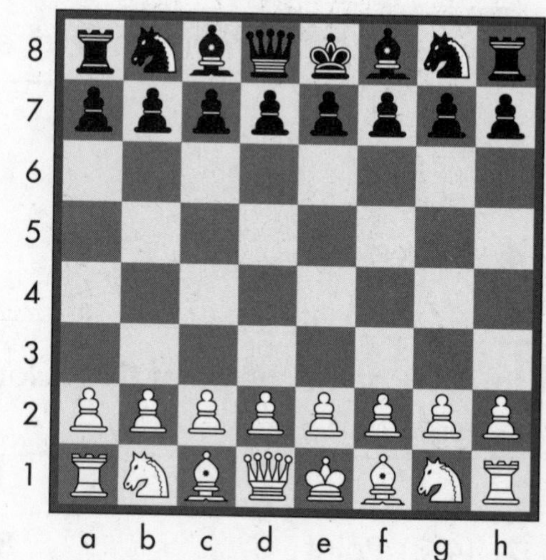

Assessment Practice

24. Point *D* is 2 units away from the origin along the *x*-axis and 4 units away along the *y*-axis.

What could be the coordinates of Point *D*?

Ⓐ (4, 2)

Ⓑ (2, 2)

Ⓒ (2, 4)

Ⓓ (6, 0)

Name ______________________

Additional Practice 14-2
Graph Data Using Ordered Pairs

Another Look!

Graph the following four points and connect them to form a parallelogram.

M (2, 1)   *N* (4, 1)   *O* (5, 4)   *P* (3, 4)

Graph (2, 1) first. Start at (0, 0). Move 2 units to the right from the *y*-axis. Then move one unit up. Draw a dot to represent (2, 1) and label the point *M*.

Graph the remaining 3 points in the same way. Then draw line segments between the points to form a parallelogram.

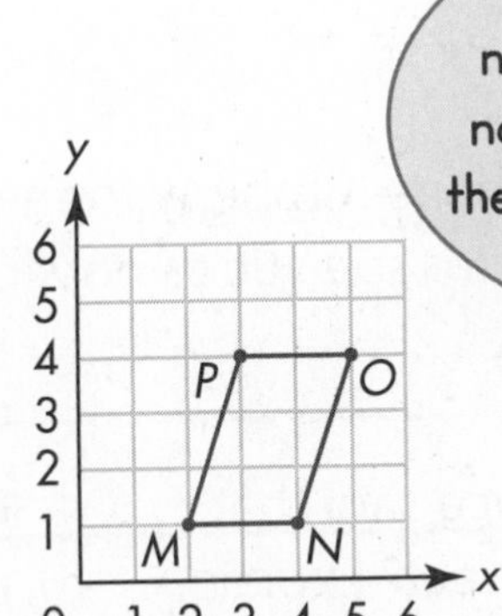

Remember that the first number in an ordered pair names the *x*-coordinate and the second number names the *y*-coordinate.

1. Explain to a friend how to graph the point (1, 5).

In **2–13**, graph and label each point on the grid at the right.

2. *A* (1, 2)   **3.** *B* (0, 7)

4. *C* (3, 3)   **5.** *D* (8, 9)

6. *E* (6, 0)   **7.** *F* (5, 4)

8. *G* (2, 8)   **9.** *H* (1, 6)

10. *I* (7, 4)   **11.** *J* (0, 0)

12. *K* (1, 4)   **13.** *L* (4, 1)

y
10, 9, 8, 7, 6, 5, 4, 3, 2, 1
0 1 2 3 4 5 6 7 8 9 10 x

14. Explain the difference in how you graphed points *K* and *L* on the coordinate grid.

15. Graph the points below on the grid at the right.

$D(1, 1)$ $E(4, 1)$ $F(3, 3)$ $G(2, 3)$

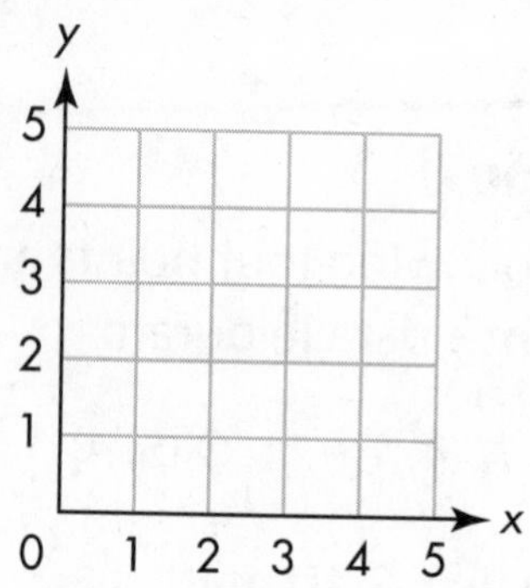

16. Kimberly wants to draw line segments to connect the points to form a shape. What would be the most appropriate tool for her to use?

17. What is the name of the shape Kimberly forms by connecting the points? Be as specific as possible.

18. Critique Reasoning Franco said that $5 + 2 \times 30 = 210$. Is he correct? Explain.

19. At a ski lift, 47 people are waiting to board cars. Each car can hold 6 people. How many cars will be completely filled? How many people are left to board the last car?

20. Higher Order Thinking One side of a rectangle is parallel to the *x*-axis. One vertex of the rectangle is located at (5, 2) and another vertex at (1, 4). What are the coordinates of the other two vertices?

21. Andi needs $5\frac{1}{2}$ yards of fabric for a project. She has a piece that is $3\frac{1}{4}$ yards at school and a piece that is $1\frac{1}{2}$ yards at home. How much more fabric does she need?

Assessment Practice

22. Connor visits the following locations: museum at $M(4, 0)$, sports center at $S(5, 2)$, and bookstore at $B(7, 8)$. Graph and label each location on the grid at the right.

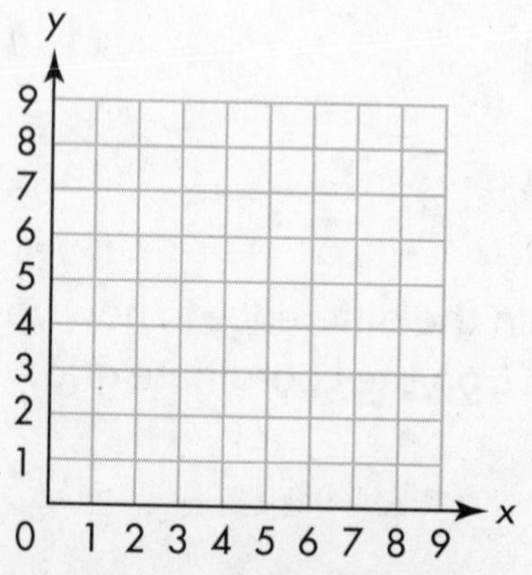

Name ______________________

Additional Practice 14-3

Solve Problems Using Ordered Pairs

Another Look!

Allison can hike 2 miles in an hour. At that speed, how far would she walk in 7 hours?

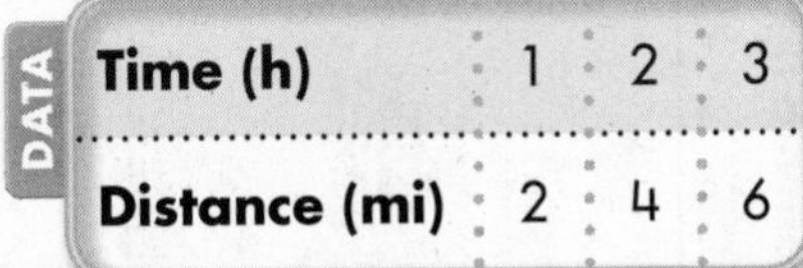

Time (h)	1	2	3
Distance (mi)	2	4	6

Plot the ordered pairs from the table. Draw a line to show the pattern. Then extend the line to where the *x*-coordinate is 7. Read the *y*-coordinate when the *x*-coordinate is 7. The *y*-coordinate is 14.

So, Allison can hike 14 miles in 7 hours.

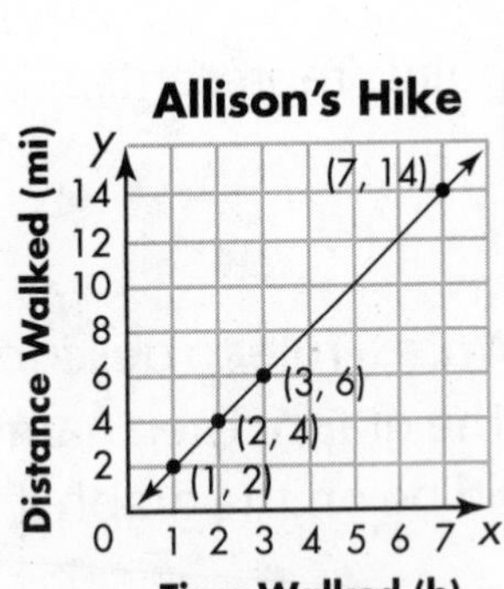

Let *x* be the number of hours Allison walks and let *y* be the number of miles she walks.

In **1** and **2**, find the missing coordinates and tell what the point represents.

1.

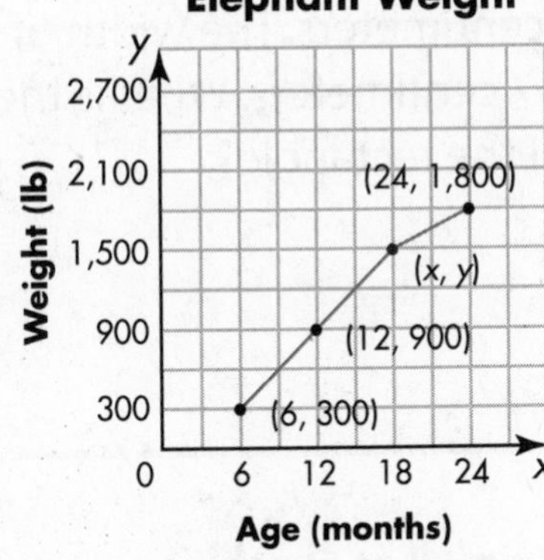

2.

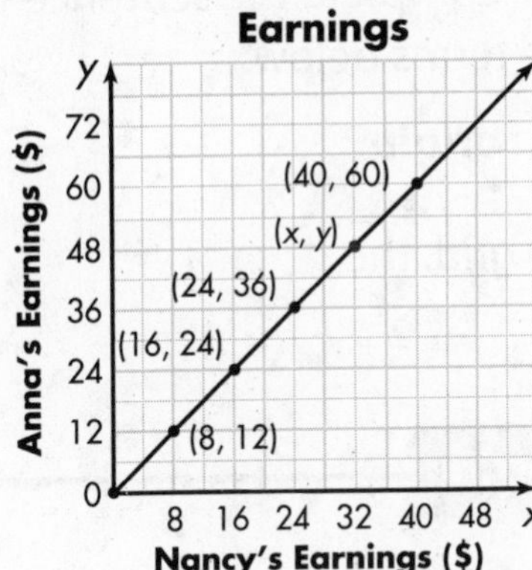

3. Write the coordinates of another point on the line in Exercise 2. Then plot and label the point on the graph.

4. What does the ordered pair for the point you found in Exercise 3 represent?

In **5–7**, use the graph at the right.

5. Jamie is making a graph to show her total earnings, *y*, after babysitting for *x* hours. Graph Jamie's first four points below on the grid at the right. Use a ruler to draw a line connecting the points.

(1, 6) (2, 12) (3, 18) (4, 24)

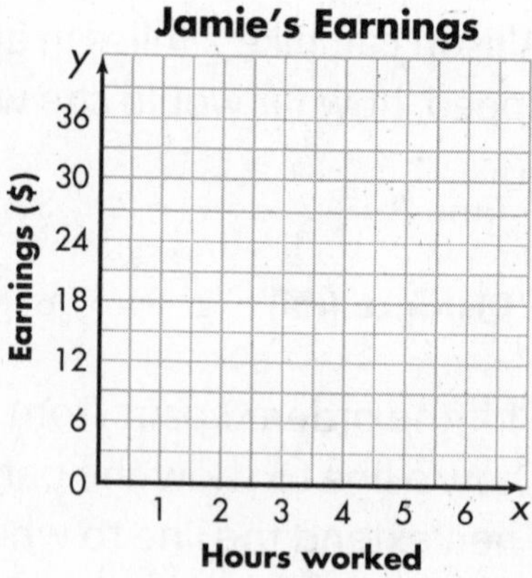

6. Describe what one of the points represents.

7. Higher Order Thinking Write a rule to describe the relationship shown in the graph. Then name two other points that would be on the graph if the line were extended.

8. **Vocabulary** Complete the sentence using one of the terms below.

***x*-axis** ***y*-axis** **origin**

On a coordinate grid, the ______________ is horizontal.

9. Be Precise The area of a rectangle is 105 square centimeters. The width of the rectangle is 7 centimeters. What is the perimeter of the rectangle?

Assessment Practice

10. What does the point (3, 10) represent on the graph at the right?

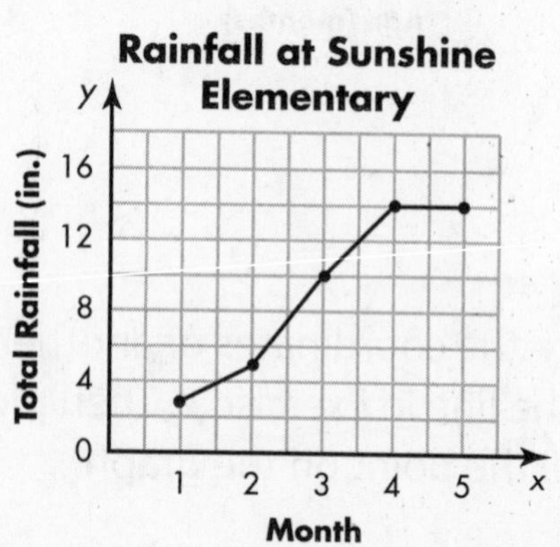

Ⓐ After 3 months, the total rainfall was 7 inches.

Ⓑ After 3 months, the total rainfall was 10 inches.

Ⓒ After 10 months, the total rainfall was 3 inches.

Ⓓ After 10 months, the total rainfall was 7 inches.

Name ______________________

Additional Practice 14-4
Reasoning

Another Look!

A blue swimming pool contains 5 inches of water. It is filled with 2 more inches of water each hour. A red swimming pool contains 25 inches of water. The water is drained 3 inches each hour. How much water will be in the red pool when the blue pool has 19 inches of water?

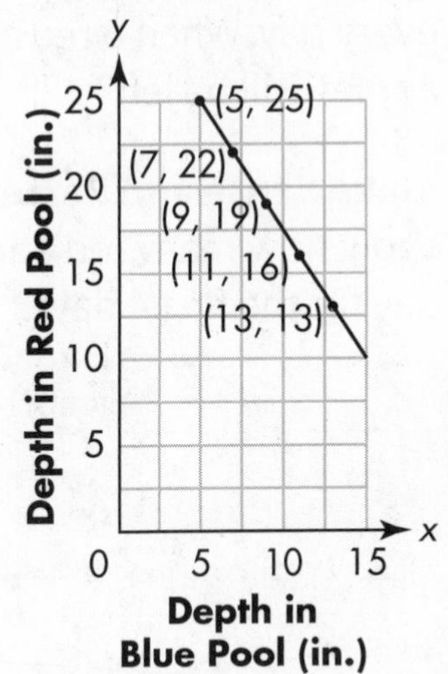

You can use a table and graph to model the math.

DATA

Depth of Water (in.)

Hour	Start	1	2	3	4
Blue Pool	5	7	9	11	13
Red Pool	25	22	19	16	13

The ordered pairs show a pattern. Each hour, the *x*-coordinate increases by 2, and the *y*-coordinate decreases by 3.

Extend the pattern until the *x*-coordinate is 19:
(15, 10), (17, 7), (19, 4)

When the blue pool has 19 inches of water, the red pool will have 4 inches of water.

Reasoning

A tree farm owner uses a grid to mark where to plant trees in the spring. The first tree is planted at (2, 3). Each of the other trees is planted 3 feet east and 2 feet north of the previous tree.

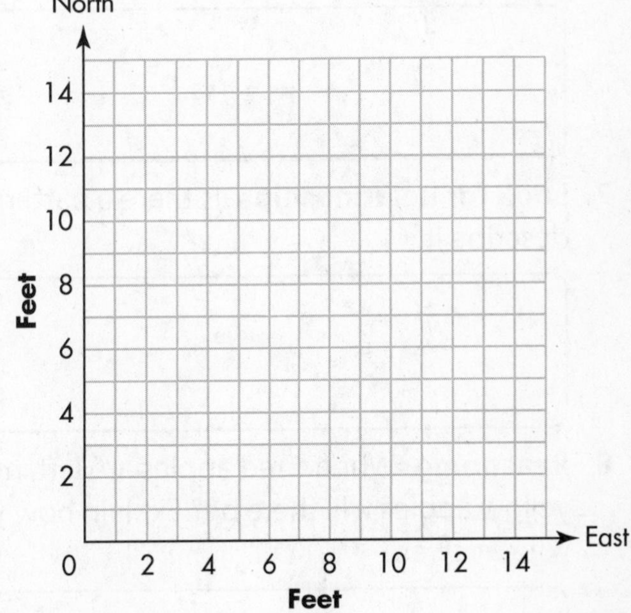

1. Draw and label the locations of the first four trees on the grid.

2. Describe the pattern of the points that represent the tree's locations.

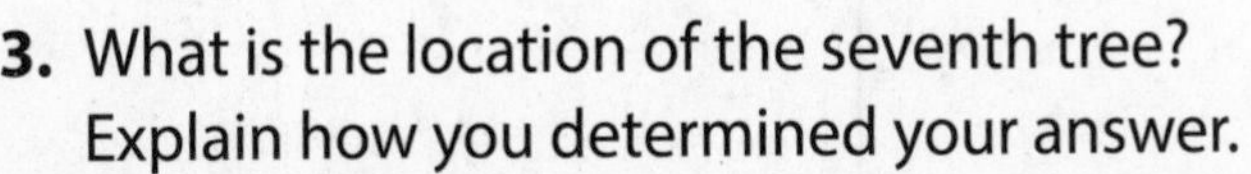

3. What is the location of the seventh tree? Explain how you determined your answer.

Performance Task

Apple Picking

The Bransen Family picked 20 red apples, 28 yellow apples, and $\frac{1}{2}$ bushel of green apples. Starting the following day, they ate 2 red apples and 3 yellow apples every day. When 6 red apples are left, how many yellow apples will be left?

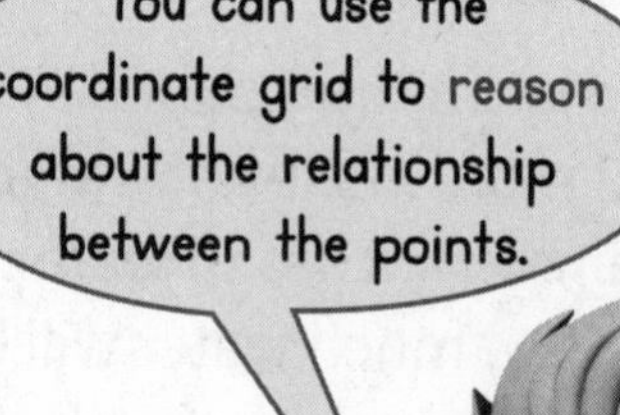

You can use the coordinate grid to reason about the relationship between the points.

4. Make Sense and Persevere Complete the table to show how many red and yellow apples there are every day for the first 4 days.

Number of Apples					
Day	Start	1	2	3	4
Red Apples	20				
Yellow Apples	28				

5. Label the graph and then plot the data points from your table.

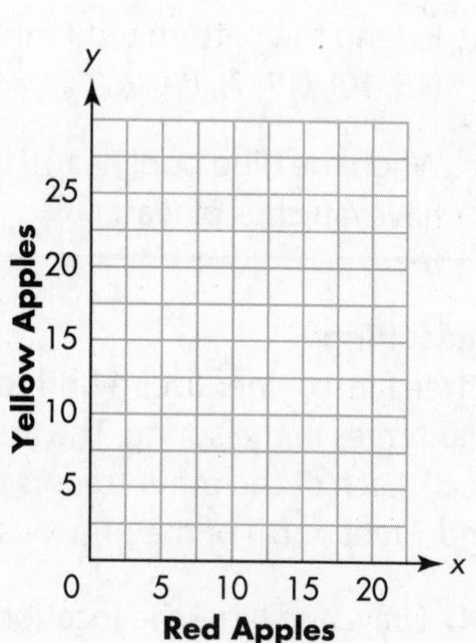

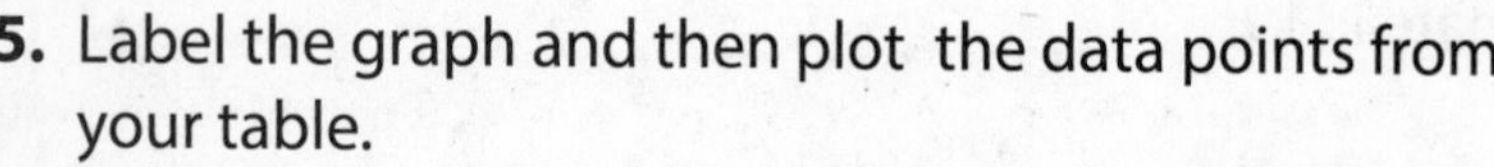

6. Reasoning Can you draw a line through the plotted points? If so, what does that mean?

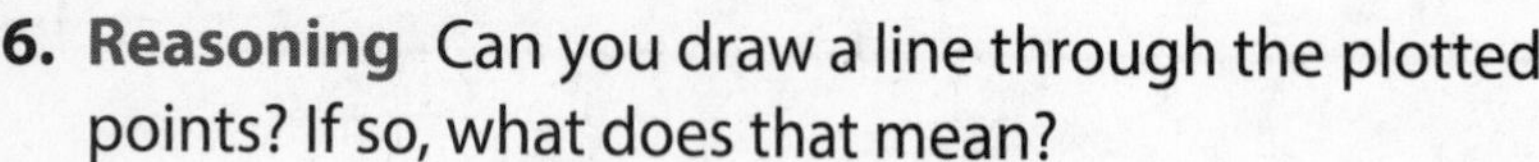

7. Look for Relationships Is there a pattern? If so, describe it.

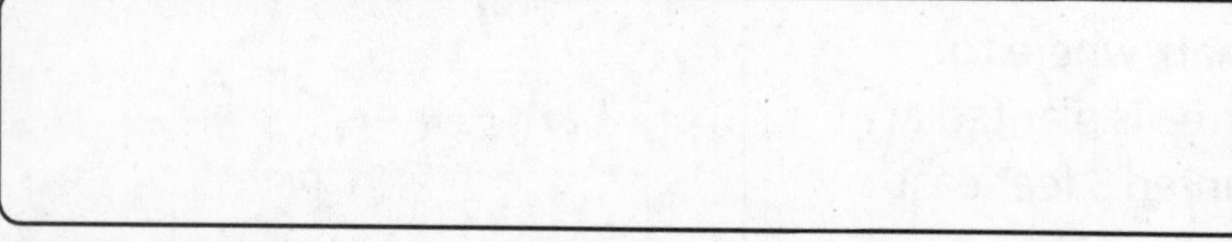

8. Reasoning When 6 red apples are left, how many yellow apples will there be? Explain how you determined your answer.

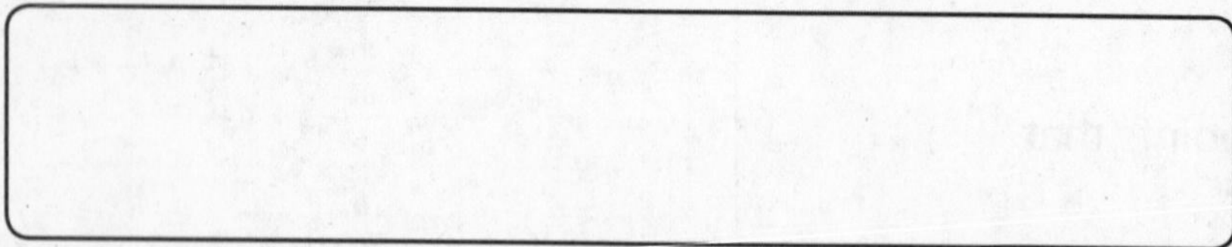

Name ___________________________

Additional Practice 15-1
Numerical Patterns

Another Look!

Cara started with $2. Her sister Chloe started with $7. Both will earn $2 each day for doing chores. How much will each have after five days? What relationship do you notice between how much each sister has after each day?

Step 1

Complete the table. Use the rule "add $2" to help you.

Total Earnings		
Day	Cara	Chloe
Start	$2	$7
1	$4	$9
2	$6	$11
3	$8	$13
4	$10	$15
5	$12	$17

So, after five days, Cara has $12 and Chloe has $17.

Step 2

Look at each row to compare corresponding terms.

After each day, Chloe has $5 more than Cara.

In **1** and **2**, use the table.

1. Becky and Anton work at an apple orchard. At noon, Becky had picked 75 apples and Anton had picked 63 apples. Each of them picks 20 more apples each hour after noon. How many apples will each of them have picked at 5 P.M.? Use the rule "add 20" to help you complete the table.

Total Apples Picked		
	Becky	Anton
Noon	75	63
1 P.M.		
2 P.M.		
3 P.M.		
4 P.M.		
5 P.M.		

2. Construct Arguments What relationship do you notice between how many apples Becky has picked and how many apples Anton has picked at the end of each hour? Explain.

3. Susie had received 9 text messages when she turned her phone on. She received 15 text messages each hour after that. Victor had received 27 text messages when he turned his phone on. He received 15 text messages each hour after that. How many messages did each person receive after 4 hours? Use the rule "add 15" to help you complete the table.

Total Text Messages Received

Hour	Susie	Victor
Start	9	27
1		
2		
3		
4		

4. **Higher Order Thinking** What relationship do you notice between the total number of text messages each person had received after each hour? Explain.

5. **Number Sense** Mr. Kim has a pitcher that contains 16 cups of juice. How many one-third cup servings are in 16 cups?

6. Pierre is using centimeter cubes to build a model. He makes a rectangular prism that is 20 cubes long, 8 cubes tall, and 12 cubes wide. What is the volume of Pierre's model?

Assessment Practice

7. Brian and Christina started keeping track of their workouts. Brian did 85 sit-ups the first week and 90 sit-ups each week after that. Christina did 65 sit-ups the first week and 90 sit-ups each week after that.

How many sit-ups will each person have done after 5 weeks?

Ⓐ Brian: 425 sit-ups
Christina: 325 sit-ups

Ⓑ Brian: 450 sit-ups
Christina: 450 sit-ups

Ⓒ Brian: 425 sit-ups
Christina: 445 sit-ups

Ⓓ Brian: 445 sit-ups
Christina: 425 sit-ups

8. Which of the following are true statements about the relationship between the numbers of sit-ups Brian and Christina have done after each week?

- ☐ Christina has always done 20 more sit-ups than Brian.
- ☐ Brian has always done 25 more sit-ups than Christina.
- ☐ Christina has always done 20 fewer sit-ups than Brian.
- ☐ Brian has always done 20 more sit-ups than Christina.

Name ______________________________

Additional Practice 15-2

More Numerical Patterns

Another Look!

Ira makes a table showing the relationship between the number of yards, feet, and inches. How many feet and inches are in 6 yards? What do you notice about the number of feet and inches?

Step 1

Complete the table.

Yards	Feet	Inches
1	3	36
2	6	72
3	9	108
4	12	144
5	15	180
6	18	216

There are 18 feet or 216 inches in 6 yards.

Step 2

Compare the number of feet to the number of inches to find a relationship.

$3 \times 12 = 36$
$6 \times 12 = 72$
$9 \times 12 = 108$
$12 \times 12 = 144$
$15 \times 12 = 180$
$18 \times 12 = 216$

So, there are 12 inches for every foot.

In **1** and **2**, use the rules "add 12" and "add 6" to help you.

1. Each team in a youth hockey league has 12 forwards and 6 defensemen. Complete the table to show how many forwards and defensemen are on 6 teams.

Team	Forwards	Defensemen
1		
2		
3		
4		
5		
6		

2. What relationship do you notice between the number of forwards and the number of defensemen?

3. Jamie makes a table to show the relationship between meters, centimeters, and millimeters. Use the rule "add 100" to complete the column for the number of centimeters. Then use the rule "add 1,000" to complete the column for the number of millimeters. How many centimeters are in 15 meters? How many millimeters?

Meters	Centimeters	Millimeters
1	100	1,000
2		
3		
4		
5		

4. Higher Order Thinking The distance between Jamie's house and her friend's house is 75 meters. If Jamie walks to her friend's house and back, how many centimeters does she walk? Explain.

5. Look for Relationships What relationship do you notice between the number of centimeters and the number of millimeters?

6. A recipe for bread uses $5\frac{3}{4}$ cups of white flour and $3\frac{1}{3}$ cups of wheat flour. How many more cups of white flour than wheat flour are used in the recipe? Write an equation and complete the bar diagram to solve.

Assessment Practice

At Ashley's Nursery, there are 12 rows of trees. In each row, there are 21 pine trees and 7 spruce trees. Make a table to help you solve the following.

7. How many of each type of tree are there in all?

Ⓐ 252 pine trees; 84 spruce trees

Ⓑ 231 pine trees; 74 spruce trees

Ⓒ 84 pine trees; 252 spruce trees

Ⓓ 33 pine trees; 19 spruce trees

8. Which of the following are true statements about the relationship between the number of pine trees and spruce trees?

- ☐ There are always 14 more pine trees than spruce trees.
- ☐ There are always 3 times as many spruce trees as pine trees.
- ☐ There are always 3 times as many pine trees as spruce trees.
- ☐ There are always $\frac{1}{3}$ as many spruce trees as pine trees.

Name ______________________

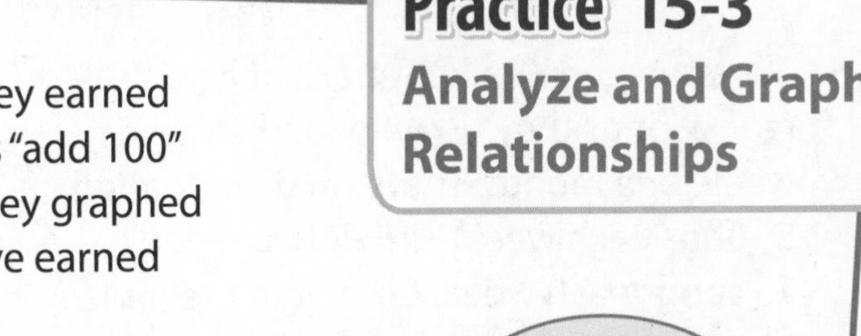

Another Look!

Mary and Sasha kept track of the money they earned at their jobs each week. They used the rules "add 100" and "add 50" to complete the table. Then they graphed ordered pairs of the total amounts they have earned after each week.

Total Amount Earned ($)		
Week	**Mary**	**Sasha**
1	100	50
2	200	100
3	300	150
4	400	200

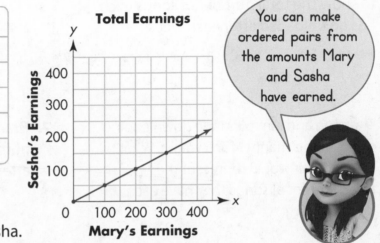

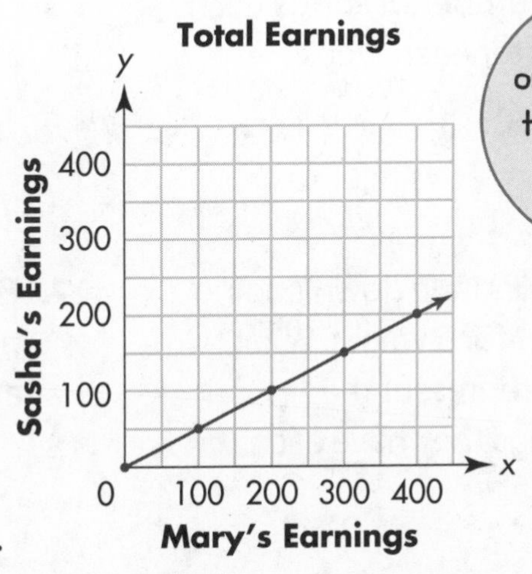

You can make ordered pairs from the amounts Mary and Sasha have earned.

Mary earned $400 after 4 weeks.
Sasha earned $200 after 4 weeks.
Mary earned twice as much as Sasha.

In **1–4**, use the rules "add 6" and "add 12" to help you.

1. Every hour at his bakery, Dennis makes 6 everything bagels and 12 blueberry bagels. Complete the table to show how many of each bagel he makes in all after each hour.

Total Bagels Made		
Hour	**Everything**	**Blueberry**
1		
2		
3		
4		

2. What ordered pair would represent the total number of each type of bagel Dennis makes in 8 hours?

3. What relationship do you notice between the total number of everything bagels and the total number of blueberry bagels made after each hour?

4. Graph the ordered pairs of the total number of each type of bagel made after each hour.

In **5–7**, use the rules "add 5" and "add 15" to help you.

5. Thurston and Kim kept track of how many songs they downloaded each week for a month. Thurston downloaded 5 songs each week. Kim downloaded 15 songs each week. Complete the table to show the total number of songs each has downloaded after each week.

Total Number of Songs Downloaded		
Week	Thurston	Kim
1		
2		
3		
4		

6. Thurston and Kim continue downloading songs in this manner for 8 weeks. What ordered pair would represent the total number of songs they have each downloaded?

7. Graph the ordered pairs of the total number of songs each has downloaded after each week.

8. Model with Math Diego makes a rectangular prism that is 2 cubes long, 2 cubes wide, and 2 cubes tall. Each dimension of June's rectangular prism is twice as many cubes as Diego's prism. What is the volume of June's prism? Use an equation to show your work.

9. Higher Order Thinking There are 347 students going on a field trip. Each bus holds 44 students. If the school pays $95 per bus, will they need to spend more than $1,000 for the buses? How can you decide without using division?

Assessment Practice

10. Claire makes bracelets using blue and red beads. Each bracelet has 20 red beads and 5 blue beads. Write an ordered pair to represent the number of red beads and blue beads Claire will use to make 8 bracelets.

11. What relationship do you notice between the number of red beads and blue beads Claire uses to make all the bracelets?

Name ______________________

Additional Practice 15-4
Make Sense and Persevere

Another Look!

Simon has 28 baseball cards and 16 soccer cards. Each month he plans to get 6 more baseball cards and 4 more soccer cards. Will he ever have the same number of baseball cards and soccer cards? Explain.

To make sense and persevere, graph ordered pairs then analyze the graph.

For each type of card, write a rule and make a table. On the same grid, graph the ordered pairs in each table.

Baseball Cards: Start at 28 and add 6.

Months	Start	1	2	3	4	5	6
Baseball Cards	28	34	40	46	52	58	64

Soccer Cards: Start at 16 and add 4.

Months	Start	1	2	3	4	5	6
Soccer Cards	16	20	24	28	32	36	40

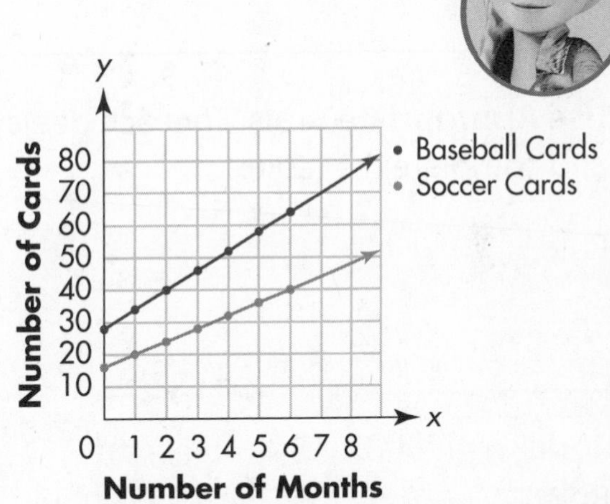

He will never have the same number of baseball cards and soccer cards. The lines are getting farther apart, so the number of soccer cards will never catch up.

Make Sense and Persevere

The stingray tank contains 6 inches of water. The shark tank is empty. Each hour, 4 inches of water are added to the stingray tank and 6 inches are added to the shark tank. Will the water in the shark tank ever be as deep as the water in the stingray tank? Explain.

Hours	Start						
Depth (in.)	6						

Hours	Start						
Depth (in.)	0						

1. Write a rule and complete each table.

   Rule: ______________________

   Rule: ______________________

2. Graph the ordered pairs in each table.

3. Explain whether the depth of water in the two tanks will ever be equal.

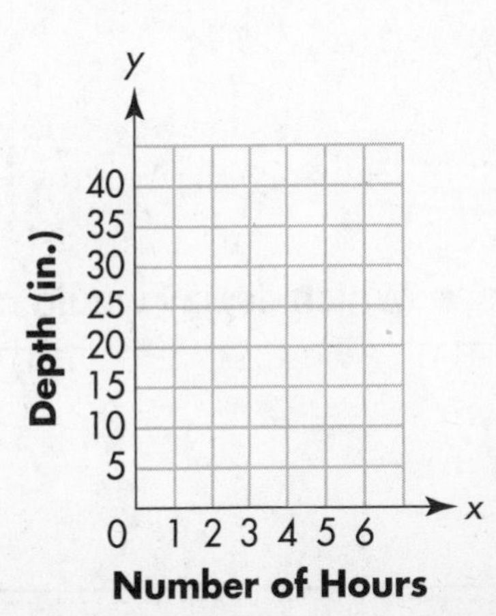

Performance Task

Fall Festival

The park district wants to hire a deejay for the Fall Festival. They expect the festival to last no more than 6 hours. Which deejay would be less expensive?

4. **Make Sense and Persevere** How can you use tables and a graph to solve the problem?

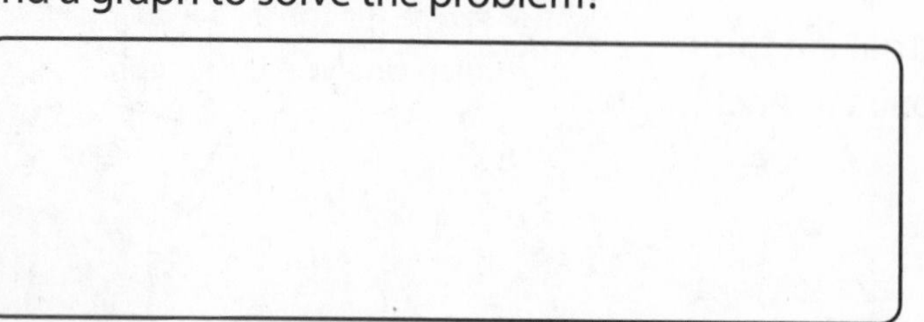

5. **Use Appropriate Tools** For each deejay, write a rule and complete the table.

Rule: ______________________

Hours	Start						
Cost ($)	90						

Rule: ______________________

Hours	Start						
Cost ($)	20						

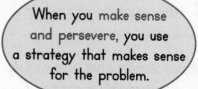

6. **Use Appropriate Tools** On the grid, graph the ordered pairs in each table.

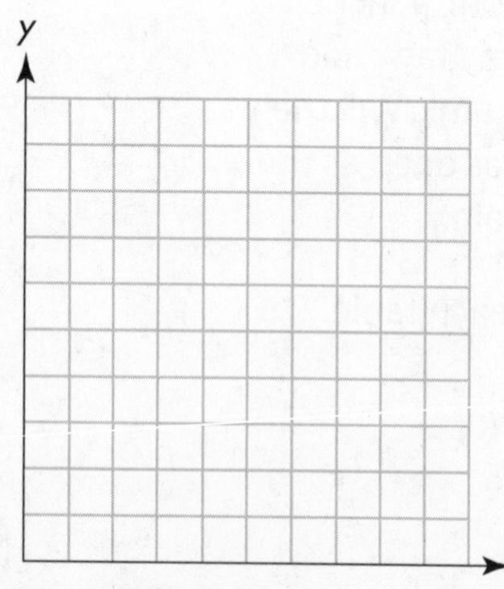

When you make sense and persevere, you use a strategy that makes sense for the problem.

7. **Be Precise** Which deejay would be less expensive?

Name ______________________

Additional Practice 16-1
Classify Triangles

Another Look!

You can classify triangles by the lengths of their sides and the measures of their angles.

Measures of Angles		**Lengths of Sides**
Acute All angles are less than 90°.	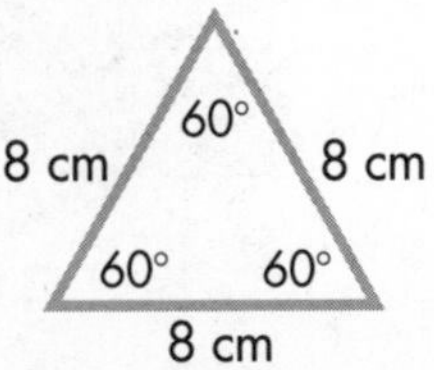	**Equilateral** All sides are the same length.
	This triangle is both equilateral and acute.	
Right One right angle	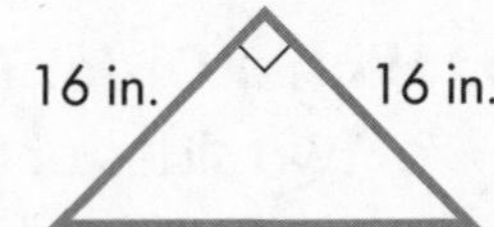	**Isosceles** Two sides are the same length.
	This triangle is both isosceles and right.	
Obtuse One obtuse angle	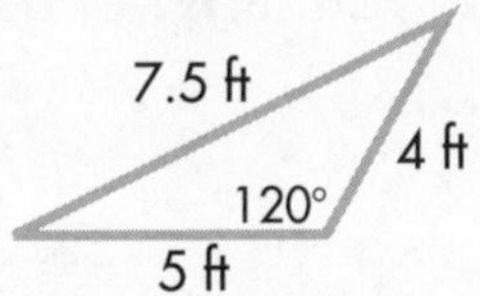	**Scalene** No sides are the same length.
	This triangle is both scalene and obtuse.	

Remember that the sum of the angle measures in a triangle is 180°.

In **1–9**, classify each triangle by its sides and then by its angles.

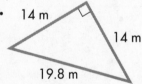

1. 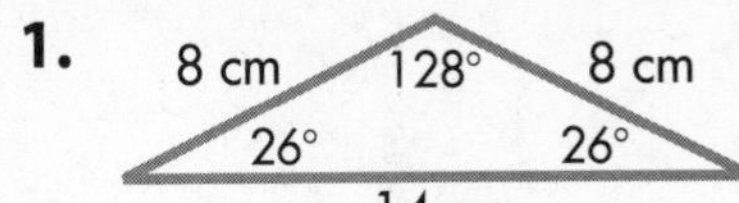

2. 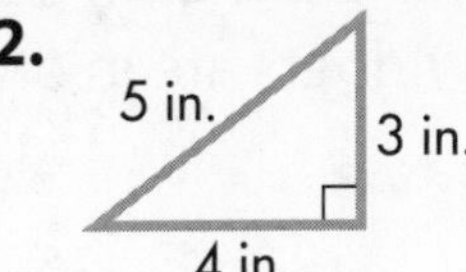

3. 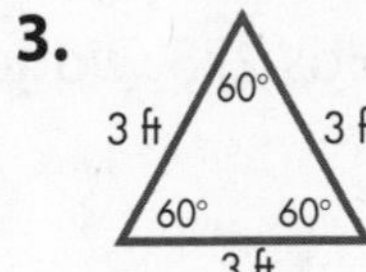

4.
14 m
14 m
19.8 m

5. 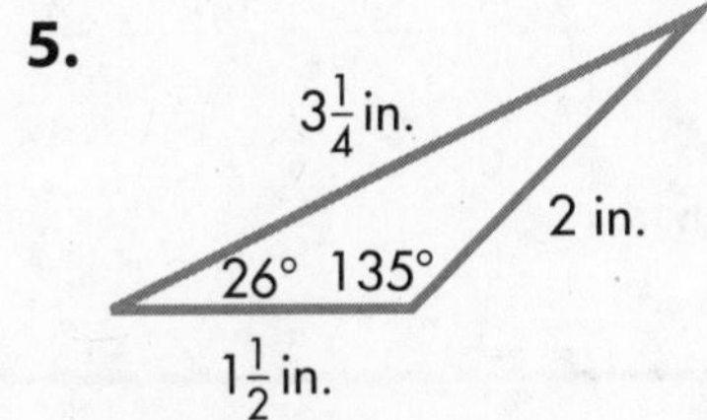

6. 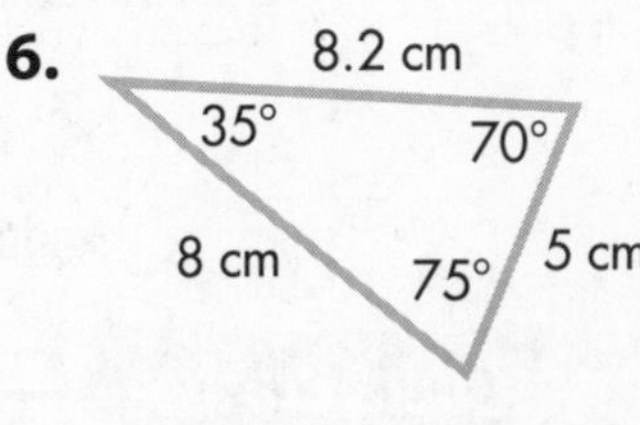

7. 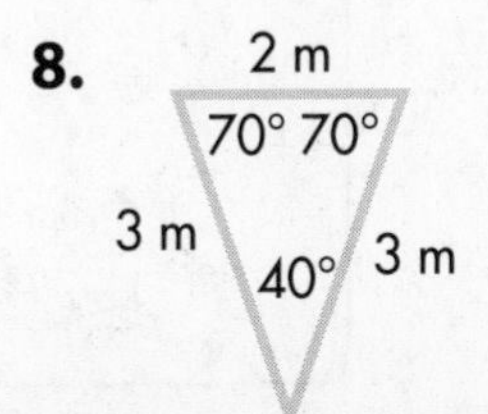

8.
2 m
70° 70°
3 m
3 m
40°

9. 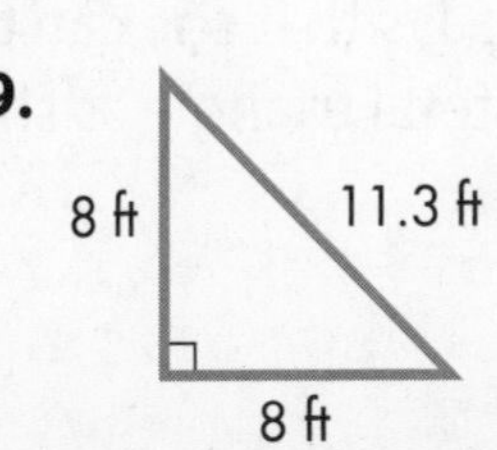

10. Judy bought a new tent for a camping trip. Look at the side of the tent with the opening. Classify the triangle by its sides and its angles.

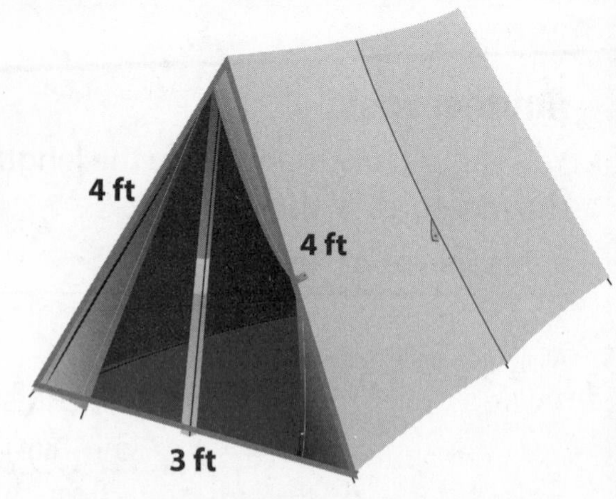

11. Judy bought her tent on sale. The sale price was $70 off the original price. Judy also used a coupon for an extra $15 off. If Judy paid $125 for the tent, what was its original price? Write an equation to show your work.

12. **Critique Reasoning** Ted says that the triangle below cannot be classified because all sides are different lengths. Is Ted correct? Explain why or why not.

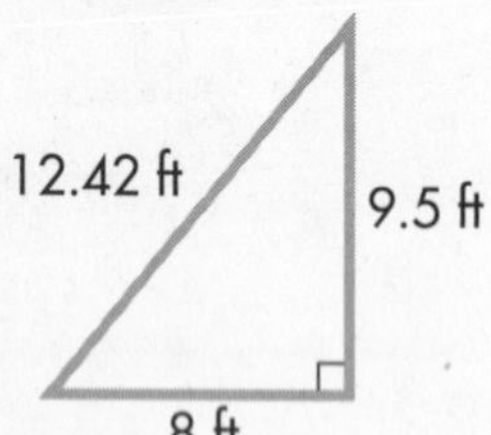

13. **Higher Order Thinking** The lengths of two sides of a triangle are 15 inches each. The third side measures 10 inches. What type of triangle is this? Explain your answer using geometric terms.

14. A factory ships widgets in crates. There are 12 boxes in each crate. Each box holds 275 widgets. How many widgets are in one crate?

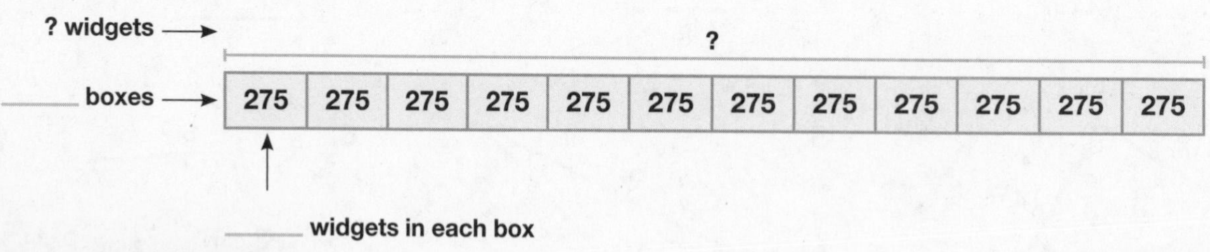

Assessment Practice

15. Claire says that she can draw an obtuse equilateral triangle. Is she correct? Explain.

Name ______________________________

Practice Video Tools Games

Additional Practice 16-2
Classify Quadrilaterals

Another Look!

Some quadrilaterals have special properties.

A **trapezoid** has one pair of parallel sides.

A **parallelogram** has two pairs of opposite sides parallel and equal.

A **rectangle** is a parallelogram with 4 right angles.

A **rhombus** is a parallelogram with 4 equal sides.

A **square** is a parallelogram with 4 right angles and 4 equal sides.

In **1–6**, identify each polygon. Describe each polygon by as many names as possible.

1.

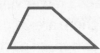

2.

3. 

4. 

5. 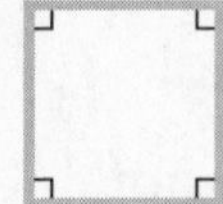

6. 

7. A parallelogram has one side that is 4 centimeters long and one side that is 6 centimeters long. What is the perimeter of the parallelogram? Explain.

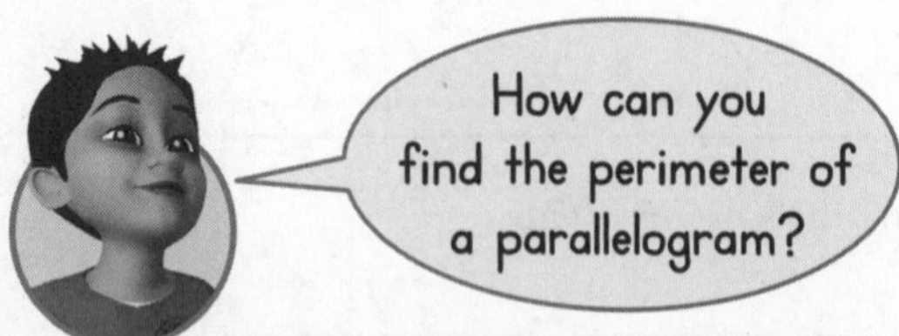

How can you find the perimeter of a parallelogram?

8. **enVision**® STEM In 2013, a wildfire near Yosemite National Park burned about 400 square miles of forest. If one square mile equals 640 acres, about how many acres of forest were burned? Show your work.

9. **Higher Order Thinking** Marvin says that all rhombuses are squares. Aretha says that all squares are rhombuses. Who is correct? Explain.

10. **Construct Arguments** What characteristics help you tell the difference between a rhombus and a rectangle? Explain.

11. Bella is putting 576 cicadas into 8 different terrariums. The same number of cicadas will be put into each one. How many cicadas will be in each terrarium?

576 cicadas

?	?	?	?	?	?	?	?

12. A store has caps on display. Five of the caps are red. There are 4 more blue caps than green caps. There are 3 fewer yellow caps than green caps. If there are 24 caps in all, how many caps are there of each color?

Assessment Practice

13. Which shape could **NOT** have side lengths 9 mm, 9 mm, 9 mm, 9 mm?

Ⓐ trapezoid
Ⓑ rectangle
Ⓒ parallelogram
Ⓓ rhombus

14. Which of the following statements is **NOT** true?

Ⓐ A trapezoid is a rectangle.
Ⓑ A square is also a rectangle.
Ⓒ A rectangle is a quadrilateral.
Ⓓ A square is also a rhombus.

Name ______________________

Additional Practice 16-3
Continue to Classify Quadrilaterals

Another Look!

You can use a Venn diagram to classify quadrilaterals and understand their relationships.

All squares are rectangles.
All squares are rhombuses.
All rectangles are parallelograms.
All rhombuses are parallelograms.
All parallelograms are quadrilaterals.
All trapezoids are quadrilaterals.

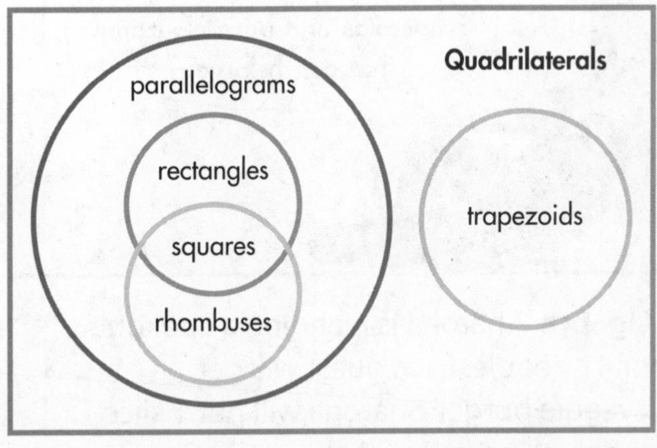

In **1–4**, write whether each statement is true or false. If false, explain why.

1. All trapezoids are parallelograms.

2. Every trapezoid is a rectangle.

3. Squares are special parallelograms.

4. All quadrilaterals are squares.

5. The figure shown below is an isosceles trapezoid. The two sides that are not parallel have the same length. How could you add this shape to the Venn diagram?

6. Why is a parallelogram not the same type of quadrilateral as a trapezoid? Explain how you know.

Look at the relationships in the Venn diagram to help you answer.

7. **Construct Arguments** Harriet says that it is not possible to draw a quadrilateral that is not a trapezoid and not a parallelogram. Is Harriet correct? Explain why or why not.

What do you know about trapezoids and parallelograms that can help you?

8. The table shows Henry's savings over several weeks. If the pattern continues, what will Henry's savings be in Week 10? Tell how you know.

DATA

Week	Savings
0	$6.50
1	$7.50
2	$8.50
3	$9.50

9. **Algebra** Sharona is planning a cookout for 42 people. Each guest will get 1 veggie burger. Sharona will put 1 slice of cheese on half of the burgers. Cheese slices come in packs of 8. Write and solve an equation to find the number of packs of cheese, p, that Sharona needs to buy.

10. **Higher Order Thinking** Suppose a trapezoid is defined as a quadrilateral with at least one pair of parallel sides. How would the quadrilateral Venn diagram change?

Assessment Practice

11. Below is the Venn diagram of quadrilaterals.

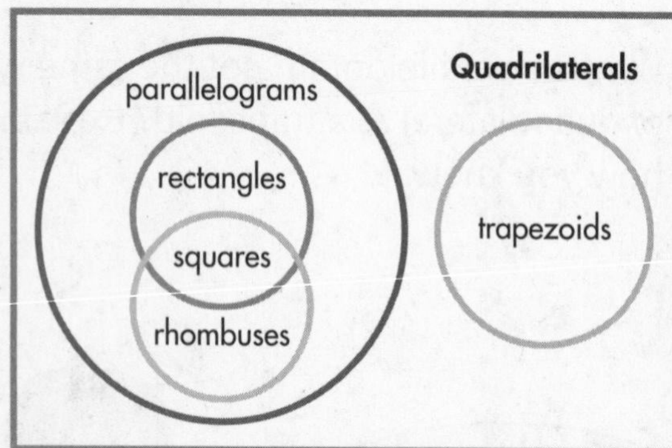

Part A

Are squares also rectangles? Explain.

Part B

What are all of the names that describe a square?

Name ______________________

    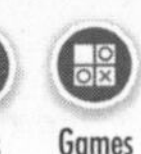

Practice Video Tools Games

Additional Practice 16-4

Construct Arguments

Another Look!

If two angles in a triangle each measure 40°, the triangle is an obtuse triangle.

Tell how you can construct a math argument to justify the statement above.

- I can make a drawing to support my argument.
- I can make my explanation clear and complete.

To help you find the measure of the third angle, remember that the sum of the measures of the angles in a triangle is 180°.

Construct a math argument to justify the statement.

The sum of the measures of two angles is $2 \times 40° = 80°$. The measure of the third angle is $180° - 80° = 100°$. An angle that measures more than 90° is an obtuse angle, so the third angle is obtuse. Since the triangle contains an obtuse angle, it is an obtuse triangle.

100°
40°
40°

Construct Arguments

Samantha says, "A triangle can have three right angles."

1. List some properties of a triangle. How does knowing the properties of a triangle help in constructing your argument?

Think about whether properties, definitions, and diagrams would help you construct arguments.

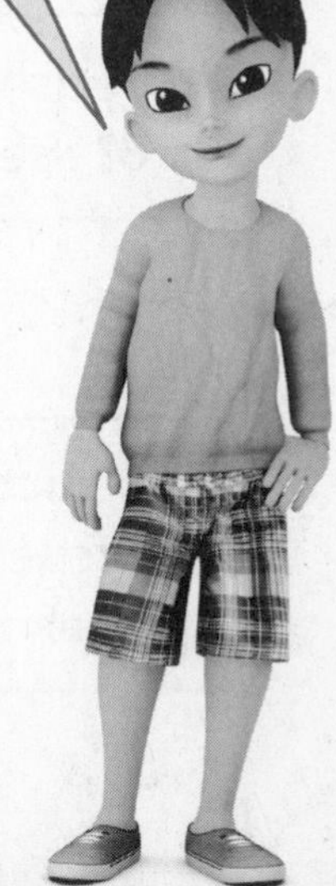

2. How can you use a drawing to construct an argument?

3. Is Samantha correct? Construct a math argument to justify your answer.

Performance Task

Stained-Glass Window

Quentin took a picture of a stained-glass window he saw at the library. He is using what he has learned about triangles to classify the triangles in the window.

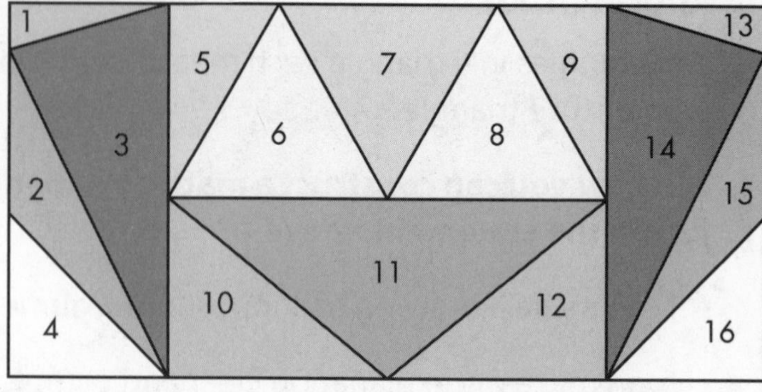

4. **Construct Arguments** Which triangles are right triangles? Construct a math argument to justify your answer.

5. **Construct Arguments** Which triangles could be right isosceles triangles? Construct a math argument to justify your answer.

6. **Construct Arguments** Which triangles are obtuse isosceles triangles? Construct a math argument to justify your answer.

7. **Be Precise** How should Quentin classify Triangles 6, 7, and 8? Use the most precise name you can.

8. **Use Structure** Choose a triangle that was not listed in Exercises 4–7. Use structure to classify it by both its angles and sides.

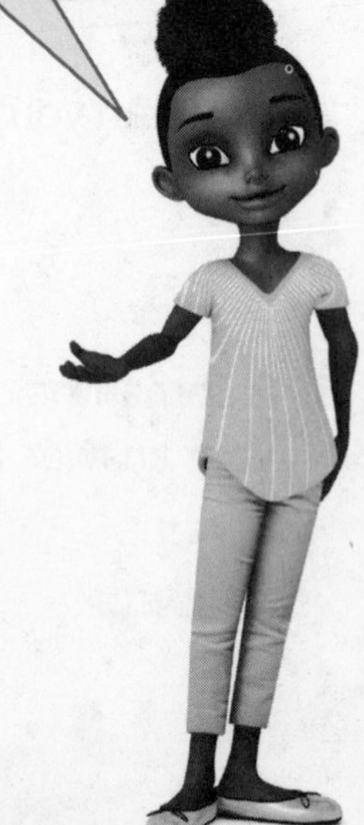

Using definitions of geometric figures can help you to construct arguments.

enVision® Mathematics

Photographs

Every effort has been made to secure permission and provide appropriate credit for photographic material. The publisher deeply regrets any omission and pledges to correct errors called to its attention in subsequent editions.

Unless otherwise acknowledged, all photographs are the property of Savvas Learning Company LLC.

Photo locators denoted as follows: Top (T), Center (C), Bottom (B), Left (L), Right (R), Background (Bkgd)

116 Bikeriderlondon/Shutterstock.